PSYCHOLOGICAL ASPECTS OF LEARNING AND TEACHING

EDITED BY KEVIN WHELDALL
AND RICHARD RIDING

CROOM HELM
London & Canberra

© 1983 Kevin Wheldall and Richard Riding
Croom Helm Ltd, Provident House, Burrell Row,
Beckenham, Kent BR3 1AT

British Library Cataloguing in Publication Data

Psychological aspects of learning and teaching.
  1. Learning, Psychology of   2. Educational
  Psychology
  I. Wheldall, Kevin   II. Riding, Richard
  370.15'23'019   LB1051
  ISBN 0-7099-0460-6

Printed and bound in Great Britain by
Biddles Ltd, Guildford and King's Lynn

CONTENTS

Contributors

Michael Beveridge, Department of Education, University of Manchester.

Geoffrey Brown, School of Education, University of East Anglia.

Margaret Clark, Department of Educational Psychology, University of Birmingham.

Ruth Clark, Queen Margaret's College, Edinburgh.

David Fontana, Department of Education, University College, Cardiff.

Ted Glynn, Department of Education, University of Auckland, New Zealand.

Roy Griffiths, Department of Education, University of Manchester.

Richard Riding, Department of Educational Psychology, University of Birmingham.

Kevin Wheldall, Department of Educational Psychology, University of Birmingham.

PREFACE

This book is designed to introduce a carefully chosen series
of psychological perspectives to education students. Our
rationale for selecting the topics covered is outlined in the
Introduction. Suffice it to say at this point that our aim
has been to present what we feel are vital, pertinent and
relevant topics within educational psychology which have
direct bearing on the processes and practice of teaching and
learning. The chapters have been written with the beginning
student in mind, but not with the aim of supplanting the
traditional introductory test which we tend to assume
education students will already have read. Our intention is
rather to take further, or 'unpack', topics which will,
necessarily, have received only limited coverage in an all-
encompassing introductory text. In some respects, then, this
book may be seen as a bridge between the traditional
introductory overview text and the 'literature'. Our aim is
to guide the education student, new to psychology, along paths
which he or she will find most relevant to teaching and
learning.

We would like to thank Patricia Riding, Margaret Pallant and
Susan Colmar for their generous help in the production of this
book.

Kevin Wheldall and Richard Riding

INTRODUCTION

Talking to education students over the years, we have frequently heard students question the value of much of the psychology they were taught; in large part, we agree with them. As we have said elsewhere (Riding and Wheldall, 1981), "Teachers frequently complain that educational psychology has little to offer them that is of real value in the classoom. We think that it is important to admit that, to some extent, they are right." As psychologists we are interested in so - called 'pure' psychology, especially where it informs our thinking about the applied use of psychology in education. But there is no reason why teachers and students of education should necessarily be similarly interested. What they are interested in is psychological theory and content which directly informs them as teachers, and which is manifestly useful to them in the classroom.

Not all aspects of psychological research have findings that are practical and useful in the school situation, nor is this confined to education. It is true of most applied areas of other disciplines, in that only part of the pure study is useful. One could think, say, of agriculture. The farm manager is not necessarily going to be interested in the whole of such subjects as botany or zoology or chemistry. Only certain aspects of these subjects are going to have practical relevance. The important thing is to identify those aspects of psychological research that provide practical information for the teacher, and which will help the teacher to be effective. So when we come to the problem of deciding what psychology has to offer to the teacher, we have to begin by asking what does the teacher need to know that is going to be relevant and useful.

In many books there is a great deal of material which has no practical use or application to the teacher; topics like the percepton of visual illusions, the learning of lists of words and nonsense syllables which are very untypical of what really

1

happens in school, and work to do with animals such as rats and pigeons whose behaviour bears little resemblance to that of human pupils. All of this may be of interest to the pure psychologist, and may even in time produce knowledge that will be helpful in understanding more fully how everyday learning takes place. However, at present it has no immediate value for the teacher and its inclusion in educational psychology texts only serves to confuse the teacher and student. This is particularly unfortunate when there is much psychological work that has been done recently which is already useful, relevant and which could be applied to the practical situation if teachers knew about it.

Our policy for this book, therefore, is to select carefully those areas which we know from our own experience and research have useful, practical applications to the everyday classroom environment. Ideally this will help teachers to understand better how to plan and present their teaching and thereby enable pupils to learn more effectively. Consequently, this book is not an introductory text in the all encompassing, traditional sense but nor does it assume that the reader has a great background knowledge of psychology. Each chapter focusses on a specific topic, specially written for this book by an expert in that area with the aim of providing the reader with a contemporary perspective.

The book consists of three parts. Part one represents a fairly major departure from most educational psychology texts since it is devoted to a consideration of the behavioural approach to teaching. This approach is swiftly gaining a wide acceptance. Chapters demonstrate the usefulness of the behavioural approach in terms of improved classroom discipline and also in academic achievement. Part two focusses on how language and thinking operate in the classroom focussing on both teachers and pupils and their individual differences. Chapters discuss the importance of language and communication in the classroom, the processes by which children typically learn in school, and the factors influencing the thinking of both teachers and children. Finally part three presents important, if not essential, background knowledge for teachers on the developing child. We have included chapters on the development of thinking, how language is learned, and the nature of individual differences between children.

All of this has led to a book with a more specific remit than most other texts in educational psychology. We have attempted to include only chapters on topics which we consider it important for teachers to know about. We have excluded areas traditionally stressed and have emphasised areas typically neglected. We hope the result is a book that is relevant and which fulfils its aim of informing you and improving your teaching.

REFERENCES

Riding, R.J. and Wheldall, K. Effective educational research. Educational Psychology, 1981, 1, 5-11.

SECTION ONE. CLASSROOM MANAGEMENT

Some children present a major problem to teachers. They may appear to be 'developmentally delayed', 'ill prepared for school', or even 'operating under a totally different value system'. These are only other ways of saying that they behave differently from so-called 'normal' children. They may not talk much, or perhaps worse, they may listen less; they may refuse to pay attention; they may well not find school work rewarding; they may indulge in anti-social behaviours; they may swear or fight. In fact they may not do many of the things you expect normal children to do and yet they may do many things you do not want them to do! A behavioural psychologist would view these problems as being primarily due to the child's learning experiences i.e. as a result of the systems of reward and punishment operating in his environment. In attempting to solve these problems we would define goals specifying behaviours or skills which are appropriate for the classroom setting and of benefit to the child. As a behavioural teacher you too can define appropriate behavioural goals for the children in your care and then use your knowledge of behavioural psychology to structure your teaching and your classroom environment to facilitate the learning of, and maintenance of, appropriate desirable behaviour and to reduce, or even eliminate, undesirable behaviour.

The first section of this book is concerned with 'Classroom Management' and serves as an introduction to the behavioural approach to teaching. In the two chapters which follow we are concerned with the mechanics of classroom teaching and we hope to demonstrate that the theories underlying behavioural psychology have direct, practical applications in the classroom. The two chapters are concerned with both children's social and academic behaviour in the classroom which cannot be entirely separated from each other. In the first of the two chapters, Kevin Wheldall considers how, by employing a behavioural approach to teaching, satisfactory classroom discipline can be achieved in a positive, nonpunitive way. In the second chapter, Ted Glynn discusses the ways in which the behavioural approach can be employed to teach children academic skills and content more effectively. Both chapters assume some familiarity with the general behavioural approach which will be reviewed briefly here.

What then is the behavioural approach? Before attempting to discuss what the behavioural teacher can achieve in the classroom, we must first consider what characterises a behavioural perspective and briefly outline its origins in the school of psychology known as behaviourism. A more thorough, but still introductory, review of this is given in 'Social Behaviour' (Wheldall, 1975), upon which parts of the following theoretical and historical sections are based.

PAVLOV'S CLASSICAL CONDITIONING

The roots of behaviourism lie in the work of the Russian physiologist I.P. Pavlov, on what came to be known as classical conditioning. Since Pavlov's work is so well known ("Pavlov, that rings a bell!"), and since its applications to education are limited, we need provide only a brief mention of it here. It is important to emphasise, however, that it had considerable influence on both J.B. Watson, the 'founding father of behaviourism' and B.F. Skinner, the man who took up his mantle to produce 'radical behaviourism', which is currently accepted by many as providing the most adequate descriptions so far of the operating principles of human behaviour. However, Pavlovian conditioning procedures are also important in their own right to an understanding of some aspects of human behaviour, especially emotional behaviour, and are applied clinically in various forms of behaviour therapy such as the desensitisation of obsessive fears and various forms of aversion therapy aimed at reducing undesirable behaviours.

WATSON'S 'BEHAVIOURIST MANIFESTO'

The unchallenged father of behaviourism was J.B. Watson who pioneered this radically different approach to human psychology in the United States at the beginning of this century. After working with animals and developing methods for studying animal psychology, he became convinced that such methods were not only equally applicable to the study of human psychology, but that they were also the only scientifically reputable way of doing so. Watson's behaviourism was based largely on Pavlovian classical conditioning. In 1913 he published what became known as the 'Behaviourist Manifesto' in which he stated the case for a new human psychology based on extreme objectivity and the importance of learning. Brushing aside introspection of inner mental life, he demanded that

5

psychology concentrate purely on what could be observed, i.e. behaviour. He insisted that concepts be both carefully defined and experimentally demonstrable. Freudian notions and instinctual theories were rejected on both of these grounds; they were vague and virtually untestable. Alternative explanations, many highly speculative, were offered by Watson in terms of learning based primarily on extrapolations from Pavlov's work on conditioned reflexes. He attempted to explain even the most complex aspects of human personality by 'millions of conditionings' of basic reflexes.

Watson was personally so convinced of the importance of learning at the expense of hypothesised, but unproven, innate behaviours that he once made the following statements:

"The behaviourists believe that there is nothing from within to develop. If you start with a healthy body, the right number of fingers and toes and eyes, and the few elementary movements that are present at birth, you do not need anything else in the way of raw material to make a man, be that man a genius, a cultured gentleman, a rowdy or a thug" (1928), and similarly - "Give me a dozen healthy infants, well formed, and my own specified world to bring them up in and I'll guarantee to take any one at random and train him to become any type of specialist I might select - doctor, lawyer, artist, merchant-chief, and, yes, even beggar-man and thief, regardless of his talents, penchants, tendencies, abilities, vocation and race of his ancestors," (1913).

This is extreme environmentalism - the belief that human behaviour is totally learned from the environment in which the person is reared, as opposed to nativism -the belief that a person's potential is biogically fixed at birth. Few of even the most fervent behaviourists would argue so extreme an environmentalist view today since it has been convincingly demonstrated that heredity exerts a powerful influence which effectively sets the limits on an individual's potential. In fact even Watson admitted that he was exaggerating when he made his claims and Skinner has subsequently said, "I have never known any behaviourist, with one exception, who has denied the very considerable role of genetic endowment," (Cohen, 1977). As Huxley (1964) has powerfully declared, extreme environmentalists such as Watson "forget that even the capacity to learn, to learn at all, to learn only at a definite stage of development, to learn one thing rather than another, to learn more or less quickly, must have some genetic basis."

Acknowledging the role of heredity and genetic endowment, however, does not necessarily mean accepting that, for example, 'intelligence' (whatever that is) is inherited - what is inherited may be something much more basic, such as susceptibility to different forms of reward and/or punishment. Nor is accepting the role of heredity to deny for one moment the essential plasticity of human behaviour, which allows considerable and continual remoulding by the environment. So called 'low' or 'poor' intelligence in a child, which may in part be (in some as yet unknown way) genetically determined, may possibly prevent the Watsons of today turning out "doctors or lawyers" but this restriction is only at the upper end of complex skilled behaviours which still allows considerable scope for changing the child's behaviour. In fact, it is probably true to say that few children are prevented from achieving their goals by genetic limitations since their potential is so rarely maximised by efficient manipulations of their environment to optimise appropriate learning. Furthermore, applied learning theory in the form of behaviour modification techniques has allowed genetically and otherwise flawed, severely retarded children to achieve levels of skill far in excess of anything that would previously have been expected from such children whose apparent future was summed up by the label 'untrainable vegetative retardates'.

SKINNER'S OPERANT CONDITIONING

The work of B.F. Skinner is frequently misunderstood. Many, otherwise well educated, people dismiss his ideas without clearly understanding what they are, often confusing them with classical conditioning and believing that he is a strong advocate of the use of punishment. As Skinner himself has said in interviews: "Its quite surprising how little the world in general knows about operant conditioning, and that world includes many psychologists."

Unlike classical conditioning, operant conditioning is not restricted to physiological (autonomic) responses. It does not build on innately established stimulus-response links but can be used to build up complex behaviours by the conditioning of simple discrete responses which the animal is observed to make.

Skinner's theory of learning basically argues that most behaviour consists of the emission of responses usually in the absence of <u>known</u> stimuli. The rate of responding will increase if responses are '<u>reinforced</u>', for example, by giving a 'hungry' animal food. Reinforcers are very difficult to define. In the strict technical sense they refer to any things or events which when following a certain behaviour lead to an increase in the frequency or probability of that behaviour. But basically reinforcers are things that the animal will seek out.

7

"Good things are positive reinforcers. The food that
tastes good reinforces us when we taste it. Things that
feel good reinforce us when we feel them. Things that
look good reinforce us when we look at them. When we say
colloquially that we 'go for' such things, we
identify a kind of behaviour which is frequently
reinforced by them." (Skinner, 1971)

Hence, food will reinforce a 'hungry' (food deprived) animal
and sexual gratification and the alleviation of thirst may
also function as reinforcers. These are examples of
unconditioned positive reinforcers; in that they appear to be
innate, they may be said to be unconditioned, and in that the
animal will seek them out, they may be said to be positive.
Negative reinforcers consist of stimuli that the animal will
seek to avoid, the termination of which will be reinforcing.
An example of a negative reinforcer is an electric shock which
will reinforce behaviour by its removal. Hence an animal's
behaviour could be reinforced positively by giving it food or
negatively by terminating an electric shock. Negative
reinforcement has the effect of increasing responses by the
termination of an aversive event whereas punishment consists
of presenting the aversive consequence in an attempt to reduce
the frequency of responses. Skinner considers punishment to
be a rather unreliable and time consuming way of preventing
responses from occurring and does not give it much emphasis in
his writings. We should note that removing positive
reinforcers is also a form of punishment.

Some teachers react adversely when they hear that the
behavioural approach to teaching has its origins in work with
rats and pigeons. They protest that it demeans man to attempt
to reduce his behaviour to the level of animal behaviour. But
of course man is an animal and it would be rather odd if these
simple laws of nature were not equally applicable to man,
albeit in more sophisticated form. Few would deny the
benefits of medical advances initially pioneered with simpler
animals and, in fact, we would expect new procedures at the
experimental stage to be tried out with animals before human
life was risked. Similarly, it makes sense that behavioural
procedures were initially pioneered with animals where there
is less (potential) risk and where greater control can be
achieved within simpler experimental paradigms, although these
would not be directly applicable in the study of human
behaviour. None of this is meant to suggest, however, that we
are, or should be, trying to apply the same procedures
directly with children in schools. Nor need we concern
ourselves further with studies carried out in the rat lab.,
since there is now a wealth of material reporting research
with human subjects and countless demonstration studies of
effective behavioural interventions carried out with children

in classrooms and similar environments.

There are many other aspects of operant theory which we have not yet described but it is preferrable to pass on to the classroom setting and introduce any further new concepts as necessary. We are now in a position to review the lessons learned from our brief historical perspective on behaviourism and to clarify exactly what we mean by 'the behavioural approach to teaching.'

REFERENCES

Cohen, D. Psychologists on Psychology. (Routledge and Kegan Paul, London, 1977).

Huxley, A. Essays of a Humanist. (Harper and Row, New York, 1977).

Skinner, B.F. Beyond Freedom and Dignity. (Jonathan Cape, London, 1977).

Watson, J.B. Psychology as the behaviourist views it. Psychological Review, 1913, 20, 158-177.

Watson, J.B. The Psychological Care of Infant and Child. (Allen and Unwin, London, 1928).

Wheldall, K. Social Behaviour: Key Problems and Social Relevance. (Methuen, London, 1975).

Chapter 1

A POSITIVE APPROACH TO CLASSROOM DISCIPLINE

Kevin Wheldall

It is a source of amazement that, whilst courses of training for teaching universally lay great stress on curriculum design and content, on the philosophical, historical, sociological and psychological perspectives on education, and on the in-depth study of one's main academic subject, relatively little time is spent in preparing the teacher-to-be in the art or, as we would prefer it, the science of teaching. Very little instruction is given in what the teacher actually ought to do in the classroom, how she or he should behave. This is particularly noticeable in the context of handling troublesome or disruptive behaviour in the classroom. Many student teachers are still told the myth that, provided you have spent enough time preparing your lessons properly, you will never have discipline problems. The falsity of this advice is exposed by the countless number of both student and practising teachers who have had lessons, which were impeccably prepared, destroyed beyond redemption. Many have been reduced to tears by classes of children which no amount of prior lesson preparation could control.

Teaching practice itself is a curious idea whereby student teachers are left alone for large periods of time to cope, as best they can, with whole classes of children, with little or no guidance as to how to proceed once they are actually in the classroom. The lucky ones may receive useful (or otherwise) tips from more experienced staff. The most common advice given is "Give them hell for the first week, show them who's boss, and then you can relax." Others rapidly acquire the skills of sarcasm and 'put down', learned from teaching colleagues (who should really know better) or perhaps dimly remembered from their own school days. Many will fervently wish that an effective model of teaching was available which offered practical advice about what one should actually do in the classroom. We believe that the behavioural model is the answer to that wish. The behavioural approach to teaching offers a theoretical basis for understanding what is happening

10

in classrooms and, perhaps more importantly, it has an accompanying methodology for approaching and analysing problems and a technology for solving them. As we hope to show, the behavioural approach offers a positive alternative for classroom discipline. We believe that the behavioural approach to teaching can, if seriously studied and the necessary skills learned, yield both more effective teaching and a more rewarding teaching experience. It is first important to spell out, however, exactly what the behavioural approach to teaching implies. The following section is based on chapter two of a forthcoming book by Wheldall and Merrett (1982).

THE BEHAVIOURAL APPROACH TO TEACHING

The behavioural approach to teaching is based on behavioural psychology, a school of thought which is sometimes referred to as behaviourism. Behaviourism, and hence the behavioural approach to teaching, is based on several general assumptions, which may be summarised as follows:-

1. The concern of psychology (and hence teaching) is with the observable.

    This means that teachers who adopt the behavioural approach (behavioural teachers) concern themselves with what a child actually does, i.e. his behaviour, rather than speculating about unconscious motives or the processes underlying his behaviour. The behavioural approach is objective and is concerned with the observable facts of life. For example, a teacher might report that "Sally worked well for the first half of the lesson but then her concentration lapsed." In behavioural terms what happened was that Sally completed ten sums correctly in the first twenty minutes of the lesson, but only two in the last twenty minutes. The teacher's reference to her concentration lapse is an attempt at explanation based purely on speculation.

2. For the most part, and certainly for most practical purposes, behaviour is learned.

    In other words behaviour, what people do, is assumed to have been learned as a result of the individual interacting with his environment, rather than being inherited at birth. This does not mean that behavioural psychologists and teachers do not believe in genetic inheritance or that they do believe that anybody can be taught to do anything given time. Rather they believe that genetics or biological endowment may set the limits for what an individual can learn, but that behaviour is still the result of learning. In other words they take the practical view that there is very little you can do about a child's genetic inheritance or the biological state of his nervous system, but that you can make it easier for him to learn behaviours by exercising control over his environment.

3. Learning means change in behaviour.

This follows from the first point really. The only way we know (that we _can_ know) that learning has taken place is by observing a change in a child's behaviour. The _behavioural_ teacher will not be satisfied with claims such as "I think she has a better attitude to school now"; he will only be satisfied if the child now displays behaviour(s) which she was not showing before. For example, this might be reflected in her increased attendance and/or punctuality figures.

4. Changes in behaviour (i.e. learning) are governed primarily by the 'law of effect.'

In simple terms this means that children (and adults, and other animals for that matter) learn on the basis of tending to repeat behaviours which are followed by consequences which they find desirable or rewarding; similarly they tend not to repeat behaviours, the consequences of which they find aversive or punishing. In other words the consequences of behaviour are critical to learning.

5. Behaviours are also governed by the contexts in which they occur.

In any situation some behaviours are more appropriate than others and we learn which situations are appropriate for which behaviour. If a child's behaviour is appropriate for the circumstances in which it occurs it is likely to be rewarded; if it occurs in inappropriate circumstances reward is less likely and the behaviour may even lead to punishing consequences. As a result of this we rapidly learn not only how to perform a certain behaviour, but _when_ and _where_ to perform it. For example, the new boy in the secondary school will soon learn to cheer on the school team from the touchline but merely to clap politely when the result is announced in assembly.

The five points set out above may be seen as the essential features of the behavioural approach to teaching. In large part they derive from the psychology of B.F. Skinner, whose operant learning theory has been very influential. Operant psychology is a science of behaviour which looks for functional, that is to say, causal relationships between behaviours and factors in the environment. As we have already said, this approach assumes that almost all of the behaviour with which we are likely to be concerned is learned, and that it is learned and maintained by environmental consequences. The direct application of this to teaching lies in the fact that if we can change or control environmental consequences, then we can change or control children's behaviour. It is important to emphasise, however, that the situations in which a child finds himself will also influence his behaviour and that we can also change the child's behaviour by altering other aspects of the child's environment. This point is frequently overlooked but is, in fact, extremely important as we shall see.

Teaching is about Changing Children's Behaviour

If we believe that teaching is concerned with helping children to learn new skills and gain new information, and if we believe also that learning implies a change or changes in behaviour, then it follows logically that teaching is about changing children's behaviour, whether we are talking about the acquisition of appropriate social skills or the learning of new academic information. Moreover, if teaching is about changing behaviour then the role of the teacher is, quite simply, to bring about changes in the behaviour of the children in her class.

There are many points which we will need to discuss which follow directly from this premise but let us initially establish the remit of this chapter, what we are trying to cover and what we are not attempting to present in the context of this short introductory overview. Basically, our concern is with the classroom management of children's social behaviour. The behavioural approach may also be applied in curriculum design and in the teaching of academic skills and subject matter but this is dealt with in more detail in the following chapter. We must immediately stress, however, that improved social behaviour in the classroom has enormous implications for children's academic progress. Our aim will be to present a positive approach to the perennial problem of classroom discipline and to demonstrate how the behavioural approach yields benefits for teachers and children. By employing effective, positive behavioural methods of establishing control in the classroom, the teacher is freed in large part from the often time-consuming chore of chiding children for disrupting lessons or for not getting on with their work. The teacher is then able to spend more of his time planning and directing effective lessons and advising and explaining with individual children. As a result of this we might also expect children, once they have become consistently more successful at their lessons, to begin to find their schoolwork rewarding in its own right. This is a change in behaviour of a different order and is the ultimate aim of all good teaching.

At this point, however, it is important to consider briefly some of the basic operating principles underlying the behavioural approach. Remember that in this chapter we can only provide an overview. Readers who become interested in this approach should read an introductory text on this topic (e.g. Wheldall and Merrett, 1982).

The Behavioural Teacher's ABC

The behavioural approach to teaching is based on several principles, some of which we have already referred to briefly. The basic model embodying the crucial elements of the behavioural approach is known as the three term analysis of behaviour or the ABC model.

A refers to the <u>antecedent</u> conditions, i.e. the context in which a behaviour occurs or what is happening in that environment prior to a behaviour occurring.

B refers to the <u>behaviour</u> itself, i.e. what a child is actually doing in real physical terms (<u>not</u> what you think he is doing as a result of inferences from his behaviour).

C refers to the consequences of the behaviour, i.e. what happens to the child after the behaviour.

ABC is a convenient way of remembering the constituents of the three term analysis of behaviour and also the logical sequence of antecedent, behaviour and consequence. For reasons other than sheer perversity, however, we will not consider them in this order here, but will start with B, the behaviour, since behaviour is the primary concern of the whole approach.

Behaviour. What do we mean when we talk about a child's behaviour? And why do we place such great emphasis on specifying exactly what behaviour a child is producing? These questions are fundamental to the behavioural approach. As we said in the introduction to this section behaviourism as a philosophy of science arose as a reaction to the highly speculative approach of early psychologists who attempted to 'explain' man's behaviour by recourse to inborn 'instincts' and to irrational, uncontrollable, unconscious forces within man. Watson, rejected such notions and demanded that the study of man should be based on the observable. Consequently he advocated that behaviour should be studied directly since

14

it could be observed objectively.

We have already said that a child's behaviour refers to what she is actually <u>doing</u> and we attempt to say what a child is doing in as precise a way as possible. If we observe a child building a tower with bricks, we would not write down 'creative play' since another observer or someone else reading our notes might interpret 'creative play' differently. It is too vague and imprecise. We would record that the child constructed a tower of four bricks. To say that it is 'creative' and/or that it is 'play' is to interpret, is prone to inaccuracy and vagueness and is unlikely to be useful. Similarly, if a teacher tells us that Jason is always 'messing about' in class, we have to ask the teacher to define the behaviour more clearly. What you regard as 'messing about' may not be what he regards as 'messing about'. Moreover, if we use a vague definition there is no guarantee that it is the same sort of behaviour we are categorising in this way two days running. So we would ask the teacher to list any of Jason's behaviours which he finds objectionable and then to define them as precisely as possible. A behaviour which is frequently found at the top of many teachers' lists is 'talking out of turn'. If we define this as "any talking by a child when the teacher has requested the class to get on with set work in silence", then we are moving closer towards an objective definition. The more objective our definition, the easier it is for two observers to agree that a certain behaviour has occurred and the easier it is to count instances of such behaviour. Counting instances of behaviour can be an extremely useful, if not essential, component of the behavioural approach to teaching.

Precise definition of behaviour also helps us to avoid the danger of over-interpretation and giving non-explanations as causes of behaviour. Non-explanations sometimes take the form of what are known as 'explanatory fictions'. These are generally unhelpful whilst providing a veneer or gloss of 'scientific' explanation. They can also be dangerous insofar as they can be used to label a child. Labelling is often coupled with the assumption that little can be done about it; the problem is seen as the child and not his behaviour. For example, if Darren keeps hitting other children his teacher may describe him as being aggressive, but if we ask her how she knows this, she may reply "He keeps hitting other children". The word 'aggressive' is simply a label for a child who frequently hits other children but is sometimes used as if it were an <u>explanation</u> of this behaviour.

Consequences. The next item in the three term analysis is C, for consequences. As we said earlier, this refers to the fact that we tend to repeat behaviours which bring us what we want and to refrain from repeating behaviours leading to occurrences which we want to avoid. This appears to be a characteristic of all animals but we differ from animals, and also from each other, in terms of what we seek out and what we seek to avoid. In common with other animals, we tend to seek out food and will repeat behaviours which have led to the provision of food when we are deprived of it. Moreover, many, if not most of us, will work for money. Similarly, the majority of people find praise and approval rewarding and tend to behave in a way which is likely to be followed by praise or approval. On the other hand, perhaps few of us go out of our way to collect train numbers and, thankfully and more seriously, even fewer seek out and behave in a way likely to secure the 'reward' of drugs such as heroin. A major concern within the behavioural approach to teaching is with the identification of things and events which children find rewarding and to structure the teaching environment so as to make access to these rewards dependent upon behaviour which the teacher wants to encourage in his class. Since this is obviously a major issue we will return to it in more detail later. At this stage, however, it is important to attempt to provide a summary of the effects of the various types of consequence upon behaviour.

In simple, everyday language consequences may be described as 'rewarding' or 'punishing'. Rewarding consequences, which we call positive reinforcers, are events which we seek out or 'go for', whilst we try to avoid punishing consequences; neutral consequences are events which affect us neither way. Behaviours followed by positive reinforcers are likely to increase in frequency. Behaviours followed by punishers tend to decrease in frequency whilst neutral consequences have no effect. In the behavioural approach to teaching, infrequent but desired behaviours (for example, getting on with the set work quietly) are made more frequent by arranging for positive reinforcers, such as teacher attention and approval, to follow their occurrence. Undesired behaviours may be decreased in frequency by ensuring that positive reinforcers do not follow their occurrence, i.e. a neutral consequence is arranged. Occasionally it may be necessary to follow undesired behaviours with punishers (for example, a stern 'telling off') in an attempt to reduce the frequency of behaviour rapidly but there are many problems associated with this procedure. Contrary to popular belief, punishment plays only a minor and infrequent role in the behavioural approach, not least because what we believe to be punishing could, in fact, be reinforcing to the child. For example, the child who receives little attention from adults may behave in ways which result in adult disapproval. This child may prefer disapproval to being ignored and will continue to behave like this because adult attention is positively reinforcing. This is known as attention-seeking behaviour.

We should note that terminating a punishing consequence is also reinforcing and can be, and often is, used to increase desired behaviours. This is known as negative reinforcement. Again this has problems associated with its use since the child may rapidly learn other, more effective, ways of avoiding the negative consequence than you had in mind. For example, a teacher may continually use sarcasm and ridicule with his pupils. He ceases only when they behave as he wishes. Another way of avoiding this unpleasant consequence, however, other than by doing as the teacher wishes, is to stay away from school.

Finally one can punish by removing or terminating positive consequences (for example, by taking away a child's sweets). This is known as response cost but again there are similar problems associated with this approach. The following diagram shows the relationships between these various consequences and their effects.

	TO INCREASE BEHAVIOUR(S)	TO DECREASE BEHAVIOUR(S)
DELIVERY OF	'Good things' i.e. rewarding with smiles, sweets, toys, praise, etc. Technical term: Positive reinforcement	'Bad things' i.e. punishing with smacks, frowns, reprimands, etc. Technical term: Punishment
REMOVAL OF	'Bad things' i.e. allowing escape from pain, noise, nagging, threats, etc. Technical term: Negative Reinforcement	'Good things' i.e. losing privileges, house points, money, opportunities to earn 'good things' etc. Technical term: Response Cost

It is important to remember that we are only attempting to provide an overview of the general behavioural approach. We will have more to say about consequences and the technical definitions of what constitutes a punisher or reinforcer later in this chapter. We must now, however, turn to the remaining aspect of the ABC model, A or the antecedent conditions.

Antecedents. It is not sufficient to attempt to examine behaviour simply in terms of behaviours and reinforcers. As well as considering what happens after a behaviour occurs (the consequence) we must also consider what happened before the behaviour occurred. We must examine events which precede as well as events which follow behaviour. Antecedent stimuli or conditions i.e. events which precede behaviour, may also influence its occurrence. They can serve to prompt a certain behaviour. Take the example of when a teacher leaves the room and his class is left alone. For some classes this occurrence will have become a cue for noisy, disruptive behaviour since there is no-one around to reprimand the children. Some classes even post a look-out to give a warning of when the teacher is returning! When he does return the noisy disruptive behaviour will cease. We can see here that this specific antecedent condition has control over this particular behaviour. This control is derived from its association with certain consequences. Take another example which highlights how this might occur.

The teacher asks a child a question in class (antecedent stimulus), the child gives a silly answer (the behaviour), and his classmates laugh (the consequence). If this consequence is positively reinforcing, we may expect the child to produce silly answers upon subsequent similar occasions. He will probably be less likely to do so, however, when his classmates are not there. The presence of his peers has become a stimulus for his misbehaviour. This example gives some of the idea behind the need to consider the context in which behaviours occur. The relationships between A, B and C, the antecedent conditions, the behaviours and the consequences are known as the contingencies of reinforcement. Another important consideration which we must bear in mind, however, is the frequency of reinforcement.

Frequency of Reinforcement

When we want to teach a child to do something new, or to encourage him to behave in a certain way more frequently than he normally does, it is important that we ensure that he is positively reinforced every time he behaves as we want him to. This normally leads to rapid learning and is known as continuous reinforcement. When he has learned the new behaviour and/or is behaving as we want him to do regularly, then we may maintain this behaviour more economically by reducing the frequency of reinforcement. Another important reason for wanting to reduce the frequency is that the child may become less responsive if the positive reinforcer becomes too easily available. Consequently, once a child is regularly behaving in a desired way we can best maintain that behaviour by ensuring that he is now reinforced only <u>intermittently</u>. Intermittent reinforcement can be arranged so that a child is reinforced every so often (i.e. in terms of time) or, alternatively, after so many occurrences of the behaviour. These different ways of organising the frequency of reinforcement are known as <u>reinforcement schedules</u>.

Following this brief summary of basic behavioural theory, we can now turn to a consideration of what the behavioural approach to teaching is all about. With some children the behaviour that concerns us has not yet been learned, with others the behaviour is learned but does not occur frequently enough whilst other children frequently behave in inappropriate ways. The behavioural approach to teaching is about changing the frequencies of behaviour. It can be used to teach new skills or to increase or decrease existing rates of behaviour. It is important to emphasise that the behavioural approach to teaching is primarily concerned with increasing the frequency of <u>desirable</u> behaviour in the classroom.

USING POSITIVE REINFORCEMENT EFFECTIVELY

The basic theory, if it is a theory, seems painfully obvious.

"When he behaves as we want him to behave, we simply create a situation he likes, or remove one he doesn't like. As a result the probability that he will behave that way again goes up, which is what we want." (Skinner, 1948).

What could be simpler? But if it is common sense and we all already know it, why do children not behave in the way we want them to? The main reason is that parents and teachers, whilst sometimes claiming to use the behavioural approach, are often hopelessly inconsistent. It is commonplace to see people using methods of reward and punishment totally unsystematically and then wondering what went wrong.

Sometimes it proves difficult to convince people of the damage they are doing or where they are going wrong. A good example is the behaviour we call 'showing off' in young children; grandparents are often the arch-villains here. Not only do grandparents tend to shower children with edible reinforcers (sweets, cakes, 'pop', etc.) and social reinforcers, they also reinforce either non-systematically or, worse, systematically but upon behaviour which is not desired by the parent. After countless lectures on behavioural methods to my own mother, I finally persuaded her that although my (then young) son, Robin's 'showing off behaviour' amused her as being 'cute', it did not evoke the same response in others, especially his parents! Later she told me proudly that now she did not pay him attention every time he was showing off, only sometimes. As you will probably realise, far from being an improvement, she had effectively changed his reinforcement schedule from continuous reinforcement to an intermittent schedule - a schedule which is far more powerful in maintaining the behaviour!

Similarly, few parents seem to realise that they often bring tantrum troubles upon themselves. How often have we observed the following incident in a shopping precinct. A toddler passing a shop window with his mother sees a toy or lollipop and shouts, "I wannit, I wannit!" Mother says, "Not today dear" and moves on. The child stays behind, begins to stamp his feet and repeat his demand more volubly. The mother again refuses and there follows a series of increasingly vociferous demands, each followed by refusal. At this point the mother often smacks the child in desperation which immediately results in a tearful, screaming fit. The mother embarrassed by the noise and the looks of the passers-by (nearly all of whom sympathise with the child) eventually gives in and buys the child the toy or lollipop. The child stops crying, beams triumphantly and the mother is only too glad that the incident is over. Unfortunately, of course, the problem has only just begun. The mother has quite definitely reinforced the screaming and demanding by giving the child a reward. The next time they go shopping the same situation is more likely to occur as the child has learned that screaming in public brings 'goodies', or that long term 'pestering' will eventually bring a reward.

The best solution to the problem is not to reinforce that behaviour in the first place, but given that the problem exists the only remedy is to employ an <u>extinction</u> procedure, i.e. stop reinforcing the child by refusing to buy goodies in such situations. An ingenious mother will make "goodies" contingent upon good behaviour throughout the shopping trip i.e. the child will only get a present at the end if he behaves satisfactorily throughout. She might also, however, sensibly use praise to reinforce his continuing good behaviour during the trip. An even more ingenious mother who has read up on reinforcement schedules will realise that if she then later only reinforces "being good at the shops" with sweets <u>occasionally</u>, then she will not only save money spent on lollipops but will also have brought good behaviour under greater control.

Lollipops are a fairly safe bet as a reinforcer with most young children, but on occasions it may prove difficult to determine or define appropriate reinforcers. We should remember that reinforcers can be defined post hoc as any event which when following a response increases the probability of that response. Such a definition, however, although it avoids 'explanatory fictions' is open to criticisms of tautology and is less than useful in a practical setting. Skinner has also suggested that what an animal or child will 'go for' is also a good indicator of a reinforcer. This is very useful in practice, as is an extension of this idea known as the Premack principle or colloquially as 'grandma's rule', i.e. "you can go out to play after you've done the chores." More specifically, this principle states that a more frequent behaviour can be used to reinforce a less frequent behaviour by making the more frequent behaviour contingent upon the performance of the less frequent behaviour. For example, you may want a child to practise the piano, which he only does rarely in preference to listening to rock music on the radio. In order to shape up piano practice you merely make listening to rock contingent upon piano practice i.e. he can listen to the radio only after he has completed his practice session.

In determining reinforcers the golden rule is "if it works use it" (within reason!). The most unlikely things can sometimes prove reinforcing; on the other hand, 'obvious' reinforcers may not always work. It is important to remember that reinforcers are defined by their consequences - do they increase behaviour(s) or not? Tom Crabtree, in an article in the Guardian, once described how a hyperactive six year old's extremely distractible (and distracting) behaviour was rapidly reduced over seventeen days by reinforcing "sitting still, keeping quiet, getting on with his work." Reinforcers employed included being allowed to water the plants or ring the bell for morning break and, more creatively, a token system whereby ten stars could be exchanged "for the privilege of feeding the guinea pigs"! Similarly a correspondent to the Observer, a few years ago, apparently ignorant of behavioural methods, nevertheless provided a delightful example of a highly successful behavioural programme she had inaugurated. Driven to distraction by her two children's incessant T.V. viewing during school holidays, she devised a system whereby television time had to be 'bought' by doing jobs around the house, each of which had a certain value ranging from ten minutes to one hour's T.V. viewing time. Not only did helping in the house increase dramatically, including the taking on of jobs which their mother would not have believed them capable of carrying out, but also the co-operation between the two children increased and they became much more discriminating about what they watched on television. This procedure is an almost classic demonstration of the 'Premack Principle', i.e.

making a more frequent behaviour dependent upon the performance of a less frequent behaviour and thereby increasing the frequency of the latter.

Some years ago we were working with a non-verbal four year old - Tim. He had a simple understanding of language but no speech. His disability had been worsened, if not created, by his mother who had, in the vernacular, 'spoilt him', by continually giving in to his gestural or grunted demands and not requiring verbal requests from him. Tim controlled her, rather than she him. Consequently his behaviours were rather idiosyncratic and we had problems finding appropriate reinforcers. Smarties were no good - he would only accept them occasionally and only when given by his mother and only out of a small tube and not from a large box! Observation of his play, however, revealed a passion for jigsaws. Consequently, we used his more frequent jigsaw playing behaviour to shape up less frequent behaviour such as imitation of gestures, (the first step in our language programme). We made the receipt of a piece of jigsaw dependent on his first imitating a behaviour such as clapping or 'hands on head.' This proved highly effective.

Another interesting point about Tim was his reaction to jelly which has often been found to be a convenient, easily dispensed, easily consumed and powerful reinforcer. For Tim, however, it proved to be a totally aversive stimulus! It must be remembered that what is reinforcing for one child is not necessarily reinforcing for another. Not all children will work for Smarties - 'One man's reinforcer is another man's punisher.' The same applies to punishment - what might be punishing for you might not be punishing for a child. Being told off, as previously mentioned, is a good example. For a child who is constantly ignored, the attention involved in being chastised for bad behaviour is preferable to no attention. Consequently, one may observe 'attention seeking behaviours', such as self mutilation or hurting other children, which are maintained by the attention it brings the child as he is being reprimanded.

Serbin and O'Leary (1976), provided a good example of this in their reported case of John, a five year old 'bully'. "When someone did not follow his instructions or give him the toy he wanted, John lost his temper. He pushed, shoved, shouted and threw things." This would cause the other children to complain and his teacher would then intervene. "She strode across the room, pulled John away and spent the next two minutes telling him why he shouldn't hit people. Five minutes later he was hitting another classmate." This demonstrates how a teacher can reinforce exactly the behaviour which is causing the problem. "For John, as for many children, being disruptive is a more effective way of attracting attention than if he behaved well .... Bullies like John are made not born." They were able to extinguish this bullying behaviour quite easily by explaining to the teacher that she must "ignore his aggressive acts except to prevent the victim from being harmed. We suggested that instead she concentrated on the child John was bullying, by saying something warm like, 'I'm very sorry you are hurt. Let me find you a nice game to play with.' When children learn that they will be ignored for their misbehaviour, they stop it almost immediately. John soon stopped bullying." Alongside this ignoring, of course, children like John should be praised when they are playing non-aggressively and behaving well.

Before moving on to consider the applications of positive reinforcement, and other aspects of the behavioural approach, in actual classroom teaching, let us consider the more traditional form of achieving classroom discipline, punishment.

PUNISHMENT AS A MEANS OF SOCIAL CONTROL IN SCHOOLS

By punishment we mean the presentation of an aversive event following the occurrence of a behaviour which has the effect of reducing the frequency of occurrence of that behaviour. There is a misconception regarding negative reinforcement, which is alarmingly common, especially in the writings of those criticising behaviourism, which insists that negative reinforcement and punishment are the same thing. There is no problem, however if you remember that the word 'reinforce' means to strengthen behaviour; a negative reinforcer strengthens behaviour by its removal. One frequently comes across phrases such as "negative reinforcement, that is some kind of punishment, may be effective in extinguishing a response in a child." Such a confusion has serious consequences and amounts to a travesty of what we advocate. For example, Skinner specifically argues against punishment as an effective means of controlling behaviours, but rightly emphasises, whilst also deploring, the use of negative reinforcement in maintaining many behaviours in every day life. He argues that most people go to work, not because they are positively reinforced by the job or the pay, but in order to avoid getting the sack or starving. He has consistently argued for the harnessing of the power of positive reinforcement to produce a better world (Skinner, 1948; 1971).

When I was writing this chapter in a crowded library I was disturbed by two students talking in loud stage whispers. I pointedly looked across at them and their irritating behaviour ceased. What had happened? Presumably, I had delivered a 'conditioned' punisher, (an angry look presumably having been paired at some point in their lives with physical punishment perhaps or some other aversive circumstance). However, within a few minutes the whispering had started up again, albeit at a quieter level. This illustrates one of the problems associated with punishment, that the punished behaviour is merely temporarily suppressed and is likely to recur once the punishment or fear of punishment is removed. Consequently, one needs to continue punishing to suppress a behaviour over a period of time and the mere fact of repeating the punishment is likely to lessen its effectiveness, possibly precipitating the escalation to more severe punishments.

Many schools still seem to be based on the principle of punishing unwanted behaviours whether those behaviours are failures to learn or anti-social acts. School rules invariably consist of a list of 'thou shalt nots', whilst appropriate behaviour is expected rather than encouraged and is rarely specified. A few years ago one of my students showed me the results of a small survey he had conducted in a large urban, comprehensive school. Nearly three quarters of the fifth year boys reported being both hurtfully hit by teachers and officially caned (of these over 65% felt it was deserved!). Only half of this proportion of second year boys had been officially caned but just as large a proportion had been hurtfully hit. Figures were generally much lower for girls (20% of fifth year girls hurtfully hit, 12% officially caned). John Holt (1962) in 'How Children Fail' has written of "why intelligent children act unintelligently at school." The simple answer, he claims, is "because they're scared ..... most children in school are scared most of the time, many of them very scared." Scared not only of physical punishment as detailed above, but of being verbally abused, sarcastically scored off, shown up in front of peers and generally demeaned. None of this is conducive to learning appropriate behaviours but will result only in forms of escape/avoidance behaviours which may sometimes include doing what the teacher wants but may more frequently include opting out of his area of influence whenever possible. As Becker, Thomas and Carnine (1969) remark:
"Avoidance and escape behaviour often have names such as lying, hiding, truancy, cheating in exams., doing things behind one's back, etc. Accompanying such avoidance and escape behaviours are negative feelings for the persons who use punishment. For the most part, the teacher is wise to find other means for influencing children."

I have often wondered why people, especially perhaps parents, continue to use punishment since it is so ineffective and has so many drawbacks. One possibility is that parents continue to punish because occasionally, in the past, punishing the child has led to the immediate (but temporary) cessation of an unwanted behaviour. Insofar as this reinforces the parent (he got what he wanted) he will continue to indulge in punishing behaviour even though he is only occasionally reinforced by it having the desired effect. In other words the parent's behaviour is under the control of an intermittent schedule of reinforcement - one of the most powerful means of maintaining a behaviour and highly resistant to extinction. The parent and child are thus, literally, in a <u>vicious</u> circle.

A moment's thought reveals the nonense of attempting to teach by means of punishment. Consider a simple learning situation where the teacher wants the child, Gavin, to get on with his work ('studying behaviour') and not to chatter, not to look out of the window, not to get out of his seat, not to disturb other children, etc. Remembering that punishment constitutes an attempt to eliminate a certain behaviour by making aversive consequences contingent upon that behaviour, the teacher decides to punish Gavin whenever he does anything other than get on with his work. She decides to deliver a very definite punisher and smack him whenever he engages in anything other than studying behaviour. Gavin pinches his neighbour, she smacks him. He gets up, she smacks him again. He looks out of the window, she smacks him again, harder this time. He begins to wail, she smacks him yet again. Gavin wails louder than ever; the teacher feels exhausted and miserable. All of her attention has been focussed on only one child, ignoring the other twenty nine who are now all watching her and Gavin, and still she has failed to teach him to get on with his work. All of this points to the simple fact that it is far more efficient to reinforce desired behaviour than it is to punish all the unwanted behaviours; for example, by remarking "Look how well Gavin is getting on with his work."

Delivering punishment also has another danger; it paves the way for shaping up other unwanted behaviour by means of negative reinforcement. By definition, we do not like or 'go for' punishment, we attempt to avoid it. Consequently, as noted earlier, avoiding the teacher, running out of the class or staying away from school are behaviours which will be rapidly learned if the child is continually punished in school as they constitute an escape from punishment and are hence (negatively) reinforcing. It seems reasonable to suggest that truancy, school phobia, school refusal, or whatever new name we have for it, may often be simply the product of a school environment which the child finds either aversive or lacking in positive reinforcements compared with what is available outside. The behavioural teacher would argue that in order to be successful, schools must be places where the desired behaviours are carefully specified and positive reinforcement is made contingent upon them. The main emphasis should be on positive reinforcement in order to maintain an efficient and effective learning agency and which will, as a result, also be a happy one.

As a postscript to this section it is worth noting that corporal punishment finally appears to be on the way out in British schools. The results from schools which have abandoned these barbaric, and as we have argued, inefficient methods are encouraging. The number of physical attacks on teachers by pupils dropped dramatically following the decision to outlaw corporal punishment in inner London schools. In Scotland it was shown that schools which had abolished corporal punishment did not suffer a decline in discipline and that none of these schools wanted to re-introduce corporal punishment. As this evidence accumulates it will become increasingly hard to justify Britain's place as the only European country which continues to beat its children in schools. Are British children so badly behaved in comparison with their European peers or are British teachers so much poorer than their European colleagues, that such primitive methods are still necessary in Britain? Whatever the reasons, we would argue that the behavioural approach offers both a more positive and a more efficient alternative. Let us now turn to some of our demonstration studies of successful behavioural interventions carried out in schools. These studies provide examples of how the behavioural approach is applied in practice.

A GAME APPROACH TO INCREASING THE FREQUENCY OF DESIRABLE CLASSROOM BEHAVIOUR IN THE PRIMARY SCHOOL

Disruptive behaviour in the classroom is widely acknowledged as being one of the major problems facing many teachers. Such problems are not confined to Secondary schools as the results of a recent survey of Primary school teachers has shown (Merrett and Wheldall, 1978). A survey of nineteen Primary schools in the 'inner ring' of a West Midlands borough was carried out in 1976. Of the 196 teachers approached, 60% replied to the questionnaire and of these, 62% replied 'yes' to the question, "Do you feel that you spend more time dealing with problems of order and control than you ought?". The survey went on to obtain opinion as to which disruptive behaviours caused the most trouble in class. It was shown clearly that teachers regard 'talking out of turn' (defined as carrying on a conversation with other children, blurting out when not called upon, making comments and remarks) as the most troublesome behaviour followed closely by non-attending and disobeying, and disturbing others, which includes 'aggression'. Talking out of turn accounts for almost a third of the misbehaviour in classrooms according to this survey of teacher opinion. A common awareness of the problems associated with disruptive behaviour in the classroom is, however, unfortunately matched by widespread ignorance regarding behavioural techniques of classroom management. Only a minority of teachers will have encountered the behavioural approach based on operant learning theory. Very few Colleges of Education provide training in behavioural principles and procedures and the only teachers likely to have encountered the technique during the course of their work are those in Special Schools.

The ways of maintaining control in an unruly classroom are many and various, but the key principle is basically praise the good, and try to ignore the bad. Becker, Madsen and Thomas (1967) and Madsen, Becker and Thomas (1968) in classic studies on this, compared "rules, praise and ignoring", i.e.

a) set a series of simple rules which are made known to the class, e.g. "we sit quietly while working",

b) ignore all behaviour contravening these rules where possible.

c) catch the children being good and reinforce them.

They compared various combinations of these three basic procedures. The first condition, rules only, had little effect in reducing undesirable behaviour. The results were still inconsistent when 'ignoring' was added. But the third combination in which praise was added to 'rules' and 'ignoring' was shown to be a highly effective procedure for maintaining classroom control. Hence they concluded that "praise for appropriate behaviour was probably the key teacher behaviour in achieving effective classroom management".

Similarly, an experiment by Thomas, Becker and Armstrong (1968) showed how 'good' teachers who normally maintain a well ordered classroom by ignoring inappropriate behaviours and by consistently reinforcing appropriate behaviours, can, by altering these contingencies, produce dramatic deterioration in classroom behaviour. In one study disruptive behaviour was raised from the normal low level of around 8-9% to over 40% accompanied by an appreciable rise in noise level. This was 'achieved' by the teacher frequently expressing disapproval for inappropriate behaviours. Thus it has been shown experimentally that whilst reinforcing (by expressing approval of) desirable behaviours leads to increased good behaviour, attending to inappropriate behaviour, even by expressing disapproval, may increase the very behaviours it is attempting to reduce. It has similarly been shown that increasing the number of 'sit down' commands _increases_ the amount of out of seat behaviour, whilst praising for in seat behaviour _reduces_ out of seat behaviour.

In our own study demonstrating one approach to behavioural classroom management, we want to devise a positive approach which the children would actually find enjoyable. Consequently, rather than concentrating on trying to eliminate undesirable behaviours which is known to be ineffective, we decided to concentrate on the behaviour we wanted, i.e. getting on with school work or 'studying behaviour' and to try to raise the frequency of what was in the class we studied, relatively infrequent behaviour. As we make clear in our paper (Merret and Wheldall, 1978), the approach was not totally original, being based on several other studies employing 'game' strategies, but it was highly successful.

The subject was a young, relatively inexperienced, female teacher, who was having a lot of trouble in controlling her class of 30 intellectualy below average 10 - 11 year olds attending a state primary school. Classroom seating was arranged around four tables and we decided to make use of this in our intervention strategy.

However, initially we needed more specific and accurate information about the childrens' behaviour in the classroom. A cassette-tape was prepared to give a clear 'ping' on a 'variable interval' schedule of sixty seconds i.e. at irregular intervals but on average once per minute. On hearing the sound the teacher would look at one of the four tables of children, indicated in random order on a pre-prepared sheet, and note the behaviour of the target child for that table by ticking the appropriate column. The target child was chosen afresh for each observation session on a random basis and thus all children in the class were observed during the study. Every time she heard the 'ping' the teacher had to glance at the schedule to see which table was next and record the behaviour of the target child by ticking appropriately. She could do this whilst working at her desk and, with experience, whilst walking around the room advising individuals and commenting on their work. The reliability of the teacher's results was checked from time to time by the experimenter using an identical record sheet and the same target children, and there was found to be very high agreement.

After several weeks of practice, 'baseline' data was collected i.e. data collected prior to the teacher being given any instruction in behavioural methods (she also had no prior knowledge of the behavioural approach). By averaging over sessions we calculated that the children were on task, i.e. quietly getting on with their work, only 44% of the time. The teacher was then given some basic instruction in the

behavioural approach and an intervention strategy was
suggested to her. She readily agreed since she was well aware
of the rather 'chaotic' state of her classroom.

Briefly, the children were told the rules of a 'game' which
were:

    a)   we stay in our seats whilst working,
    b)   we get on quietly with our work,
    c)   we try not to interrupt.

Whilst the game was in progress, the cassette would be
switched on and every time the 'ping' sounded the teacher
would look at one of the tables. If everyone on the table was
keeping the rules, then each child on the table would score a
house point. (They were assured that all tables would get
equal turns but that the order would be random). Each time a
team point was given it was accompanied by verbal praise.
This procedure lasted for five weeks when an amendment was
announced. In future points would be awarded on only 50% of
the signals (pings), again on a random basis. The pings
continued to serve the teacher as a signal for observing and
recording the behaviour of the target children as well as a
signal for reinforcement.

The results were remarkable and immediate. From the baseline
on task behaviour of only 44%, it rose to 77% following the
intervention. Moreover, when the amendment to the schedule of
reinforcement was made, after five weeks, the on task
behaviour rose even higher to between 80 and 100%.
Interestingly the quality of 'off task' behaviour also
changed. Whereas before the intervention disruptiveness was
mainly shown in loud talking and quite a lot of movement
around the room, after intervention off task behaviour
consisted mainly of passive inattention, daydreaming, watching
other children etc.

A purely subjective estimate of the classroom after the
intervention was of great improvement in terms of orderliness
and quiet during classroom work periods. An attempt was also
made to measure academic output both before and after
intervention. For example, samples of written work taken from
the class during the collection of baseline data showed a mean
output of approximately 5 written words per minute. During
one of the first intervention sessions this had improved to a
mean of approximately 13 written words. However the number of
spelling errors, despite the big increase in output, had
hardly changed.

Comment was invited from the teacher once the project was
completed. She used the term 'harrowing' to describe her

problems with class control in her first (probationary) year. The recording of baseline data had proved "tedious and time-consuming" at first but she thought that it became easier and less distracting after practice. She said she "felt silly" about putting up the wall chart of rules, but she agreed that the effect of the intervention was immediate and very effective and said that she would continue using behavioural techniques especially in providing positive reinforcement for good behaviour. Some of the children were also asked their opinion of the game. Of the thirteen who responded, twelve were approving. All of those approving commented upon the fact that the quietness that prevailed enabled them to concentrate and get on with their work without interruption. Eight referred to the chance of earning house-points. The one child, a girl, who did not approve of the game, found the 'ping' distracting, but liked the idea of working for house points.

One issue which surprised both authors was the effectiveness of house-points. It had been supposed that some stronger back-up reinforcement would be needed to make the game effective. Perhaps the house-points worked so well because the intervention took place shortly after the system had been introduced and because it, in turn, was backed up by the award of badges to be worn in school. What remains a mystery is the great reluctance of this teacher, who is not atypical, to use verbal reinforcers, in spite of having been impressed by the effectiveness of behavioural techniques. It remains a question for our future research to determine why teachers typically praise desired behaviours only infrequently, whilst continually commenting upon undesired behaviour. Could it be that teachers are more certain of what they do not want than of what they do want? Or is that unfair?!

THE BEHAVIOURAL APPROACH IN A SECONDARY SCHOOL

A common reaction to reports of studies such as the one described above is that such an approach would only work with young children. We have recently completed a study to demonstrate the effectiveness of behavioural approaches to classroom management with a class of older children. Few of the mass of studies reporting behavioural interventions in schools referred to secondary schools, a view recently endorsed by McNamara and Harrop (1979). Many are sceptical of success in such settings, believing that at best it would necessitate a highly complicated, powerful procedure. Consequently this study evolved to demonstrate that control could be achieved equally well in a secondary classroom using only 'light' behavioural procedures.

We selected a large comprehensive in a deprived, urban area and located a difficult class of 25 fourteen year-olds from the lowest three of ten 'streams'. Since all teachers involved with this class admitted difficulties privately, but were reluctant to admit this publicly by volunteering, the headmaster, who taught the class remedial maths for five lessons per week, volunteered himself. Our observations of him and the class revealed that he was an impressive teacher who rarely shouted and who, relatively speaking, used a lot of praise. The class appeared to like and respect him but our eleven days of baseline observation showed that they were on task only 55% of the time. Many of the students were often off task because they had finished the set work (usually a set of 'sums' put up on the board) and did not know what to do next, whilst others had not finished but were being disturbed by those who had. Consequently we suggested that a few more problems be put up on the board for the quicker ones to get on with while the slower ones caught up (i.e. a manipulation of an antecedent condition for on task behaviour).

The Head agreed and the observations for the next seven lessons showed improved on task behaviour by nearly 15% to an average of around 70%. We decided that this could be improved still further and a comparison was made between a 'light' strategy of using only a simple 'rules, praise and ignore' procedure and a 'heavier' alternative, whereby points could be earned which gained free time. This resulted in what is known as an alternating conditions design in which simple contingent praise alternated daily with the other strategy whereby, on a group contingency basis, the class could earn one minute's free time each time they were all on task when a timer sounded (variable interval two minutes), as judged by the teacher. Free time was taken during the Friday afternoon lesson; 25 points winning the whole 40 minute lesson off.

The head agreed to these procedures and the results were dramatic. The design of our study clearly showed further improvement in on-task behaviour to over 80% produced by the rules, praise and ignoring strategy and to over 90% during timer game sessions. The two strategies finally merged at around 95% 'on-task'. The study thus provided:

1) a clear demonstration of successful behavioural approaches in a secondary school,

and 2) proof of the power of simple procedures such as contingent praise and the manipulation of antecedent conditions ('more sums' in this case).

In this study (reported in more detail in Wheldall and Austin, 1980) some reference was made to the notion of changing the antecedent conditions for behaviour. In the final example of our demonstration studies, we report another more overt manipulation of an antecedent event, i.e. classroom seating arrangements.

CHANGING CHILDREN'S BEHAVIOUR BY CHANGING THE CLASSROOM ENVIRONMENT

Most teachers will have noticed how the behaviour of a certain class varies depending on who is teaching them or even depending on where they are being taught. In other words, the behaviour of classes of children comes under what behavioural psychologists call stimulus control, whereby different stimulus conditions are followed by different forms of behaviour. Being in Softy Simpson's room may become the stimulus for unruly behaviour, for example, whilst few would dare even to breathe loudly in Biffer Barnes' class. Similarly, academic lessons, held by necessity in the art and craft room by the same teacher, may lead to more off task or disruptive behaviour than when held in a regular classroom. Being in the art and craft room has become associated with a different form of behaviour, involving more movement around the room perhaps.

As we said earlier, it is not enough to attempt to analyse children's behaviour merely in terms of responses and reinforcers. As well as considering what happens following a behaviour (the consequence) we must also consider what happens before the behaviour occurs, the antecedent conditions.

It has been shown, for example, that location, where children sit in class, dramatically affects the number of questions they are asked, (Moore, 1980). Other studies have shown that during story sessions and demonstrations, kindergarten children's 'on task' behaviour (paying atention to the teacher) was higher when the children were placed so as to allow space between each child and his neighbours, than when they clustered around their teacher. On task behaviour was also higher if the session was preceded by a rest period rather than by a session of vigorous activity, giving the lie to the common sense view of children being quieter after "having got 'it' out of their systems", (Krantz and Risley, 1977).

In Britain, classroom seating whereby desks or tables are arranged in rows is the norm in secondary schools and this was also the case in primary schools until the sixties. The influential Plowden report advocated a generally less formal aproach to primary education favouring learning by discovery via topic and project work. This appears to have been acompanied by a move towards less formal seating arrangements, away from rows to a preference for table formations. In this latter arrangement, desks or tables are arranged so that four to eight children sit around a common work area. This new seating arrangement was widely adopted and is still the most commonly found arrangement, being employed for overtly academic, individual, task orientated work (e.g. workcards), as well as group work. To our knowledge, however, no empirical evidence was ever adduced to support this change of seating arrangement. Our own research comparing the effects of different seating arrangements in classrooms was inspired by, and replicates and extends, recent work by Alexrod, Hall and Tams (1979).

We have recently carried out two parallel studies comparing 'tables' and 'rows' type seating arrangements in two state junior schools, (Wheldall et al., 1981). In both schools a fourth year class of 10-11 year old children was chosen. One class consisted of 28 mixed sex and ability children attending a school in an urban residential area whereas the other class consisted of 25 similar children from a school on a council housing estate. In both classes the children normally sat around tables in groups of 4, 5 and 6, except for end of term tests when they sat in rows. The design, procedure and, indeed, results of the two studies were very similar.

The children were initially observed for two weeks (ten days) in their normal seating arrangements around tables. An observation schedule using a time sampling procedure (described below) was employed to obtain estimates of on task behaviour. This was defined, by the teachers, as doing what the teacher instructed i.e. looking at and listening to her when she was talking to them, looking at their books or work cards when they were required to complete set work, only being out of seats with the teacher's permission, etc. In the second study observations were carried out at different times including all lessons except P.E., Art and Music, whereas in the first study observations were only made during purely academic lessons when the children had been given specific work to complete. Calling out, talking to neighbours, interrupting, etc. were regarded as off task by the teachers in both studies.

The observation schedule required each child to be observed twice per lesson in random order for 30 seconds. This was broken down into six, five second periods. If the child was on task for the whole five seconds he scored one point; if off task for any of the five seconds he did not score. Hence, this yielded a score out of six for each 30 second period and a score out of twelve for the two observation periods per child per lesson combined, which was subsequently converted to a percentage. This gave us an estimate of percentage on task behaviour for each child for each lesson which, when averaged, gave an estimate of on task behaviour for the whole class.

After observing the class for two weeks sitting around tables (baseline data), the desks/tables were moved into rows without comment from the teacher and the children were observed for a further two weeks (eight days in the first study, ten days in the second study) using the same procedure. Finally, the desks were moved back to their original positions, again without comment, for a further two weeks of observation (seven days in the first study; ten days in the second study). This time there were a few complaints from the children since they preferred sitting in rows.

In short, on task behaviour rose by around 15% overall when the children were placed in rows and fell by nearly as much when they returned to tables. Note how similar the general picture is for the two classes.

Average percentage on task behaviour in each phase

	Tables	Rows	Tables
Study 1	72	88	69
Study 2	67	84	72

Looking at individual children, the most marked improvements in on task behaviour occurred within those children whose on task behaviour was previously very low. As we might expect, the effect was lessened in the case of children with high initial on task behaviour. One or two children in each study showed higher on task behaviour in groups; especially one child in the second study, the noisy ringleader of an anti-school group, who spent most of his time in rows trying to regain contact with his group!

We have also carried out a more detailed (as yet unpublished) study on seating arrangements in a special school for E.S.N. (M.) children with behaviour problems. In this study we also included observations of disruptive behaviour and teacher behaviours. A huge amount of data was collected in this study of which only a brief report can be presented here.

Three classes were observed for four phases of 10 observations spread over approximately two week intervals. Again, seating was normally arranged around tables. In the first phase, observation was carried out in the usual (tables) conditions to provide baseline data, followed by phase 2 in which the class was moved into rows. Phase 3 constituted a return to the tables seating arrangement followed, by phase 4, in which seating was again arranged in rows. All lessons took place in the same room and were maths lessons given by the same teacher to all three classes: a junior class of 11 children, a middle class of 11 children and a senior class of 12 children.

The results dramatically confirmed and extended our previous findings. For every class on task behaviour doubled during rows and fell during tables conditions. Similarly, rate of disruptions trebled during tables and fell during rows.

Average percentage on task behaviour in each phase

	Tables 1	Rows 1	Tables 2	Rows 2
Junior Class	27	72	32	68
Middle Class	34	72	37	71
Senior Class	37	73	36	69

Average number of disruptions in each phase

	Tables 1	Rows 1	Tables 2	Rows 2
Junior Class	49	10	28	9
Middle Class	25	9	24	7
Senior Class	18	6	19	8

We also observed changes in teacher behaviour. Positive comments consistently went up during rows conditions whilst negative comments decreased. Thus the teacher apparently found it easier to praise and to refrain from disapproval when the children were seated in rows.

Before commenting on the conclusions to be drawn from our studies we must attempt to answer the question "Why does seating around tables lead to more disruption, less on task behaviour and less desirable teacher behaviour?". We believe that the answer is quite simple. A table arrangement is geared towards enhancing social interaction. It facilitates eye contact, a prime means of initiating a social encounter, and provides a setting for increased participation in such encounters by involving the whole group. After all, we engineer such seating arrangements in precisely this way when we wish to encourage social interaction, in committees or when playing bridge, for example. Moreover, tables provide ideal cover for covert aggression or teasing, by means of kicking or pinching under the table, thereby increasing disruption. Rows formations, on the other hand, minimize either form of social

35

contact, allowing fewer occasions for the teacher to comment adversely and more instances of desirable behaviour for him or her to comment upon favourably. In short it could be argued that it amounts to little short of cruelty to place children in manifestly social contexts and then to expect them to work independently.

We must immediately emphasise, however, that we are not advocating a return to rows for all work. We offer it only as a possible strategy to encourage academic work which requires the child to concentrate on the specific task in hand without distractions. Rows would be totally inappropriate, for example, for small group discussions or group topic work, where table arrangements might prove more effective. Alternatively a horse shoe arrangement of desks around the room facing inwards might well facilitate our class discussion sessions as well as allowing children to get on with individual work when necessary. These are empirical questions which we hope to tackle in our future research.

These results on seating arrangements constitute just one lesson to be learned from the behavioural approach to teaching. Certainly they should cause us to doubt our current pre-occupation with fixed classroom seating arrangements and to encourage us to experiment with seating so as to optimize the appropriate behaviour for the task in hand and to discourage inappropriate behaviours. Further studies, and also commentary on various aspects of the behavioural approach to teaching, are reported in Wheldall (1981) and Wheldall and Merrett (1982).

BUT THAT'S WHAT I DO ALREADY

Many teachers on first hearing about the behavioural approach understandably react by saying "But that's what I do already!" It is unlikely that many teachers are employing behavioural techniques effectively, however, otherwise there would be fewer harassed teachers! The confusion arises as a result of teachers sometimes dismissing the behavioural approach as 'obvious' or 'common sense' based on a failure to have paid sufficient attention to, and to utilize, certain key principles which underpin the whole system. The techniques advocated are very similar, if not identical, to the procedures utilised by skilled teachers; nor is this surprising since few children would learn very much that is useful and desirable if these principles were not sometimes being followed. But there are differences which it is easy to gloss over in a spirit of self-righteousness. The most important of these is undoubtedly consistency. How many teachers could put their hands on their hearts and claim to reinforce desired behaviours and ignore undesirable behaviours consistently? Nor is this a cause for shame, since few teachers have been trained to do so, but this is the ultimate key to success. One cannot expect to achieve success with the behavioural approach unless the principles are followed consistently.

Another bone of contention is the nature of reinforcement. How many teachers actually enthusiastically reinforce desired behaviours, rather than giving a begrudging tick or a "that's O.K." Remember the teacher does not define the reinforcer - it defines itself by its effect on behaviour. It could be that you, the teacher, are not a very powerful source of social reinforcement since you have little to offer the child. It is comforting to believe that your approval is desired and is reinforcing, but is it? Ask yourself whose approval is valued by the children in your school and attempt to determine why. What have you got to offer children that will make your approval desirable? In other words you should attempt to build up your approval into a powerful social reinforcer by pairing it with known desirable consequences (existing reinforcers), i.e. make sure you become associated with events which your children really 'go for'.

What about immediacy of reinforcement? Do you wait until the end of the week to tell Jones that his handwriting has improved? Delay between the behaviour and the presentation of the reinforcer has been shown to weaken its effect. Similarly, are you structuring the classroom situation so as to encourage desirable behaviour to occur by re-arranging the seating, for example? These points are raised to serve as reminders of the sort of care needed to teach effectively using the behavioural approach. No-one is claiming that it is an easy fool-proof method. It is dependent upon skills being learned so well that they become automatic; skills which it is unlikely that you were taught at college or which were, at least, never presented within a cohesive conceptual framework, such as that provided by behavioural psychology. It is an approach well worth studying and a programme of skills well worth learning since, whilst it does not provide you with a curriculum of what to teach, it provides you with the most efficient method of teaching and a truly positive approach to classroom discipline.

REFERENCES

Axelrod, S., Hall, R.V. and Tams, A. Comparison of two common classroom seating arrangements. Academic Therapy, 1979, 15, 29-36.

Becker, W.C., Madsen, C.H. Jnr, Arnold, C.R. and Thomas D.R. The contingent use of teacher attention and praise in reading classroom behaviour problems. Journal of Special Education, 1967, 1, 287-307.

Becker, W.C., Thomas, D.R. and Carnine, D. Reducing Behaviour Problems: An Operant Conditioning Guide for Teachers. (National Laboratory on Early Childhood Education, Urbana, Illinois, 1969).

Holt, J. How Children Fail. (Penguin, Harmondsworth, 1969).

Krantz, P.J. and Risley, T.R. Behavioural ecology in the classroom. In O'Leary, K.D. and O'Leary, S.F. (Eds.), Classroom Management: the Successful Use of Behaviour Modification (second edition). (Pergamon Press, New York, 1979).

McNamara, E. and Harrop, L.A. Behaviour modification in the secondary school: a cautionary tale. Occasional Papers of the Division of Educational and Child Psychology of the British Psychological Society, 1979, 3, 38-41.

Madsen, C.H., Becker, W.C. and Thomas, D.R. Rules, praise and ignoring elements of elementary classroom control. Journal of Applied Behaviour Analysis, 1968, 1, 139-150.

Merrett, F. and Wheldall, K. Playing the game: a behavioural approach to classroom management. Educational Review, 1978, 30, 391-400.

Moore, D. Location as a causal factor in the unequal distribution of teacher questions: an experimental analysis. Proceedings of the Third Australian Conference on Behaviour Modification. (A.B.M.A., Melbourne, 1980).

Serbin, L. and O'Leary, D. First lessons in inequality. Psychology Today, 1976, 2, 12 - 15.

Skinner, B.F. Walden Two. (MacMillan, New York, 1948).

Skinner, B.F. Beyond Freedom and Dignity. (Cape, London, 1971).

Thomas, D.R., Becker, W.C. and Armstrong, M. Production and elimination of disruptive classroom behaviour by systematically varying teacher's behaviour. Journal of Applied Behaviour Analysis, 1968, 1, 35-45.

Wheldall, K and Austin, R. Successful behaviour modification in the secondary school: a reply to McNamara and Harrop. Occasional Papers of the Division of Educational and Child Psychology of the British Psychological Society, 1980, 4, 3-9.

Wheldall, K. (ed.). The Behaviourist in the Classroom: Aspects of Applied Behavioural Analysis in British Educational Contexts. (Educational Review Publications, Birmingham, 1981).

Wheldall, K., Morris, M., Vaughan, P. and Ng, Y.Y. Rows versus tables: an example of the use of behavioural ecology in two classes of eleven year old children. Educational Psychology, 1981, 1, 171-184.

Wheldall, K. and Merrett, F. Positive Teaching: the Behavioural Approach. (Allen and Unwin, Hemel Hampstead, 1982).

Chapter 2

BUILDING AN EFFECTIVE TEACHING ENVIRONMENT

TED GLYNN

A key behavioural principle that appears to be little
appreciated and greatly under-utilized in classroom teaching
is the principle that learning can be facilitated and
inhibited by altering the stimulus conditions or "setting
events" within the physical and social context of the
classroom. As was made clear in the previous chapter, a
behavioural approach should utilize not only consequent
events, which follow behaviour, but also antecedent events, or
conditions which precede or accompany learning in the
classroom This is not to deny the importance or power of
procedures based on positive reinforcement but it is argued
that such procedures should be used more selectively and
discriminatingly in classroom teaching. This chapter draws on
contemporary applied behavioural research to illustrate how
both stimulus conditions (setting events) and selective
reinforcement procedures may be used to enhance children's
learning in the classroom.

Some of the common features of a behavioural approach to
teaching include the need for gathering objective and
systematic information, the need for continuous measurement
and the need for instructional decision-making to be data-
based. Teachers employing such behavioural procedures may be
characterized as being responsive to data. They change or
modify their teaching behaviour in response to objective
information about their own and their children's performance.
In this chapter various ways of teachers changing their
behaviour in response to information on child and teacher
behaviour will be discussed. These are grouped according to
the two principles of manipulating setting events and the
selective use of reinforcement procedures.

MANIPULATING SETTING EVENTS

The concept of setting events, their identification and use is
of major importance in the behavioural approach to teaching.

Bijou and Baer (1978) note that

"a setting event influences an interactional sequence by altering the characteristics of particular stimulus and response functions involved in an interaction " (p. 26)

Within the classroom environment it is known that a wide range of stimulus conditions will influence behaviour. These range from physical events like noise level and seating arrangements (see previous chapter) or the presence or absence of particular curriculum materials, to social events such as the presence or absence of an audience of adults or peers. These social-environmental variables or setting events can strongly influence the quality of teacher-child interaction that can take place. Knowledge of their operation is thus vital to a behavioural approach to classroom teaching.

Research by Risley (1977) and Krantz and Risley (1977) within the general context of ecological psychology illstrates the importance of classroom environmental variables on the on-task behaviour of children (see previous chapter). Further research by Hart and Risley (1975) demonstrates the strength of naturally occurring adult-child interactions as particularly important setting events for academic learning. McNaughton (1980) argues that the structuring of learning settings for academic tasks including the way curriculum materials are presented, organized and sequenced, and the use of instructions, are setting events which influence specific interactions among instructional materials, instructor and learner. Research from these four perspectives will now be examined.

1. Classroom Environmental Variables as Setting Events

Much of the classroom research investigating environmental variables as setting events has been concerned with the management of children's social behaviour and was referred to in the preceding chapter. Consequently we provide here examples concerning other aspects of behaviour which might concern teachers.

Baker (in an unpublished study supervised by the author) was able to increase dramatically the amount of food eaten at lunch by a problem eater in a day care centre. In a multi-element (or alternating conditions) design, Baker either sat with the child and conversed with him while he ate, or merely supervised from a distance (normal routine). At no time did she reinforce the child for eating or punish him for not eating, rather she merely engaged him in conversation. Under normal routine supervision this child ate approximately seven spoonsful of food, while in the company of the day care supervisor, he ate approximately 21 spoonsful. The conversation of the supervisor appeared to operate as a powerful setting event for eating. This finding supports those of Glynn, Glynn and Lawless (1978) in which the presence or absence of parents during mealtimes clearly affected the amount of food eaten by a family of five children. Children ate more when parents were present.

An unpublished study by Frewin (also supervised by the author) in a University day care setting, demonstrated that the presence of an adult near the jig-saw table greatly increased the number of children participating in that activity. This effect was clear whether the jig-saws were displayed openly on the table, or stacked together. Similarly O'Rourke and Glynn (1978) found that playground participation increased and inappropriate behaviour decreased more permanently, when participating adults were introduced into an intermediate school playground, than when additional equipment, static and moveable, was provided. Participating adults were a more powerful setting event for a high rate of playground participation by children than the additional equipment.

2. One-to-one Interactions as Setting Events

The presence or availability of an interacting adult is a major setting event exerting a powerful influence on children's learning in the classroom. Brief periods of individual attention within the classroom context set the occasion for an important type of teacher-child interaction which rarely occurs during class or small-group instruction.

This one-to-one interaction allows the teacher to monitor and to provide immediate feedback to individual children on their current performance on academic tasks. However, the one-to-one setting can occasion behaviours that are either productive or counterproductive for children's learning. If teachers use one-to-one interaction entirely as a setting for evaluative assessment, concerned only with detecting errors and making critical comments, then one-to-one interaction may function as a setting event for poor task performance and even avoidance and withdrawal behaviours. This could be the case for children who are poor readers and who actively avoid being called on to read to the teacher.

Alternatively, teachers may use one-to-one interaction as a setting for providing children with individualized qualitative feedback on the effectiveness of their performance on academic tasks. Teachers may also use the one-to-one setting as an opportunity for monitoring their own teaching strategies. McNaughton, Glynn and Robinson (1980) for example emphasize the importance of the one-to-one setting in oral reading for both reader and tutor, for both these reasons and for the reason that this setting provides an opportunity for the teachers to monitor and reinforce important self management behaviours in children, (e.g. self correction of errors).

In the area of oral language skills, Hart and Risley (1975) demonstrated the efficiency of spontaneously occurring adult-child interactions for the incidental teaching of language skills (labelling and describing). Incidental teaching situations were interactions initiated by children, usually when requesting adult assistance for help with obtaining materials or handling clothing. These child-initiated interactions provided a powerful setting event for the practice and refinement of oral language skills. Since appropriate use of language leads in these settings to the child obtaining the desired object or activity, there is little need for additional external reinforcement. The naturally occurring setting events sufficed to modify children's oral language.

In these oral reading and incidental teaching situations the one-to-one context can be viewed as a setting event for mutually rewarding interaction, leading to gains in skill for both child and teacher. Perhaps this is the case when interested children line up eagerly wanting to read aloud to their teacher or to show a piece of completed work.

Teachers employing a behavioural approach will monitor whether all children in their class receive sufficient opportunities for such one-to-one interaction. Data from an unpublished study by the present author and his colleagues suggested that one special class teacher spent progressively more individual time with those children making greatest progress under a behavioural programme to improve oral reading accuracy. The child showing lowest progress received proportionately less individual teacher time.

It is possible that the high rate of progress from hither-to low-progress readers became a setting event for more mutually rewarding teacher child interaction. Quite unintentionally, this teacher appeared to be calling on the high progress readers more often for one-to-one oral reading sessions. Low progress children need more opportunities than high progress children for individual feedback on their academic performance, not less.

It will take close and careful monitoring for teachers to establish whether for each particular child their one-to-one interaction functions as a setting event for avoidance, or for positive interaction and whether some children are being denied access to this opportunity.

3. Curriculum Materials as Setting Events

Another type of setting event in classroom learning concerns the presentation of instructional materials. The importance of this type of setting event can also be illustrated within the context of oral reading instruction. Providing a beginning reader with a set of cards each containing an individual word, or with a list of separate words is likely to be a setting event for teacher questions such as "what's this word?" and for examining words in isolation, and making single word responses. This may in turn limit teacher feedback to a simple indication of correct or incorrect. Such teacher child interactions are unlikely to provide qualitative feedback to child or teacher.

Providing a beginning reader with a natural language text, however simple the sentences, is likely to be a setting event for a much wider range of child and teacher behaviour. The teacher may require the child to point to separate words while hearing the sentence read. The child may be asked to predict the meaning of an unknown word from the information available either from graphic cues in letters or words or from the semantic and syntactic cues in the remaining words. The teacher might provide the child with information about the usefulness of his strategies for predicting or solving unknown words, whether or not the attempt was correct in a particular instance.

Thus, two sets of curriculum materials can function as different setting events for quite different teacher-child interaction. The style of teacher-child interaction occasioned by the use of meaningful texts is consistent with contemporary theories on the nature of reading (Clay, 1979; Smith, 1978). McNaughton et al (1980) consider that for older low-progress readers the most important setting event is sufficient opportunity to read meaningful passages from interesting books to an interacting adult. Ironically, this is the very setting event which is denied to low progress readers by remedial programmes which emphasize opportunities to practise letter and sound identification skills with isolated words.

Three further setting events can be illustrated within the context of one-to-one oral reading. These are the opportunities available for children to self-correct errors, the difficulty level of the book, and the provision of oral introductions to stories.

The behaviour of the teacher during one-to-one oral reading interaction itself functions as a setting event for specific behaviour. Clay (1969) has identified the reader behaviour of self-correction of errors as an important predictor of high rate progress in learning to read. Self corrections occurred more frequently with high progress rather than low progress beginning readers. McNaughton and Glynn (1980) in a within-subjects replication design showed that child self corrections were greatly reduced under conditions of immediate teacher attention to errors. Removal of immediate error attention by requiring the teacher to wait for a period of up to five seconds (or until the child reached the end of the sentence) resulted in increased self correction of errors and in increased reading accuracy. The withholding of immediate teacher attention appeared to function as a setting event for the child to detect and attempt to correct the error. By contrast, immediate teacher attention precluded all opportunity for such behaviour to occur. Two studies of parent home tutoring programmes for remedial readers report increased self corrections and accuracy using procedures which included delay of tutor attention to errors. (McNaughton et al 1980).

It is interesting to speculate whether high progress and low progress children function as setting events for differential teacher behaviour. In this way, a teacher may be more likely to intervene immediately, in the interests of "helping" a low progress child but in so doing may deny him the opportunity to self correct. Such teacher behaviour would then be reinforced by the child's imitation of the teacher correction of the error. In the case of a high progress child, a teacher may be more likely to wait to see whether the child would self correct the error, and in so doing may then reinforce the child for self correction.

Books that are too difficult present so many new words that they function as setting events for word by word reading, excessive attention to graphic cues, and offer severely limited opportunities for children to employ semantic and contextual strategies to solve unknown words. Books that are too difficult may impair the quality of teacher-child interaction. They restrict opportunities for the teacher to observe and reinforce children's problem solving behaviours, especially self correction of errors. The high error rate may set the occasion for an aversive style of teacher-child interaction during oral reading. Books that are too easy may also impair the quality of teacher-child interaction. The very low error rate affords little opportunity for the child to employ problem solving behaviours for the teacher to observe and reinforce. However, for a low progress child who typically receives minimal reinforcement for oral reading, performance on an easy book could serve as a setting event (high accuracy performance) for teacher reinforcement. This may be one reason why teachers select only very easy books for children to take home to read to parents. These teachers may be trying to provide a setting event that will ensure a positive parent-child interaction.

The other additional setting event in learning to read easily manipulated by teacher is providing a preparatory introduction and discussion for stories to be read. Wong and McNaughton (1980) provide data to demonstrate that a 7.5 year old low-progress reader improved in accuracy and in self-correction of errors on occasions when the teacher supplied in advance simple introductions to identify events, outcomes and unfamiliar words and concepts.

A behavioural approach to teaching emphasizes the continual monitoring of performance. Frequent checks on the accuracy of a child's oral reading will provide data on whether the current book level is appropriate or inappropriate, and whether, for some children, their high error rate functions as setting events for aversive teacher behaviours. A simple procedure for recording and analysing child and adult interaction in oral reading is provided in Glynn, McNaughton, Robinson and Quinn (1979). This involves the analysis of either live or tape-recorded samples of children's reading, scoring for types of error, incidence of self correction of errors, and adult response to these errors. Where data indicate that the interaction is aversive or unhelpful a set of procedures for changing the timing and quality of the adult response to errors has been successfully implemented (Glynn, 1980). These procedures include the use of a set of written instructions intended to cue the instructor or teacher to respond differentially to children's errors. Instructions are themselves a class of setting event which can be shown to affect children's behaviour in classrooms.

4. Instructions as Setting Events

Teachers frequently issue instructions which are intended to alter children's behaviour e.g. "Everyone stop work and watch me", or "Put down your pencils" "Start work!" These examples are stimulus events intended to occasion quite different behaviours. The effectiveness of these instructions in controlling behaviour depends upon the consistency with which they signal that the specified classes of behaviour will be reinforced. Confusion arises when teachers issue too many instructions in a short time, without reinforcing sufficient examples of the behaviour specified, and when teachers do not indicate how long an instruction is to be in effect before it is replaced by another. Glynn and Thomas (1974) found in one primary school written language lesson a teacher frequently changed his instructions from those specifying individual written work to those specifying stop and look at the teacher

46

while he gave information. These instruction changes occurred so often that children were unable to operate a self management procedure. The self management procedure required them to assess their own behaviour as on-task or off-task contingent on a random tone sounding. After a teacher instruction to stop and listen, there would not be an instruction to return to work. When the tone sounded at these times the children had difficulty in deciding whether or not they were on task. Similarly children who continued writing after the teacher's instruction to stop, tended (not unreasonably) to assess themselves as on-task. The confusion was overcome by providing a two-sided chart, one specifying individual work, the other specifying stop and listen to the teacher. The teacher was required to turn this chart over to the appropriate side everytime he changed his instructions. This had the effect of cueing both the children and teacher about which of the two instructions was currently in effect, and thus which behaviours qualified for reinforcement. The procedure specified an important change in teacher behaviour (turning the chart) which brought consistency to his use of instructions. Under these conditions children were always certain about which behaviours were expected, and were able to implement the self management procedure quite effectively, with a resultant clear increase in on-task behaviours. The procedures resulted in the different sets of instructions becoming effective setting events for different child behaviours.

Obviously, as the number of different instructions increases, the more difficult it will be to provide simultaneously for the differential reinforcement of behaviours appropriate to each - i.e. their effectiveness in changing behaviour will be diminished. The number of instructions should be kept to a minimum, and new instructions or changes in instructions should be introduced individually to allow time for the reinforcement of sufficient examples of appropriate behaviour.

Another feature of many classroom instructions and more frequently, school rules, is that they are negatively stated, (in terms of prohibitions) rather than in terms of specifying appropriate behaviour. Such sets of rules may function as setting events to occasion aversive teacher-child interactions. Teacher behaviours appropriate to negatively stated rules are those of observing and reporting transgressions. This may frequently initiate a teacher-child contact in the form of a criticism or complaint. Similarly, positively stated rules and instructions may be viewed as setting events for positive teacher child contact and interaction, and for teacher behaviours of observing and reporting on appropriate child behaviours.

Setting events such as crowded classroom environments, sequencing of lesson activities, provision of appropriate or inappropriate curriculum material, and clear and consistent use of instrtuctions have all been found to influence children's learning in classrooms through altering the quality of possible teacher child interaction. Teachers following a behavioural approach will adopt an experimental stance to identify for themselves which particular setting events are functional - i.e. can be shown in their classroom to have a clear effect on children's learning. Given that several functional setting events can be established for particular learning tasks teacher time spent in direct instruction and administering social or tangible reinforcement contingencies can be reduced.

The major setting event for academic learning introduced in this section is that of brief periods for one-to-one teacher-child interaction, particularly those initiated by the child (Hart and Risley, 1975). Such setting events however can be utilized only when the classroom organization and management allows sufficient time for a teacher to detect and respond to these initiations.

Classroom programmes which schedule the teacher in extended periods of direct instruction engaging the whole class, or large or small groups, severely limit opportunities for extended one-to-one interaction, particularly child-initiated incidental teaching. Classroom programmes which timetable for several different but simultaneous child activities, through the provision of a range of curriculum materials for children to choose from (e.g. the traditional infant class "developmental" lesson), would appear to maximize opportunities for one-to-one interaction, or child initiated incidental teaching. Such programmes provide a range of stimulus materials (learning activities) which occasion a variety of child behaviours. A high rate of engagement in appropriate task behaviour could be expected where children have a choice of activities.

Under these conditions the teacher is free to observe and detect opportunities for incidental teaching interactions, as well as opportunities to reinforce appropriate behaviour. Under these conditions also, the child behaviour of initiating adult interaction in the context of academic task performance would be classed as appropriate behaviour, and is likely to be reinforced by the resulting positive interaction. In the context of a whole class or small group direct instruction lesson, such educationally important behaviour would be clearly inappropriate, and unlikely to be reinforced.

SELECTIVE USE OF REINFORCEMENT

It was noted earlier that the principle of positive reinforcement needs to be applied much more selectively and discriminatingly. Discussion among teachers and educators who are more acquainted with the notion of positive reinforcement typically centres around two issues. The first concerns the relative merits of particular reinforcers (e.g. is time at a chosen activity a more acceptable or defensible rewarding event than earned points which are exchanged for consumable items, such as sweets?). The second issue concerns practical procedures or techniques for administering reinforcement - e.g. the use of weekly token cards, contract cards, token currencies, or pupil self recording of rewards. While both the choice of appropriate reinforcing events, and the devising of practical procedures for implementing reinforcement in the classroom are important, extensive discussion of these issues often precludes discussion of a prior and educationally more important issue of contingency. What is reinforcement to be contingent upon?

While it could be argued that technical questions concerning the selection, scheduling, and implementation of reinforcement are the professional domain of the behavioural psychologist, decisions concerning which behaviours qualify for reinforcement in an educational context such as the classroom are surely the domain of the teacher. The same reinforcer (e.g. teacher praise) administered on the same schedule (e.g. continuous reinforcement) would be expected to have quite different learning outcomes according to the behaviour on which it is contingent. In written expression, for example, praise for accuracy of grammar and spelling may have a distinctly different long-term effect from praise for interesting content.

In this section behavioural research is discussed which bears on the selective reinforcement of specific response contingencies namely those of appropriate versus inappropriate behaviour, academic versus attentional behaviours, fluent responding versus accurate responding, (including the reinforcement of specific task components), and the reinforcement of independent rather then dependent behaviour.

1. Reinforcing Appropriate versus Inappropriate Behaviour

One of the major contributions of early applied behaviour research in classrooms was the consistent demonstration that positive reinforcement in the form of teacher attention to appropriate behaviour not only increased children's appropriate behaviour, but clearly also decreased inappropriate behaviour (Madsen, Becker and Thomas, 1968;

Thomas, Becker and Armstrong, 1968; Glynn and Quinnel, 1971; Glynn, 1972). Indeed, the strategy of "catch the children being good" (Masden et al, 1968) has become a basic component of behavioural programmes for classroom management.

While most teachers would agree that teacher praise for appropriate child behaviour is an elementary and commonplace teaching practice, available descriptive data suggest otherwise. White (1975) studied the natural rates of teacher approval and disapproval in 104 U.S. classrooms, from grades 1 to 12 and found the disapproval rate to vary between two and three times the approval rate. Heller and White (1975) report similar findings for teachers of low ability children.

Thomas, Presland, Grant and Glynn (1978) examined baseline observations from ten grade seven classrooms in three New Zealand intermediate schools. For nine of the ten teachers disapproval rates exceeded approval rates, the median ratio being 17 to one. Appropriate behaviour in these classrooms ranged from 43 to 90 percent, the lowest score being that of the class whose teacher had a ratio of disapproval to approval of 17 to one.

Heller and White (1975) suggested that teachers may find use of disapproval more reinforcing than the use of approval. Thomas et al (1975) suggest disapproval comments are maintained because it is reinforcing to the teacher to detect inappropriate behaviour. Disapproval comments may also be reinforced through their possible short term effect in terminating inappropriate behaviour. However, such a strategy will not necessarily result in any increase in appropriate child behaviour, indeed increasing teacher attention to inappropriate behaviour is likely to increase this behaviour (Thomas, Becker and Armstrong, 1968).

Successful implementation of teacher social reinforcement of appropriate classroom behaviour is linked to successful teacher observation of appropriate behaviour. Given that the reinforcement contingency is on **appropriate** behaviour, teachers need both clear specifications of behaviour that is appropriate to the task, and skills in observing and detecting the occurrence of such behaviour. Greater skill is needed in observation and detection when the target child displays only a low rate of appropriate behaviour.

Without these prior skills of observing and detecting appropriate behaviour the application of reinforcement will be clearly ineffective. It may result, for example, in an increased overall rate of teacher attention or praise. However this could be counterproductive, since such non-contingent attention may unintentionally reinforce inappropriate behaviours. The crucial skill for teachers employing a behavioural approach is to ensure that reinforcement (in whatever form) is delivered contingent upon observable appropriate behaviour, and that unintentional reinforcement of inappropriate behaviour is minimized.

2. Reinforcing Academic rather than Attentional Behaviours

Marholin and Steinman (1977) observe that one reason why so much research has focussed on the development of on-task and non-disruptive behaviours has been the assumption that those behaviours are precursors (in the sense of pre-requisites) to improve academic performance. These authors reviewed several studies which indicate that the amount of time a child spends on-task can be increased and the amount of disruption decreased by reinforcing academic achievement directly, without the need first, or concurrently, to reinforce on-task behaviour or other related social behaviours. They studied the on-task behaviour, number of maths problems attempted, and accuracy of eight fifth and sixth grade children. These behaviours were observed first under conditions where reinforcement was contingent upon on-task behaviour, and subsequently on accuracy and rate of maths problem performance. The same reinforcer (access to free time) was awarded at a similar density under both conditions. The number of problems attempted increased and the disruptive behaviour was reduced under conditions of reinforcement for accuracy and rate of maths problems, particularly during periods when the teacher was absent from the classroom.

Glendinning (in an unpublished study supervised by the author) established that in teaching four primary school under-achievers in an adjustment class for disturbed children, reinforcement (tokens) contingent on their attending behaviour had little effect on their academic work output, (written expression and maths). In contrast reinforcement contingent upon academic work output greatly increased attending behaviour as well as improving academic output. Henderson (1978) also argues in favour of increasing on-task and academic performance by reinforcing correct work alone. He describes a one-way dependency between academic performance and appropriate behaviour. Ballard and Glynn (1975) found that on-task behaviour for a class of grade three children was higher when they wrote stories under conditions of reinforcement for components of writing than when they wrote stories under baseline conditions.

It would seem that there is a clear-cut case for discarding the reinforcement of attending or on-task behaviour in favour of reinforcing academic work output in classroom settings. However, Marholin and Steinman's argument against the reinforcement of attending behaviour is in terms of the presence of the teacher being a discriminative stimulus (setting event) for such reinforcement. Hence with the teacher temporarily absent from the room (or otherwise engaged within the room) on-task behaviour would not be reinforced, whereas with reinforcement contingent upon academic output, the learning task or curriculum materials themselves will function as the setting event for maintaining on-task behaviour. This argument holds so long as the reinforcement procedures require the teacher to administer reinforcement for on-task behaviour. It is, however, quite feasible for children themselves to take over the function of observing and recording their own attending behaviour, as well as administering their own (token) reinforcement.

A series of studies employed these self-management procedures, and clearly improved the on-task behaviour of children in primary school classrooms, (Glyn, Thomas and Shee, 1973; Glynn and Thomas, 1974; Thomas, 1976). Children in these studies assessed themselves as being on-task or off-task when cued by an intermittent and unpredictable tone sounded from a tape recorder. Children entered marks on a card each time the bleep "caught them working". Points awarded earned children time at chosen activity. Children successfully increased their on-task behaviour quite independently of the teacher.

Unfortunately, these studies did not include data on academic work completed, since the children were performing a range of academic tasks that did not always lead to an observable permanent product - e.g. playing word games or number games with activity materials such as flash cards and dice. However, the pupil self-managment procedures permitted the teacher to spend the majority of her time in one-to-one instruction, and responding to approaches from individual children. Under these conditions of diminished teacher supervision, and where a permanent ,response product' outcome is not appropriate for a particular set of instructional tasks, reinforcement contingent upon on-task behaviour seems to be an appropriate and worthwhile tactic.

3. Reinforcing Fluent Responding versus Accurate Responding

When a person moves to a new environment requiring the learning of a new language, local people are usually very supportive of hesitating first attempts and very tolerant of inaccuracies. Fortunately, they typically do not comment on and immediately correct every error which occurs. Rather, it seems that they respond to what they perceive as the speaker's intended message. Even a poorly structured inaccurate request for directions is frequently responded to, with the speaker obtaining at least some of the information required.

Similarly when a young child is learning to speak, parents typically go out of their way to interpret the message the child is trying to communicate, and similarly respond in terms of that message, (e.g. provide an answer to a question, or supply a requested object).

While parents frequently take such opportunities to model a more elaborate or acceptable language structure for the child, like the local people where a stranger is learning a new language, they clearly do not demand complete accuracy of pronunciation and structure from the children before responding to their messages. Language does not have to be completely accurate in order to be functional. Given sufficient opportunity to practise using language in a context of communication with competent speakers, young children and strangers receive sufficient reinforcement for their attempts that their language becomes both increasingly fluent and accurate.

Unfortunately much academic learning which takes place in classrooms is not organized on these principles. Some school writing programmes, for example, require children to spend many months of instruction in activities such as tracing or forming individual letters and tracing or copying words before they are permitted to generate their own writing. Graves (1978) notes that schools provide few opportunities for children to practise writing. Clay (1980) argues that the power of making one's own statement and getting better at it is rewarding in itself. Clay considered this was exemplified in the case of one of the children studied by Florio. This child said that he made his own words and did not copy other people, and that the more he learned to write good letters the better they got. Florio suggested that teachers could best serve the acquisition of writing by structuring social occasions which require children to write purposefully, such as letters of invitation and request.

In an unpublished study in a special class setting for mildly retarded pupils, we found that children were spending all of their scheduled writing time in copying and transcribing tasks, and were not asked to generate any words or sentences of their own. A major feature of this study was the introduction of reinforcement for approximations of words or sentences as a starting point in modifying writing behaviour. Spelling was never an essential requirement for reinforcement, and accuracy of letter formation received only minimal attention once reinforcement was made contingent on generating approximations of words and sentences. Major improvements occurred in the number of words and sentences written, and in the complexity of these sentences. Independent assessors of this writing commented informally that these pupils appeared to produce more accurate letter formation when generating their own words than when copying or transcribing from a model.

The classroom practice of providing reinforcement contingent only on accuracy, appears to be counterproductive. Under this contingency, children in the above study produced virtually no words or sentences of their own. When reinforcement was contingent upon generating words and sentences, the teacher no longer reinforced accuracy. Had she continued to do so, it is likely these children would have ceased to write anything of their own. It is interesting to speculate whether the consistently minimal written work produced by many low achieving secondary school children could be a result of continued exposure to conditions where reinforcement was available only for accuracy, and not fluency.

Two further unpublished studies carried out under our direction are of interest on the issue of reinforcement for fluency. Espiner implemented a procedure to reinforce self-generated writing in a six year old. As in the case of our earlier study, spelling was not taken into consideration and accuracy of letter formation received very little attention. Data indicated a clear increasing trend in amount written. Also, consistent with our earlier findings, writing samples indicated progression over time from simple to more complex concepts, and an improvement in standard and accuracy of letter formation.

In the second unpublished study, Arndt measured a seven year old girl's output and legibility (accuracy) in her story writing in two settings, school and home, under baseline conditions. The girl consistently wrote more in the same ten-minute time limit at home than she did at school, but her accuracy (percentage of letters correctly formed) was similar at home and at school. Arndt next introduced at home procedures which involved discussion of ideas for story writing, and interesting words that might be used, together with adult comments responding to the ideas and content in the story. This took place immediately the story was finished. No comments were made about the number of words written nor about the accuracy of letters. Data showed that following the introduction of these procedures, there was a marked increase in the amount written at home. More importantly there was also a marked increase in accuracy, such that the accuracy of the girl's writing at home now clearly surpassed that of her writing at school. Under conditions which tended to reinforce the use of interesting words and ideas, this girl not only wrote more, but she formed her letters more accurately. This finding is consistent with those of Clay (1974).

If reinforcement for self generated words and sentences not only increases writing output but also leads over time to improvement in accuracy of letter formation, even with mildly retarded children, then the practice of restricting children to copying and transcribing tasks for such a high proportion of time available for practising writing needs to be seriously questioned.

Reinforcement can be made contingent not only on the amount written (number of words) but also upon specific components of the writing product. Brigham, Graubard and Stans (1972) reinforced fifth grade children in a remedial classroom for three different components-number of words, number of different words, and number of new words. Children's writing output increased under all three conditions, but in addition their stories were independently rated as of higher quality under conditions of reinforcement for number of words used. Similarly, Maloney and Hopkins (1973) report that children's stories written under contingencies of reinforcement for selected parts of speech (different adjectives, different action words and different sentence beginnings) were independently rated as more creative than stories written under baseline conditions. This finding was supported in a further study by Ballard and Glynn (1975) where pupil self recording procedures when introduced in conjunction with reinforcement for selected parts of speech in story writing, resulted in increased usages of those particular parts of speech. Stories written when reinforcement was contingent on use of action verbs were rated highest in terms of creativity by two independent raters.

Another important study of the power of differential reinforcement is a study of creative block building by children in a kindergarten class (Goetz and Baer, 1973). Reinforcement contingencies were experimentally altered by requiring staff to reinforce (praise) children only for use of new block construction forms occurring in each session. Under these conditions children produced an increasing number of different forms, and original forms (never used before in any session). Reinforcement contingencies were then returned to staff praise for the same stereotyped constructions, and children's production of new forms decreased. A final phase replicated the results of the differential reinforcement for different forms.

The selective or differential use of reinforcement is thus a critical variable in modifying the quantity, accuracy and quality of children's work in the classroom. In the case of expressive writing, contingencies on fluency appear to have greater promise than contingencies on accuracy.

4. Reinforcing Independent rather than Dependent Responding

Statements about educational goals frequently refer to the desirability of students becoming autonomous, "self-monitoring" learners, capable of acting independently of adults. Unfortunately, school management policies, particularly those relating to school rules and discipline do not provide many opportunities for student autonomous or independent behaviour to occur. Nor do they provide sufficient reinforcement contingencies when such behaviour does occur, as we have said earlier (Glynn, 1976). Within the individual classroom, independent learning behaviour can occur only to the extent that there are sufficient setting events, or opportunities to perform academic behaviours outside the direct control of teacher-imposed contingencies.

It has already been noted that classroom organizations which allow pupils a choice of instructional activities can free the teacher to provide individual children with brief periods of one-to-one interaction. While the teacher is engaged with individual children, the remaining children can be readily taught to monitor their own on-task behaviour (when cued by an intermittent signal) and to self administer token reinforcement contingencies as we have shown (Glynn, Thomas and Shee, 1973; Jackson and Glynn, 1974; Thomas, 1976). These studies demonstrate the usefulness of a procedure which trains children directly in some of the skills needed for self regulation. The procedure specifies and trains a specific self-monitoring response (checking whether one's behaviour is "on-task" or not) to be performed on cue from a tape recorded signal. The procedure provides children with access to immediate reinforcement (a tick or point on a token card). Reinforcement is contingent upon on-task behaviour occurring at the time the signal occurred. Since the self-monitoring is an extremely simple task, children have little difficulty in discriminating whether or not their behaviour is on-task, provided that the task specification is clear and teacher instructions are consistent (Glynn and Thomas, 1974). A high rate of on-task behaviour, independent of direct teacher control, can be achieved by these procedures.

However, these classroom studies of self regulation do not address the question of how important behaviours such as self-monitoring and self correction occur within the context of learning academic skills. The one-to-one setting in which a child performs an academic skill and interacts with a teacher is an even more important context for the learning of self-regulated or independent learning behaviour. In performing an academic skill the child has the much more complex task of discriminating both which behaviours are appropriate to completing that task, and learning which alternative behaviour to substitute when a specific behaviour is ineffective. Children learning both to monitor their own behaviour and to correct their own responding, are powerfully influenced by the behaviour of the teacher in the one-to-one setting and by the selection of appropriate learning materials.

We might consider the paradox that the long-term outcome of adaptive child behaviour that is independent of control by an external agent may, in the short term, depend upon particular types of external agent attention. We could further conceive of a child and an adult (e.g. teacher) in a learning situation in which the adult, by appropriate external monitoring and labelling of cues, facilitates the child's learning to self-monitor and self-correct. This is consistent with Kanfer's (1970) view of the role of the external agent in the child's learning to self monitor. The children's learning of these two types of self-regulatory responses in turn further enhance their performance on the learning task. Hence the behaviour of the teacher influences not only how well the child learns a particular task, but also whether or not in the process the child leans self-regulatory skills, such as monitoring and corrective behaviour.

The teacher's use of reinforcement procedures is very critical in this one-to-one context. First, it is important to recognize that an appropriately selected academic task carries its own reinforcement. Solving a problem or correctly reading a sentence produce reinforcement in the form of information. Additional or "back-up" reinforcement whether tangible or social for task performance may be superfluous, and it may even be restricting given the previous discussion of contingencies for academic behaviour. Instructor behaviour in the one-to-one oral reading setting should be such as to increase the reader's self-regulatory skills, and not to reinforce the reader for dependence on instructor-provided corrections and solutions.

The tutoring procedures developed by Glynn, McNaughton, Robinson and Quinn, (1979) include both instructor cues and prompts and selective reinforcement. Given a child's error the instructor is asked first to wait (a possible setting event for child self correction) and then to provide a cue for the child to read on to the end of the sentence (or to go back to the beginning). Next, the instructor is asked to supply one or two prompts (contextual or semantic prompts where the error does not approximate that of the correct word, and letter-sound prompts where the error does approximate that of the correct word). Only when the sequence of waiting, cueing and prompting has not lead to the error being corrected, does the instructor supply the child with the word. Thus, when a child reads the word correcty before the instructor supplies it, he has to some extent escaped from total dependence on the instructor to correct the error. Hence it is important for the instructor to detect and reinforce children's self-corrections, children's prompted corrections, and children's attempted corrections, (which result in the substitution of words of approximate meaning to that of the correct words). Reinforcement procedures employed in this way may thus increase children's problem solving strategies, and increase their performance of behaviours likely to lead to successful reading. Children can thus receive reinforcement for their attempts at some words, even though specific attempts may be unsuccessful.

In contrast, the teacher behaviour of immediately supplying the correct word when a child makes an error could be seen to reinforce the child for dependent behaviour such as stopping, and looking at the teacher to obtain the correct word. Reinforcement of the child's imitation of the teacher's correct model would then tend to reinforce the whole sequence of dependency.

Two of our recent studies trained parents of older low-progress readers to implement a tutoring programme incorporating these differential cueing, prompting and reinforcing strategies. In the first study (McNaughton et al, 1980) eight parents learned to increase the percentage of times when they delayed intervening after children's errors, to use an increased proportion of prompting rather than supplying the correct word, and to dramatically increase the number of praise statements. In the second study (Glynn, 1980), parents of four other low-progress readers increased, in addition, their use of praise specifically contingent on child self corrections and prompted corrections. In both studies, there was marked improvement in the accuracy of children's reading at home. Generalization to improved reading at school was limited in the first study due to difficulties in obtaining continuous measures of reading at school for the older children. Generalization was more clear-cut in the second study. Children showed a mean gain in reading accuracy of 6.25 months over four months of tutoring by parents. Although these tutoring procedures were developed for use at home by parents, they are readily useable by teachers in the context of one-to-one oral reading in the classrooms.

Finally, Wilson and Glynn (1978) report a study in which mildly retarded children experienced a successful behavioural programme of reinforcement for self generated words and sentences. The programme greatly increased the amount written by these children to the point where they were maximizing reinforcement for themselves by calling upon the teacher to supply them with the words they wanted (dependent behaviours), rather than first check whether the required word was on available wall charts or in personal work lists. As this increase in teacher dependent behaviour meant the teacher was literally "run off her feet" supplying individuals with words, a mild response cost procedure was introduced to counter some of the unnecessary reinforcing of dependent behaviour. Thus children now lost a point if the word they asked the teacher to supply was found to be on the wall charts or in personal lists. The teacher continued to supply genuinely new words. Under these conditions, there was a dramatic drop in the number of words 'found' by the children themselves. In this case, unproductive teacher reinforcement of dependent behaviours was countered by a mild punishment procedure.

The research presented in this section points to the value of deploying classroom reinforcement contingencies selectively. The research suggests teachers employing a behavioural approach should ensure that available contingencies of reinforcement are weighted in favour of behaviour that is appropriate (rather than inappropriate), in favour of academic task performance (rather than attentional behaviour), in favour of fluent (rather than merely accurate behaviour), and in favour of independent behaviour (rather than dependent behaviour).

The systematic deployment of such contingencies of reinforcement, together with the arrangement and manipulation of the variety of classroom setting events discussed in the previous section, constitutes a powerful behavioural approach, capable of strongly enhancing the quality of children's learning in the classroom.

REFERENCES

Ballard, K.D. and Glynn, T. Behavioural self-management in story writing with elementary school children. Journal of Applied Behaviour Analysis, 1975, 8, 387-398.

Bijou, S.W. and Baer, D.M. Behaviour Analysis of Child Development. (Prentice-Hall, New Jersey, 1978).

Brigham, T.A., Graubard, P.S. and Stans, A. Analysis of the effects of sequential reinforcement contingencies on aspects of composition. Journal of Applied Behaviour Analysis, 1972, 5, 421-429.

Clay, M.M. Reading errors and self correction behaviour. British Journal of Educational Psychology, 1969, 39, 47-56.

Clay, M.M. Reading: The Patterning of Complex Behaviour,

(second edition). (Heinemann Educational Books, Auckland, 1979).

Clay, M.M. Early writing and reading: reciprocal gains. In Clark, M.M. and Glynn, T. (Eds.), Reading and Writing for the Child with Difficulties. (Educational Review, Occasional Publications Number Eight, University of Birmingham, 1980).

Glynn, T. Verbal and token reinforcement: elements of behaviour choice in a problem class. New Zealand Psychologist, 1972, 1, 13-20.

Glynn, T. Student behaviour: a self-management approach. In Codd, J.A. and Hermansson, G.L., (Eds.), Directions in New Zealand Secondary Education. (Hodder and Stoughton, Auckland, 1976).

Glynn, T. Parent-child interaction in remedial reading at home. In Clark, M.M. and Glynn, T. (Eds.), Reading and Writing for the Child with Difficulties. (Educational Review: Occasional Publications Number Eight, University of Birmingham, 1980).

Glynn, T., Glynn, V. and Lawless, S. Nutrition: A behaviour analysis approach. How we influence what children eat. Procedings of the Nutrition Society of New Zealand, 1979, 4, 110-130.

Glynn, T., McNaughton, S.S., Robinson, V.M.J. and Quinn, M. Remedial Reading at Home: Helping You to Help Your Child. (New Zealand Council for Educational Research, Wellington, 1979).

Glynn, E.L. and Quinnell, J.T. Modification of non-task behaviour in the classroom, through contingent teacher remarks. New Zealand Journal of Educational Studies, 1971, 6, 137-50.

Glynn, E.L. and Thomas, J.D. The effects of cuing on self-control of on-task classroom behaviour. Journal of Applied Behaviour Analysis, 1975, 7, 299-306.

Glynn, E.L., Thomas, J.D. and Shee, S.M. Behavioural self-control of non-task behaviour in an elementary class. Journal of Applied Behaviour Analysis, 1973, 6, 163-71.

Goetz, E.M. and Baer, D.M. Social control of form diversity and the emergence of new forms in children's blockbuilding. Journal of Applied Behaviour Analysis, 1973, 6, 209-218.

Hart, B.M. and Risley, T.R. Incidental teaching of language

in the preschool. Journal of Applied Behaviour Analysis, 1975, 8, 411-420.

Heller, M.S. and White, M.A. Teacher approval and disapproval on ability grouping. Journal of Educational Psychology, 1975, 67, 796-800.

Henderson, M. Increasing appropriate classroom behaviour and academic performance by reinforcing correct work alone. Psychology in the Schools, 1976, 12, 195-200.

Jackson, H.J. and Glynn, T. Prior training and self reinforcement in the standard two classroom. New Zealand Psychologist, 1974, 3, 65-73.

Kanfer, F.H. Self-regulation: research, issues and speculations. In Neuringer, C. and Michael, J. (Eds.), Behaviour Modification in Clinical Psychology. (Appleton-Century Crofts, New York, 1970).

Krantz, P .J. and Risley, T.R. Behavioural ecology in the classroom. In O'Leary, K.D. and O'Leary, S.G. (Eds.) Classroom Management: The Successful Use of Behaviour Modification. (Pergamon Press, New York, 1977).

Madsen, C.H. Jr., Becker, W.C. and Thomas, D.R. Rules, praise and ignoring: elements of elementary classroom control. Journal of Applied Behaviour Analysis, 1968, 1, 139-150.

Maloney, K.B. and Hopkins, B.L. The modification of sentence structure and its relationship to subjective judgement of creativity in writing. Journal of Applied Behaviour Analysis, 1973, 6, 425-434.

Marholin, D.I. and Steinman, W.M. Stimulus control in the classroom as a function of the behaviour reinforced. Journal of Applied Behaviour Analysis, 1977, 10, 465-478.

McNaughton, S. Structuring settings for learning academic skills; applications to oral reading. Proceedings of the Third Australian Conference on Behaviour Modification, Melbourne, 1980.

McNaughton, S. and Glynn, T. Self Regulation Processes in Early Oral Reading; Controlling Accuracy via Self Correction. (Education Department, University of Auckland, 1979).

McNaughton, S. and Glynn, T. Delayed versus immediate attention to oral reading errors: effects on accuracy and self-correction. (Education Department, University of Auckland, 1980).

McNaughton, S., Glynn, T. and Robinson, V.M. Parents as Remedial Reading Tutors: Issues for Home and School. (New Zealand Council for Educational Research, Wellington, 1980).

O'Rourke, M. and Glynn, T. Play equipment and adult participation: effects on children's behaviour. In Glynn, T. and McNaughton, S. (Eds.), Behaviour Analysis in New Zealand. (New Zealand Council for Educational Research, Auckland, 1978).

Smith, F. Understanding Reading: A Psycholinguistic Analysis of Reading and Learning to Read (second edition). (Holt, Rinehart and Winston, New York, 1978).

Thomas, J.D. Accuracy of self-assessment of on-task behaviour by elementary school children. Journal of Applied Behaviour Analysis. 1976, 9, 209-210.

Thomas, D.R., Becker, W.C. and Armstrong, M. Production and elimination of disruptive classroom behaviour by systematically varying teacher's behaviour. Journal of Applied Behaviour Analysis, 1968, 1, 35-45.

Thomas, J.D., Presland, I.V., Grant, D. and Glynn, T. Natural rates of teacher approval and disapproval in Grade 7 and Grade 8 classrooms. Journal of Applied Behaviour Analysis, 1978, 11, 91-94.

Wilson, M.G. and Glynn, T. Increasing self-selection and self- location of words by mildly retarded children during story writing. The Exceptional Child, (in press).

White, M.A. Natural rates of teacher approval and disapproval in the classroom. Journal of Applied Behaviour Analysis, 1975, 8, 91-94.

Wong, P. and McNaughton, S. The effects of prior provision of context on the oral reading proficiency of a low progress reader. New Zealand Journal of Educational Studies, (in press).

SECTION TWO. COMMUNICATION, COGNITION AND INDIVIDUAL DIFFERENCES

In the first section classroom management was examined. The chapters in Section Two extend this theme by considering communication within the classroom, individual differences in learning and the social context of the classroom.

In chapter three Margaret Clark begins by considering the two basic contributors to a child's education - the home and the school, and points to the need for a partnership between them if pupils are to reach their full potential. Clearly education does not just take place at school. Not only do children begin school with a great deal of basic knowledge that they have acquired at home, but their progress will be greatly influenced by the encouragement they receive from their parents and the way in which school learning is supported by activities out of school. This can only be achieved if teachers are aware of the importance of the home and have a meaningful relationship with the parents of the children they teach.

Since the basic means of communication is language, an appreciation of the ways in which it can be developed in children is essential if teachers are to educate effectively. Here the teacher needs to consider the relationships between spoken language, written language and reading. In connection with language some very basic practical questions arise. For instance, what should a teacher do about dialect as opposed to "standard" English? How can communication between the teacher and the pupils and between one child and another be encouraged?

The final section of chapter three looks at the teacher's judgment of a child's ability. Influenced perhaps by notions of intelligence and testing some teachers are inclined to label a child as "bright" or "dull" and this categorisation then influences the teacher's view of how the pupil is likely to perform in all subjects. This approach is not only psychologically unsound but can have disturbing consequences for the child; a "dull" child may be written off as incapable of producing any worthwhile work in any subject with the effect that in areas where he has abilities these will not be developed to anywhere nearly the full extent and, just as stunting, the pupil's self-esteem will be damaged. This section prepares the reader for a detailed consideration of the ways in which instruction can be adapted to get the best from the pupil, in the next chapter.

Chapter four by Richard Riding indicates four characteristics of the human learning system which must be taken into account if learning is going to be efficient. The first of these is that the reception and analysis of the meaning of information takes time and although the system works quickly and often automatically, if the processing capacity is exceeded then information will be lost or the learning will be at a fairly low level. Research indicates that teachers frequently present information more quickly than their pupils can process it. The second is that new learning is given meaning in terms of what is already known. Consequently for efficient learning the pupil must have in memory the concepts to which the new information is to be related. Thirdly, there are differences between pupils in the way in which they represent information in thought and memory. Some use a predominately verbal mode of representation while others think in terms of images or mental pictures. This difference in mode of representation affects not only how well children learn different types of material, but also the type of presentation they prefer - verbal or pictorial. Lastly, children differ in the degree to which they discriminate or differentiate one item from another. Some are very sensitive to small differences between stimuli while others have a more global approach.

For pupils to achieve their full potential instruction must be adapted to the characteristics of each individual. The presentation must allow for a particular child to process the information to be learned, the content of the learning must match what the pupil already knows so that it can be fully understood, and it must be in a form that can be readily represented in the child's memory and is appropriate to the level of discrimation. When these conditions are met a pupil will find learning successful and statisfying.

In chapter five Mike Beveridge and Roy Griffiths focus on social aspects of the thinking of pupils and teachers. In school the children have to think about what the teacher says. The teacher has to think about the decisions that must be made to make learning efficient and effective. Both of these actions are within, and are affected by, the social context.

For <u>children</u> entering school, the quality of their thought about their work is likely to be greatly influenced by the level of reflective thinking they experience at home in social interaction with their parents. The first section begins by considering how this can be studied and continues by looking at two other social aspects of classroom learning: the tendency of some children to pretend they understand when in fact they do not, and the growth in a child's perceptions of situations.

For the <u>teacher</u>, decisions must be made almost moment by moment in the classroom about, for instance, what is to be taught, how it is to be presented, how understanding can be improved, and how behaviour can be controlled. In the school the teacher is a decision maker, and the quality of these decisions is crucial to the effectiveness of the education of the pupils. Further, in the practical situation, the teacher is often under pressure because there are several decisions demanding attention at the same time - Jim, who is still on the first part of the work, says, "Please sir, I don't understand this", while over in the far corner Bill is punching Fred, and Jill, who is very bright, finished the work ten minutes ago and is waiting for further instructions. This section considers the types of decisions that the teacher has to make, the information available on which the decisons may be based and the strategies teachers can use when faced with several features to deal with at the same time.

Chapter 3

LANGUAGE, COMMUNICATION AND LEARNING IN THE CLASSROOM

Margaret M. Clark

To those aware of the vast research in recent years in each of the topics of "Language", "Communication" and "Learning" their inclusion in a single chapter may seem an unrealistically extensive remit - even when consideration is limited to the classroom. It is, however, the wealth and complexity of the researches, the diversity of sources in which they have been reported, and the often technical (and even changing) vocabulary in which many of the reports are couched which has made their study a daunting task for all but the specialist. The non-specialist has often been content to depend on secondary sources (or sometimes even further removed simplified versions of the original studies). The aim in this chapter will be to alert the reader to the range of issues on which new evidence to education is appearing, to relate these to each other and to draw attention to a number of sources which will take the reader a step further in understanding the interaction of factors which influence the effectiveness of the classroom as an educational setting. No attempt will be made to provide simplified statements of the findings from a variety of studies on what are in many cases highly complex issues.

THE HOME AND THE SCHOOL

It is important that teachers consider the strengths and weaknesses of the institution of the school, and the social setting of the classroom, within which much of formal education takes place. Its very institutionalised nature tends to cut off this aspect of a child's experience and learning from the out of school and pre-school experiences and to distance the contribution of the home. Until recently reference to the home as a factor in research studies has tended to be not so much in terms of its educational contribution per se, but rather its supportive role to formal education. Measures of the home in studies of factors influencing school progress have often been in terms of its

66

material or attitudinal support for goals set by the school. Frequency of visits by parents to the school, numbers of books in the home, extent of assistance with homework, are examples of such measures. In other studies homes have been categorised in terms of socio-economic status based on the type of employment of the male head of the household or the number of years of schooling, or beyond compulsory schooling, of one or both parents. Average differences in progress by children in relation to one of these measures, or a group of such features - sometimes also including whether or not the mother was in employment - were studied. Assumptions were often made in studies on this type of model with regard to the dynamics of the home but seldom was this based on first-hand information from the home. Even where massive input of resources was evident, as in the Head Start programmes in the United States and to the more limited extent in the Educational Priority Area studies in Britain in the late sixties, the assumptions of the deficiencies in the homes as educational settings were mainly drawn from evidence of the greater probability of later failure in school of children from certain types of homes or geographical areas. Deficiencies in the children's apparent level of functioning, particularly in language tasks at an early age, seemed to confirm such a model of "deprivation" and the need for what was referred to a "compensatory" education to make good the deficits as early as possible - and hopefully even before the advent of mandatory schooling. Formalised educational input for young children with a particular stress on language, and in some instances instruction in the structure of language, was seen as important to ensure that these children, otherwise doomed to failure would arrive better prepared for the school setting. In most researches at that time, professionals or para-professionals were the mediators of the programmes rather than the parents whose potential as educators was often ignored and whose self-esteem would also be further lowered by the model upon which such intervention was based.

There has recently been a growing awareness of the over-simplified nature of this model of educational disadvantage, of the possibility of erroneous conclusions based on assumptions about the dynamics of the home when not based on empirical evidence. There has also been a growing awareness that to define areas of educational deprivation geographically does not reach those in greatest need. It has been realised also that the exhibited deficiencies in the language of certain children in formal settings, one of the basic assumptions from which many of these models of early intervention were derived, does not take account of the influence of the "situation" on the quality and quantity of language elicited nor the differential effect on children's exhibited language competence of their previous experience of such formalised settings. One major growth point for ther study of interaction between adults and children has been within the pre-school age group, partly growing out of language studies of "Head Start" and "EPA" where it became obvious that it was not adequate to talk in terms of the nursery school or the playgroup, but essential to compare and contrast the different settings and the role of the various adults within differently organised settings. More recently also, studies of language and interaction between parents and young children have become a part of the growing evidence on the dynamics of language development.

The importance of the home, and even the contribution of homes upon whose deficiencies previous formulations had focussed, has become apparent in more recent pre-school studies. Indeed, attention has also been drawn by a number of reviewers of the pre-school intervention programmes to the involvement of parents as an important feature in those studies in which substantial and long-term gains were evident. Useful sources to consult for discussion of the issues touched upon above are Bronfenbrenner (in Clarke and Clarke 1976) and Donachy in (Clark and Cheyne, 1979), while in Stanley (1972 and 1973) there is a review of the range of Head Start programmes.

Before turning to the classroom it is important to draw attention to a further often overlooked contribution of the home to a child's readiness for instruction. If the subjects in question are among those taught in school, it tends to be assumed that where the learning is successful it is because of the school instruction with little account being taken of readiness for instruction. This readiness is not only attitudinal but also influences by prior cognitively orientated language interaction, resulting in the ability to ask questions when in doubt and to answer questions in such a way as to indicate the limits of one's understanding.

Additionally, while the ability to use the technical vocabulary of instruction may not in the initial stages be essential, an understanding of the main technical terms and specific uses of words in more general use will greatly facilitate a child's potential to benefit from instruction in the school group setting. Even an understanding of terms such as "letter", "word" and "sentence", for reading or "large", "round" and "greater than" for mathematics and "mountain", "land" and "country" for geography may be important variables affecting ability to profit from the language of the classroom; yet for many this may have been assimilated elsewhere.

Reading is just one example of the skills taught in school and apparently learnt there by most children yet where many of the concepts of print will have been acquired elsewhere. The print in the environment and the responsiveness of the adults to the child's interest, which may have played a crucial role in the early stages, are not assessed in many tests of reading readiness, where often the more visual - perceptual aspects of the task have been the focus. Downing (1979 Chapter 1) cites growing evidence from a variety of sources on the importance of "linguistic awareness" in reading readiness - aspects to which the home may already have made an important contribution pre-school. This would include knowledge of the language of instruction, of the relationship between speech, reading and writing and features such as the beginner's ability to segment speech. While the present author's study <u>Young Fluent Readers</u> (Clark 1976) was based on children who were already reading fluently and with understanding on starting school, there are lessons which can be learnt by teachers from a study such as this both for understanding the child whose progress in learning to read appears to be entirely within the school setting and even in promoting a broader understanding of the features and needs of those who fail to learn within the school setting.

While the remainder of this chapter will focus on the classroom, it is important to remind ourselves continually that the level of performance and the range of skills shown in a particular classroom, or in school generally, is by no means the only level of performance of which these children are capable - or more important still, for which they have potential. The contribution of the home in a wide variety of ways to the attainment of the high progress child must be undervalued. In studies of children of school age, little account has been taken of the positive influence of out-of-school features on progress and it is important that the lessons from the pre-school researchers are not ignored. With the limited contact between teachers and parents and the artificial settings in which it so often takes place it is so easy for each to under-value the contribution of the other. The home is all too often expected to carry the responsibility for the failures, while the school accepts full credit for the successes. Two examples of parental involvement in which not only the children's progress was influenced by the programme but also the self-esteem of the parents were those of Donachy (1979) with parents of pre-school children and Glynn (1980) with parents of children who were failing in reading. One important further aspect in Donachy's study was the change in morale of the parents for whom educational failure had previously been seen as almost inevitable for their children, a cycle in which they had felt helpless to intervene. Their morals benefitted and an appreciation of their concern and willingness to co-operate became apparent to the school staffs with whom they came in contact and who would subsequently be responsible for the formal education of these children. In Glynn's study while some of the children who had been failing made progress when the intervention was by assistance only at home by the parents, for others a concerted effort involving both home and school was necessary before much progress was evident.

To argue for an importance contribution by, and role for, the parents in the education of their children need not be to undervalue the professional contribution of the teacher, but rather to ensure that in education, account is taken of <u>all</u> the various factors influencing educational progress. There is a long way to go yet before a full understanding of learning potential is reached and before this can be translated into teaching and learning strategies which optimise the progress of individual children. Meantime it is important to avoid over-simplifying the process or drawing hasty conclusions from limited evidence, which has all too often been the case in educational developments. Many recent studies in the home as well as school setting, in which the dynamics of intervention between adults and children have been explored, do justify a more optimistic view of educability than the previous static model of "ability", "attainment", and "teaching style" round which many researches were developed and many educational settings organised. There is evidence of changes in measured intelligence as a result of early intervention studies; or in the short-term as a result of changes in the method of administration, the acceptability of the tester, or differential influences of prompts on the level of performance. It is important that teachers are aware of the growing evidence of the complexity of features which influence even the "standard" test situation if they are to appreciate the potential for educability of their pupils - depending on the contexts of instructions and contexts in which it is presented. (see Cazden 1970 and Donachy 1979).

LANGUAGE RESEARCH: ITS IMPLICATIONS FOR THE CLASSROOM

Particularly in the early years of schooling, much of the instruction given by the teacher is through the medium of oral language; while the judgements as to its appropriateness for a particular class are also greatly influenced by the children's responses in spoken language. In a later section, focus will be on communication in the classroom, the dynamics of the situation. In this present section it is important to set a foundation for this by considering some of the recent researches into language, a number of which although they were not undertaken in classrooms, have already been shown to have important implications.

As children progress further through schooling, while oral

language still retains an important role both as a medium for instruction and a way of assessing the understanding of the class during the process of instructing, gradually written language competence takes an increasingly important part in the educational scene. The ability to read becomes a necessary skill so that the children can acquire sufficient content and range of instruction and at a more variable pace of input to suit individual children than is possible with oral instruction; likewise competence in writing for a variety of purposes becomes a necessary skill by which children both develop further competence and give evidence of how much they have absorbed; thus writing becomes not only a medium of instruction but also a tool for assessment.

In a number of recent studies of reading its relationship to spoken language has been considered with a questioning of the assumption that print is merely speech written down. Increasingly those studying the development of reading have come to appreciate the reciprocal relationship between reading and writing. Thus it is important in a chapter such as this to include reference to some studies in which instead of regarding the process as from speech to reading then to writing, their interrelatedness has been explored. Clearly it is possible only to mention very briefly and selectively researches from the massive literature on reading and writing: the importance of particular studies to the appreciation of language in the classroom will be criterion in selection.

Oral Language

It is a useful, if simple, starting point to distinguish receptive and expressive language to reinforce the extent of the difference between the level of children's development of understanding of language and their own spoken language both with regard to complexity of sentence structure and vocabulary. Parents are very quickly made aware of the ability of a young infant to understand their private dialogue even at a stage when the infant's own speech is poorly articulated and limited in vocabulary. Teachers are faced, however, with a much more complex task in assessing the level of understanding of the individual members of a class from what must, of necessity, be brief and limited interchanges with the individual children. Where misunderstanding is observed there is still the problem of determining which of their assumptions about the children's ability to comprehend were incorrect. It is therefore not surprising that for some children their level of understanding is over-estimated by their teachers, while for others their limited ability to express themselves effectively in oral language leads the teacher to undervalue their comprehension. The situation is further complicated in the classroom by the nature of the language register used for much of the instruction and the more limited range of acceptable ways of responding which may lead certain children to refrain from attempting to answer questions because of their more limited access to the appropriate language code.

In the early seventies many of the researches by linguists were detailed longitudinal case studies of very young, sometimes precocious, individual children whose language development was reported in highly technical terms and from which it was difficult for those in educationn to extrapolate to school-age children in the classroom. With the focus in educational research during those years being on educational failure and the association of this with apparent deficits in language development, it is not surprising that the formulation by Bernstein of a major language difference between middle class (more successful) and working class (less educationally successful) children in terms of access to an "elaborated code" by the former and limitation to a "restricted code" by the latter should have been so readily accepted. Since, however, the language in which Bernstein discussed his views was complex, and his terminology varied with time and since initially it had been tested by little in the way of empirical investigation, it is probably fair to say that this conceptualisation was perhaps too soon and too uncritically adopted as part of the folklore of teacher training. Assumption of access to restricted or elaborated code as a generalisable feature of language discriminating between social classes was a misleading deduction from the range of studies stimulated by Bernstein's early provocative papers - and also a dangerously negative formulation for anyone in the business of education. In order to make a fair evaluation of the influence of Bernstein it is important to go well beyond his early papers from which most quotations are taken - to study a range of the empirical work stimulated by his ideas and finally to redress the balance on Bernstein's views on educability by studying, for example, another of his early papers in which he critically evaluates the whole concept of compensatory education which at the time of his writing tended to imply intervention prior to schooling while leaving the school framework untouched, (Bernstein, 1970). Studies by the Gahagans in collaboration with infant teachers published in Talk Reform (Gahagan and Gahagan 1970), which originated from the unit with which Bernstein was associated, are an example of co-operative planning of intervention strategies for implementation in the classroom to encourage a wider and more flexible use of language by all children, appropriate to particular situations and recipients.

One source which may be consulted for a selection of empirical studies by co-workers of Bernstein is Class Codes and Controls Volume 2 (Bernstein 1973). The results of a number of these empirical studies were interpreted at the time as evidence of difference in performance in what was assumed to be a standard task, similarly perceived by the children. In the light of recent work the question might now be raised as to the extent to which any differences could be explained by differences in perception of the task; an aspect not explored in these early studies and one with very different educational implications. In a paper entitled Language Management, Socio-economic Status and Educational Progress, Robinson (1980) sets the developments over the preceding ten years in context and claims that many teachers may have over-estimated the size of the correlation between socio-economic class, speech and educational progress. He also suggests that on currently available evidence it would be possible to explain differences in attainment as resulting from "discriminating behaviour" by teachers, one factor influencing this he argues being the "language management of children".

A number of the pre-school interventions studies were, as was mentioned earlier, based on the assumption that for some children instruction in language structure was necessary at an early stage to "correct" their errors and make good their language deficits. Such a formulation would also lead teachers in the classroom to assume that they would be failing in their duty were they not to correct the speech of the children for whom they were responsible. "Dialect" would for many teachers have been included in such incorrect speech, thus there would be an insistence in the classroom on "correct" or Standard English. Attacks on this assumption of the correctness of Standard English as compared with dialect forms, of the necessity to use it as a vehicle for communication of more abstract thought and of Bernstein's conceptualisation of elaborated and restricted codes gathered momentum. A forceful criticism of the assumptions of a language deficit as an explanation for educational failure by American Negro children was to be found in the influential paper by Labov, The Logic of Non Standard English, in which he explored the intellectual and communicative power of a language which differed in grammatical structure as well as vocabulary but which he argued had as much potential as other forms to which it had been claimed to be inferior as well as different. This paper is to be found in most collections of papers on Language in Education (see, for example, Labov 1972). In an interesting and clearly written introductory text entitled Accent, Dialect and the School, Trudgill (1975) explores a number of these issues and sets them in context. Trudgill also discusses some of the problems faced by West Indian children in coping with English even although for them it is not a second language.

A different aspect of language development was explored by Tough (1973) who compared the purposes for which language was used by two groups of young children, initially of pre-school age and studied in a play situation. She found that while both groups of children used language to interact for certain purposes, there was a significant difference in the extent to which language was used for cognitively demanding purposes by the advantaged group and the difference increased with time though both groups had scored comparably, and high, on an intelligence test. The educational significance of findings such as these has been stressed in, for example, the Bullock Report, A Language for Life (DES 1975). Again it is important in considering the educational significance of findings such as these to bear in mind that while there were average differences between the groups there was still evidence in both groups of instances of use of language for a variety of purposes. Thus to interpret this within a "deficit" model would be unnecessary, it would seem important rather to explore the types of situations which can optimise the use of language for a variety of purposes. It further acts as a warning against judging the variety of language of which a child is capable from a limited example of his speech in a particular situation. As a result of her studies of young children in play situations, Tough was led to develop strategies to assist teachers in encouraging language development of a more cognitively demanding kind (See, for example, Tough 1976).

The problems of stimulating language development and interaction in a group setting with what she refers to as poorly functioning children have been explored by Blank in a number of publications - a difficulty faced by teachers of school aged and pre-school children. Blank highlights some of the problems caused by the group setting where in order to encourage the participation and co-operation of the more poorly functioning children the teacher may be faced with responses which are not just incorrect but irrelevant, which it is difficult to build upon or even to utilise and stay within the topic under discussion. She stresses the importance, with very poorly functioning children, of at least brief tutorial sessions in which the topic under discussion is drawn from shared experience. She also stresses in her writings the greater complexity of certain types of questions and their importance for cognitive development - the question of "why" and "how" rather than "where" and "what", since the latter type elicit only labelling responses. In a group situation the poorly functioning child who does manage to contribute may be continuing to respond only at this less demanding level (See Blank 1973 and Blank, Rose and Berlin 1978). The researches on language mentioned so far whether by Tough, Blank, Labov, or even those of Bernstein, could all be interpreted as illustrating the importance of the situation in influencing the quantity and quality of the oral language

74

likely to be elicited from children and the dangers of drawing conclusions from limited instances. In a valuable overview on "the Neglected Situation", Cazden (1970) discusses the importance of the task, the topic and the listener to oral language. Cazden in that article and in a more recent one (1977), makes a number of important points of significance not only to the teacher of the young child to whom the more recent paper is particularly addressed, but also to teachers of a wide range of ages and background.

Competence in oral language and understanding of spoken language are clearly important, particularly in early education, not only as a medium of instruction and means by which its success can be judged. Development of the ability to understand a wider range of spoken language and to communicate effectively by means of spoken language to a variety of recipients in a number of settings, would also be regarded as one goal in education, particularly in the early years. Gradually, however, written language as a source of information and as a means of communication begins to assume important proportions in the life of the classroom.

Written Language

Mastery of the ability to read and write at an early stage in educational process is crucially important because apart from any intrinsic worth in the skills themselves, within the classroom setting these soon become major tools whereby access to a range of instructional material is made possible and because the child is able by writing to exhibit the extent of his assimilation of the appropriate instruction. Indeed the effects of failure to acquire reading skill soon become pervasive in such a way, as compared with for example difficulty with mathematics, that what might initially have been a specific difficulty may well be interpreted by subsequent teachers as a general all round failure - or lack of potential. The extent to which reading and learning to read may helpfully be regarded as a language process has been discussed elsewhere (Clark 1975 and 1976). In Understanding Reading, a most influential book in the early seventies, Smith (1971) argues persuasively for the importance of considering reading and learning to read from the standpoint of what the skilled reader does and the beginning reader is trying to do; and the need to consider the skills the child brings to the reading situation for which he seldom has credit. While Smith does not give empirical evidence to support his stance, views such as his are important to the practitioner who may wish to re-appraise techniques of instruction in order to ensure that forms of instruction appropriate for shorter-term goals are not detrimental to longer term objectives of developing a skilled flexible reader who can cope readily with a variety of material, very different from the scheme reader in the Basal Reading Scheme. Clay, considers reading as a "Patterning of Complex Behaviour" (Clay 1972) while Goodman uses the term "A Psycholinguistic Guessing Game" for reading (Goodman 1973), stressing the need in learning to read for prediction based on a knowledge of the likely sequence of words in sentences in written form which may be very different from the way the message would be transmitted orally. While it is important not to neglect the visual perceptual aspects of the reading task, a study of the work of Smith, Goodman and Clay is of value in redressing balance for those involved in early reading instruction - or work with backward readers. Teachers may well be led to question their formulation of the task, possibly even the materials used, and the emphasis by some on training certain kinds of visual or auditory identification or discrimination skills in which a child's weakness may have been apparent and regarded as a crucial feature in the learning situation, yet in spite of which some children may have acquired reading competence. A study of these authors may help to pin-point crucial ways in which learning to read does depend on oral language and ways in which the two skills are fundamentally different. An appreciation of the language context of reading also helps teachers to appreciate the similarities and differences in the skills of reading and spelling; why for some children, even some of those who are good readers, spelling instruction may be necessary, and what are the essential features of such instruction. In reading, the ability to predict the likely sequence of words, partly developed through oral language and partly through interaction with print, is important, hence the insistence by the authors referred to above that one learns to read by reading. Such a mastery does not necessarily lead to competence in spelling, a task in which recall, with precise accuracy of each letter and in order (while concentrating on other aspects of writing) is essential. Even in spelling, however, the evidence is that good and poor spellers differ in their awareness of the likely probability of certain letter combinations appearing in the language in which they can spell efficiently, some of these being specific to a particular language; they thus have a language sensitivity. They do not, on the other hand differ in their ability to remember groups of letters which are not word-like in the order in which the letters are placed. In short, the difference between a group of good and poor spellers in the English language in recalling nonsense "words" increases, the greater their approximation to English words. Further discussion of these points and of child and teacher variables influencing progress in spelling are discussed in Peters (1970)).

With the greater emphasis now on the language of books as being somewhat different from spoken language this has implications not only for our understanding of the reading process but also with regard to the issue as to whether and for what purposes it is necessary to encourage standard English and discourage dialect in order to prepare the child for reading. In as far as it is accepted that written language has important unique features, it is possible to argue that a sensitivity to the appropriate styles for written language can be developed through a wide experience of books while leaving the least in the early stages if desired a more colloquial or "dialect" form of oral communication. Standard English in spoken form would then be regarded as a necessary skill in certain contexts for oral communcation but not as a pre-requisite for either reading or the development of written language, which would be more likely to be developed by experience of reading - and attempting to communicate in writing. In Clark (1976 p. 87-88) there is an example of a boy able to read before starting school and to write effectively who yet spoke in dialect even in a formal situation. These points are discussed further in (Trudgill 1975) and also in two books in which the inter-relatedness of reading and writing are considered - Language and Literacy: The Sociolinguistics of Reading and Writing, Stubbs (1980), and Reading and Writing for the Child with Difficulties edited by Clark and Glynn (1980). There is a growing interst by those involved in research in reading in the reciprocal relationship between reading and writing, Clay (1980 in Clark and Glynn eds.), for example, has suggested that creative writing, from which the child who has difficulty in learning to read is often debarred, may have a role to play in the development of reading competence, in addition to being a pleasurable activity in its own right.

One of the advantages of skill in writing as a form of communication is that the message can be modified, the style changed for greater precision or for enhanced effect or a more telling or persuasive argument developed in ways that is not possible in the instantaneous communication of spoken language. In the educational setting it is thus important that writing as a form of communication is open to the child. Provided written language is used in this way with the child encouraged to draft and re-draft, not merely to correct, but to modify to achieve the most effective communication, it is an invaluable medium through which the child can learn about language. As Binns (1980) has pointed out, in many cases it is only the corrective proof reading aspect of re-drafting that is permitted to children. A skill which it is important for the teacher to acquire is the ability to assist children to become self-evaluative in such a way that they improve their communicative competence in written as well as spoken language.

The crucial importance of the situation in determining the quality and quantity of both spoken and written language is being stressed in more and more of the recent research findings. Thus important skills for the teacher to acquire are a sensitivity to the variations in understanding of language of the individual children in the class and an ability to devise situations which are rich and varied enough to act as a stimulus to the development of spoken and written language.

COMMUNICATION IN THE CLASSROOM

Until recently there has been little first-hand knowledge of the dynamics of the normal classroom, and teaching has been an isolated occupation with one adult and normally a large group of children spending much of the day behind a closed door. While in the primary school most of the day was usually spent in the same classroom, in the secondary school the children would move from one room to another, but even then there was no first-hand knowledge from observation as to how the interaction of particular children varied from classroom to classroom or of the extent to which even as generalised a feature as teaching style was modified from class to class. During teacher training a student teacher would be observed, but in a setting artificial in so many ways that even long term predictions about that student's performance were not impressive, while generalisations about the dynamics of the classroom from such observations were scarcely justified. Assessment of the effectiveness of teaching was to a great extent in terms of the product of written assessment or examination results rather than by a study of the process of instruction.

The structure of schools has changed as well as the organisation of the classrooms and both have to be considered in any attempt to assess the dynamics of the setting in which formal education takes place. In the primary school after the publication of Children and their Primary Schools, the Plowden Report (DES 1967) in England and Primary Education in Scotland (SED 1965), there was assumed to be a move towards group teaching in primary classes with less and less instruction of the whole class. In a number of researches, differences in attainment were reported when more or less progressive approaches were adopted by the teacher - different classroom organisation or teaching style. Seldon, however, was there any assessment of the "dynamics" of the classroom and the extent to which these apparent changes in approach was reflected in fundamental changes in interaction in the classroom. (See for example Bennett 1976 and the discussion of this study in the book by Galton, Simon and Croll, 1980).

The Open Plan school is an architectural design which may

facilitate certain changes in organisation of the school. Here also, however, there may be no fundamental change and it is still possible to find in schools built on an open plan, classrooms very similar in dynamics to those in a closed plan except that in the former the lack of sound-proofing between the classes militates against effective communication in the classroom. At the other extreme, it may be that there are large groups of children sharing a "team" of teachers or even that individual children pace themselves consulting teachers of their choice and only when they feel the necessity. Team teaching itself again can vary depending on the relative status, knowledge and acceptability to the children of the various members of the team. Team teaching is relatively new in primary and secondary classrooms and little observational research has been based on this.

Analysis of the communication patterns between staff and children has become a major interest in the more recent researches in pre-school education. While there is normally a better adult child-ratio than in classrooms for older children, only a proportion of the adults will be teachers, and there will normally be several adults available to any group of children. There are thus enough similarities to the team-teaching and open plan situations for valuable insights to be gained from the pre-school studies both with regard to crucial variables to be investigated and possible methodological techniques - and problems. In some studies the focus has been on the adults and the factors which appear to influence the typical range of their language, such as the perceived hierarchy among the staff, the heterogeneity or otherwise of the groups of children, the types of activity which are being supervised and the organisation of the day. In other studies the target has been the children observed over time, or compared with each other, or in different settings. It is clear that while availability of additional adults may increase the possibility of extended dialogue for a greater number of children, this will not necessarily take place and there are significant managerial as well as personality features which will have a bearing on the patterns of communication within different groupings of adults and children. Thus not only have the researches been valuable in alerting staff to the findings in a variety of settings, but also some of the observational schedules are themselves of value in training staff to a greater sensitivity, to the extent of involvement of particular children, and to the features which appear to stimulate this. Some examples of studies of communication in pre-school settings are to be found in Tizard et al 1976 and 1980 and in the reports of the Oxford Pre-School Project direct by Bruner in Sylva, Roy and Painter, (1980) and Wood, McMahon and Cranston, (1980). A comparison of the interaction of children perceived as having special needs and others not so perceived in attendance at the same ordinary pre-school units is reported in Clark and Cheyne (1979) and is being further investigated using observational schedules in an on-going research also directed by the writer.

There have been surprisingly few studies of the dynamics of communication in primary school classrooms - all the more surprising in view of the assumptions which have been made about dramatic changes both in the curriculum and the organisation of classrooms as a result of reports such as the Plowden Report referred to earlier (DES 1967) with the critics assuming chaos and a move away from the basics, while others have assumed the development of an individualised approach and more extensive and creative curriculum. One of the earlier studies based on observation in classrooms in which an attempt was made to study "The Teacher's Day" in the primary school was that of Hilsum and Cane (1971). Even at that time the picture in the classroom was more fragmentary and the time devoted to instruction more limited in total than many would have expected. In a more recent series of studies "Inside the Primary Classroom" by Galton, Simon and Croll (1980), the various classroom patterns of grouping have been studied along with the types of dialogue occurring between teacher and pupils in the different contexts. In this study the communicaton has been viewed both from the teacher's perspective and from that of a number of target pupils of different levels of ability, while in a second publication these patterns of communication have been related to progress and attainment (Galton and Simon 1980). In their first publication, Galton, Simon and Croll report less evidence of group and individualised teaching than most would have expected. They stress the managerial problems such an approach involves and give evidence of the extent to which the communication between the teacher and individual pupils either alone or when in groups was managerial rather than instructional, concerned with what to do and how to do it, the talk tended to be "at" rather than "with" children in these settings. They found evidence of more cognitively stimulating talk between pupils and teachers in the class setting where the organisational problems were less. It is important, however, to look at this important situation from the perspective of the individual pupil who in such a setting would have little opportunity to contribute and even less to develop an extended communication, or to initiate.

The research workers made an extensive and elaborate analysis of the dynamics of different classrooms, and of the same classroom at different times. In the latter instance one of the points under consideration was the stability or variability of the organisation and whether or not the teachers were "frequent changers". They also compared the proportion of "intermittent workers" and "quiet collaborators" in the different settings. They did not find evidence of the chaos or departure from the basics which many critics of so called progressive education would have expected; on the contrary they found a relatively high level of work-related activity in the primary classrooms they investigated. On the other hand they found little evidence that pupils even at this stage in the school would during a day have had much interaction in the classroom either with the teacher or with other pupils. Since in studies such as this it is the research workers who tend to define instructional talk it is perhaps worth drawing attention to the work of Duthie (1970) in which an analysis was made of the teaching and "housekeeping" duties during the day in a variety of classrooms and with a range of age groups of children. This study was undertaken in an attempt to assess the extent to which and the ways in which the appointment of non-teaching auxiliaries in classrooms could assist teachers by relieving them of non-teaching duties. A striking finding was the variation in the pattern and extent of housekeeping duties or non-teaching duties undertaken by different teachers - even with the same age of children or type of school. In as far as communication in the classroom of a cognitively stimulating and extended type is seen as an important aspect of instruction it is clearly important to encourage teachers themselves to study by transcripts, for example, the nature of communication in the classroom in order to plan ways in which to maximise the time devoted to instructional language in its broadest sense.

When attention is turned to the content of the dialogue in primary classrooms, as Galton, Simon and Croll indicate, there has been very little research. The work of Barnes (1969) and others in secondary school classrooms and in a variety of subject areas attracted considerable attention, showing as it did that even when apparently open-ended questions were asked by a teacher often there were "right" answers which the teacher expected, while other equally valid answers would be rejected. In Language, the Learner and the School Barnes (1969), and in other similar studies examples of dialogue are reported and discussed in a context which is valuable for staff development and also in the pre-service training of teachers. The hidden language of the classroom becomes clear from a study of extended dialogue between teacher and the class as does the need for acceptable forms as well as content of response by pupils if their contributions are to be accepted. The register adopted in classroom discourse is discussed by Edwards in Language in Culture and Class (1976), and the evidence from researches that in general terms communication in the classroom is a one-way process with teacher dominance as one striking feature of the discourse. It is not only as pointed out by Flanders after many hours of classroom observation that two thirds of time spent in the classroom someone is talking, and the chances are two out of three it is the teacher. What is perhaps more important still is that "teachers usually tell pupils what to do, how to do it, when to start, when to stop and how well they did whatever they did" (quoted by Edwards, 1976 in Flanders, 1970 p.14). Teachers usually initiate, pupils respond. This chapter by Edwards is a valuable scene setter for anyone wishing to study the more recent classroom interaction studies. He not only draws together a number of the studies of language, but also considers some of the problems in reducing the dynamics of the classroom to fit interaction schedules such as that of Flanders, pointing out for example the importance of knowing the context in order to evaluate the significance and even the meaning of particular responses. In a recent review article McIntyre (1980) discusses the way ahead in studies of interaction in classrooms and stresses the need for "focussing on carefully selected and pre-defined facets of classroom activity", otherwise the observer may be guilty of a subjectivity of which he may not himself be aware (p.3). He claims that the early classroom interaction studies had a teacher focus and an overwhelming concern with attending and task involvement and that the assumed goal had been pupil compliance. He expresses concern that those involved with classroom interaction have tended to be more concerned with the reliability of the observations than their validity and argues that while systematic classroom observation could be most valuable in identifying "effective teaching" this is where it has so far been inadequate. For this the framework must include teachers' conceptualisation of what they are doing and what they are trying to do.

In a review article on Perspectives on Classroom Language in the same journal, Edwards (1980) claims that in the kind of analyses which McIntyre is discussing "speech is too often treated as a transparent medium for the exchange of meanings and the organisation of relationships", (p.31). He is by this statement emphasising that there is greater complexity in classroom talk than is appreciated by many of those involved in classroom interaction studies and that there are occasions for example when what is meant is left unsaid or when the participants themselves may be suspending judgment. A combination of these two review articles by McIntyre and Edwards gives a very valuable balanced perspective with a review of a range of studies, a consideration of their limitations and of the way ahead. Edwards includes in his review a section on "Language Use and Scholastic Success" in which he refers to a number of the researches discussed earlier in this chapter in which the importance of the situation was stressed as a determinant of the quality and quantity of language. It is important, he feels, that teachers and research workers, appreciate the possibility that children may fail to respond not because they cannot but because they have not understood what is expected of them by way of a response. In addition, however, he stresses the need for teachers, particularly in multi-cultural societies to appreciate that children's answering or failure to answer could be as a result of following different rules of communication. He draws attention also to the evidence that lower working class children for example are less inclined unless pushed to give answers, or at least verbally elaborated answers, to questions when they perceive the questioner knows the answer already; which it has been shown in many researches is a feature of most questions in the classroom setting. There are a number of aspects of communication in the classroom to which Edwards draws attention which are of importance, including the ratio of pupil to teacher talk and equally important the proportion of teacher directed talk. Even with systematic observation however, it is still difficult to appreciate the complexity of meanings which may be largely inaccessible to the observer - an example is in attempts to decode classroom humour.

In attempting to understand communication in the classroom it is important to include study of the "moves" and the "exchanges", that is the larger units of dialogue, and not only the frequency of contribution and the initiator. Dialogue between adults and children is often asymmetrical with the adult permitted to ignore questions, yet insist on answers, interrupt yet refuse to be interrupted. In the classroom because of the group setting, resulting in frequent interruption to teacher-pupil dialogue, and the explicit instructional context with the teacher perceived as having the answers and the child as expected to acquire them - and to respond appropriately, understanding of the complexities of the communication patterns is even more complicated than in ordinary adult-child dialogue. When there is added to that the parameters of acceptable modes of response in the classroom and by the various teachers, the success of so many children in acquiring the appropriate communicative competence becomes impressive. The significance of communicative competence to progress makes it essential that teachers and researches achieve a clearer understanding of the patterns of communication in the classroom and the purposes. According to Edwards it is only in the last ten years that researchers studying communication in the classrooms have recorded the actual words exchanged rather than codings of them and it is therefore only in recent years that the full complexity of the interactions has been apparent and the limited options for response available to pupils in many of these settings.

Before closing this section on communication it seems

pertinent to include a reference to a rather different aspect of communication also based on classroom interaction studies, that of the amount and duration of instances of reading in a range of secondary school classrooms. The evidence from this study, which is of importance to teachers in planning the contexts for reading in their classrooms, is reported in the The Effective Use of Reading, (Lunzer and Gardner 1979). This study revealed how brief and limited are the contacts with print of many pupils in the secondary school - even with a very low level definition of the act of reading. The organisational patterns of instruction were found in many instances to militate against prolonged and concentrated encounters with print in ways which would develop an understanding of, and appreciation of complex written language. For most pupils it would be difficult with these limited and brief encounters to appreciate the theme of a book, the style of an author or the complexities of a textbook. The fragmentary nature of these contacts would make access to written communication an even greater problem for the child of limited reading ability. Gardner (1980) has stressed the need, particularly with such pupils, to adapt the setting, rather than simplify the text, in such a way as to facilitate more sustained and concentrated encounters with books, to avoid what he describes as "Failure to Read" rather than "Reading Failure". Clearly this is yet another instance in which sensitive and prolonged observation in classrooms may help us to analyse the interactions but where in addition a framework for analyses of these is essential in order to relate the goals of the instruction to the potential of the setting.

LEARNING

It seems essential within a chapter such as this to explore the extent to which the thinking of teachers about educability and the potential for learning of the children for whose education they are responsible has been coloured by assumptions about the distinctness of ability and attainment and the innateness of ability, of which intelligence testing may give an approximate estimate and from which potential attainment can be predicted. Most textbooks recommended to teachers in training would until recently probably have contained a section in which ability and attainment were distinguished, with intelliigence tests as indicators of the former and scholastic tests of the latter. Much of the organisation of learning has been, and indeed still is, based on the assumptions in spite of growing evidence of a much greater interrelatedness of the two concepts. Selection for secondary education by means of intelligence tests, or aided by these, was based on the assumption of a measurable innate potential which could be judged at an early age; and while this form of clear-cut selection may be less in evidence at the present time, the establishment of the "slow learners" class is still within the same framework. The separation into special education of a certain proportion of children as a result of intelligence tests is based on similar assumptions that ability is being measured and that the results make possible a long term prediction for individual children. This categorisation of the need for special education of the ESN(M) child on account of limited intelligence could be challenged on many grounds, including the evidence that many children of similar measured levels remain in ordinary schools and in some cases achieve a degree of success which would not have been anticipated from a fatalistic assumption of their limited potential. Again, the distinction in textbooks on remedial education between the "backward" reader and the "retarded" reader identifies the former as failing to achieve a level expected of a child of that age while the latter's level of achievement would have been assessed in relation to his "mental" age. The concept of "under-achievement" which either explicitly or implicitly influences decisions such as in some instances access to remedial education or whether or not a child is regarded as having a specific learning difficulty continues to be a feature of categorisation of children's learning potential and teacher expectation. This, in spite of questioning of the whole issue of "under-achievement" for over twenty years as to some extent an artefact of the statistical features of the tests, and the evidence that there must also be a considerable number of over-achievers as a result of test construction.

It is neither possible nor appropriate in this context to explore the controversies on intelligence tests and testing nor the issues on the relative contributions of genetic and environmental influences and differences in measured intelligence between different cultural groups. For a discussion of such issues the reader is referred to Vernon (1969). From a different but equally relevant standpoint the problems in assessing the level of a child's understanding of Piagetian-type tasks is discussed in Donaldson (1978). It is also important to draw the attention of teachers to the possibility that their judgments of pupils, in addition to being coloured by the language competence exhibited in the classroom, may be influenced in such a way as to lead to over generalisations of learning capacity based on assessment of a child as "bright" or "dull", a "slow learner" or with "specific difficulties". It is possible for the organisation of the school or classroom to "confirm" these assumptions - or for the teacher to ignore evidence which does not match the expectation. In an interesting paper in which she explores this issue of terminology in relation to learning difficulties, Hunter (1980) discusses the need for teachers to learn to "read" their pupils by sensitive observation and not to adopt terminology which leads them to over-generalise. In a recent lecture on intelligence testing Vernon (1979) discussed a number of issues on the relationship between intelligence and educational testing. While concerned that we should not "throw away the baby with the bath water", he does stress the need for criterion-referenced tests to assess the stage which a child has reached in learning and where he should go next. He refers to the view of a number of writers that "IQ tests are predictive of achievement only in a monolithic educational system" - a point well worth further consideration. One writer who would certainly argue for a very different conceptualisation of learning and ability is Bloom (1979) who in considering new directions in educational research argued for a change in emphasis from the actors (teachers and students) to the study of learning and teaching and from stable or static variables to variables which are alterable either before the teaching - learning process or as part of these processes. He would argue for a focus on "cognitive entry skills" (rather than intelligence) and formative testing rather than summative (or achievement) testing and for a focus on teaching rather than teachers. Rather than becoming embroiled in issues of intelligence versus attainment or heredity versus environment in categoriation of children or in defining styles of teachers, it seems more profitable to analyse the teaching - learning process wherever it takes place. Studies of language and of communication in the classroom are already providing valuable insights of relevance to the understanding of the teaching/learning process and revealing to those in education both the complexity of the task in which they are involved and the potential of those with whom they are concerned.

REFERENCES

Barnes, D. Language, the Learner and the School. (Penguin Education, Harmondsworth, 1969).

Bennett, S.N. Teaching Styles and Pupil Progress. (Open Books, London, 1976).

Bloom, B.S. Alterable Variables: The New Direction in Educational Research. (The Scottish Council for Research in Education, Edinburgh, 1979).

Bernstein, B. "A Sociolinguistic Approach to Socialisation, with some Reference to Educability" in F. Williams (ed) Language and Poverty, pp.25-61, (Chicago, 1970).

Bernstein, B. Class, Codes and Control, Vol.2. (Routledge & Kegan Paul, London, 1973).

Binns, R. "A Technique for Developing Written Language" in Clark, M.M. and Glynn, T. (eds) Reading and Writing for the Child with Difficulties, pp.44-54, Educational Review Occasional Publications No.8, University of Birmingham, Birmingham, 1980.

Blank, M. Teaching Learning in the Preschool Charles E. Merrill, Columbus, Ohio, 1973.

Blank, M., Rose, S.A & Berlin, L.J. The Language of Learning: The Preschool Years. Grune and Stratton, New York, 1978.

Bronfenbrenner, U. "Is early intervention effective? Facts and principles of early intervention: a summary" in Clarke, A.M. and Clarke, A.D.B. (Eds) Early Experience: Myth and Evidence. pp.247-256,(Open books, London, 1976).

Cazden, C.B. "The Neglected Situation in Child Language Research and Education" in Williams, F. (ed) Language and Poverty, pp.81-101, (Markham Pub.Co., Chicago,1970).

Cazden, C.B. "Concentrated versus Contrived Encounters" in A. Davies (ed) Language and Learning in Early Childhood. pp.40-59,(Heinnemann, London, 1977).

Clark, M.M. "Language and Reading: Research Trends" in A. Davies (ed) Problems of Language and Learning. pp89-103,(Heinemann, London, 1975).

Clark, M.M. Young Fluent Readers. (Heinemann Educational, London,1976).

Clark, M.M. Studies in Pre-school Education. (Hodder and Stoughton, London, 1979).

Clark, M.M. & Glynn T. (eds). Reading and Writing for the Child with Difficulties. Educational Review Occasional Publication No.8, University of Birmingham, Birmingham, 1980.

Clay, M.M. Reading the Patterning of Complex behaviour. (Heinemann Educational, London, 1972).

Clay, M.M. "Early Writing and Reading: Reciprocal Gains" in Clark, M.M. and Glynn, T. (eds) Reading and Writing for the Child with Difficulties. Educational Review Occasional Publication No.8, pp.27-43, Birmingham University, Birmingham, 1980.

Department of Education and Science. Children and their Primary Schools. (H.M.S.O., London, 1967).

Department of Educationand Science. A Language for Life. (H.M.S.O., London, 1975).

Donachy, W. "Parental Participation in Preschool Education" in Clark, M.M. and Cheyne, W.M. (eds) Studies in Preschool Education. pp.122-149,Hodder and Stoughton, London, 1979).

Donaldson, M. Children's Minds. (Fontana, 1978).

Downing, J. Reading and Reasoning. (Chambers, 1979).

Duthie, J.H. Primary School Survey: A Study of the teacher's Day. (H.M.S.O., Edinburgh, 1970)

Edwards, A.D. Language in Culture and Class. (Heinemann Educational, London, 1976).

Edwards, A.D. "Perspectives on Classroom Language".Educational Analysis,2, pp.31-46, 1980.

Gahagan, D.M. & Gahagan, G.A. Talk Reform: Explorations in Language for Infant School Children, (Routledge and Kegan Paul, London, 1970).

Galton, M. & Simon, B. (eds). Progress and Performance in the Primary Classroom. (Routledge & Kegan Paul, London, 1980).

Galton, M., Simon, B. & Croll, P. Inside the Primary Classroom, (Routledge & Kegan Paul, London, 1980).

Glynn, T. "Parent-Child Interaction in Remedial Reading at Home" in Clark, M.M. and Glynn, T, (eds) Reading and Writing for the Child with Difficulties. Educational Review Occasional Publication No.8, pp.67--79, (University of Birmingham, Birmingham, 1980).

Goodman, K.S. "Psycholinguistic Universals in the Reading Process", in Smith, F (ed) Psycholinguistics and Reading. pp.21-27, (Holt, Rinehart & Winston, New York, 1973).

Hilsum, S & Cane, B.S. The Teacher's Day. (National Foundation for Educational Research, Windsor, 1971).

Hunter, C.M. "Becoming a better teacher of children with learning difficulties" in M.M. Clark and T. Glynn (eds.). Reading and Writing for the Child with Difficulties Educational Review Occasional Publications No.8, (University of Birmingham, 1980).

Lunzer, E. & Gardner, K. (eds). The Effective Use of Reading. (Heinemann Education, London, 1979).

McIntyre, D.I. "Systematic Observation of Classroom Activities" Educational Analysis, 2, pp.3-30, 1980.

Peters, M.L. Success in Spelling, (Institute of Education, Cambridge, 1970).

Robinson, W.P. "Language Management, Socio-economic Status and Educational Progress" in Hersov, L.A., and Berger, M. (eds) Language and Language Disorders in Childhood. pp.23-47, (Pergamon, Oxford, 1980).

Scottish Educational Department. Primary Education in Scotland. (H.M.S.O., Edinburgh, 1965).

Smith, F. Understanding Reading. Holt, (Rinehart & Winston, New York, 1971).

Stanley, J.C. (ed). Preschool Programmes for the Disadvantaged. (The Johns Hopkins University Press, Baltimore, 1972).

Stanley, J.C. (ed). Compensatory Education for Children Ages Two to Eight. (The Johns Hopkins University Press, Baltimore, 1973).

Stubbs, M. Language and Literacy: The Sociolinguistics of Reading and Writing. (Routledge & Kegan Paul, London, 1980).

Sylva, K., Roy, C & Painter, M. Childwatching at Playgroup and Nursey School. (Grant McIntyre, London,1980).

Tizard, B., Philps, J & Plewis, I. "Staff Behaviour in Preschool Centres" Journal of Child Psychology and Psychiatry, 1976, 17, pp.21-33.

Tizard, B., Carmichael, H & Pinkerton, G. "Four Year Olds Talking to Mothers and Teachers" in Hughes, M., Hersov, L.A. & Berger, M. Language and Language Disorders in Childhood, pp.49-76.(Pergamon, Oxford, 1980).

Tough, J. "The Language of Young Children: The Implications for the Education of the Young Disadvantaged Child" in Chazan, M. (ed) Education in the Early Years, pp.60-76, (Faculty of Education, University of Swansea, Swansea, 1973).

Tough, J. Listening to Children Talking: A Guide to the Appraisal of Children's Use of Language. (Ward Lock Educational, London, 1976).

Trudgill, P. Accent, Dialect and the School, (Arnold, London, 1975).

Vernon, P,E. Intelligence and Cultural Environment,(Methuen, London, 1969).

Vernon, P.E. Intelligence Testing 1928-1978 - What next? (Scottish Council for Research in Education, 1979).

Wood, D., McMahon,L. and Cranston, Y. Working with Under Fives,(Grant McIntyre, London, 1980).

Chapter 4

ADAPTING INSTRUCTION FOR THE LEARNER

Richard J. Riding

In planning instruction the teacher needs to consider both the aspects of the learning process that are common to all pupils, and also those in which they may differ. As an example, take two children, Jack and Jill, who are about to embark on learning the same topic in mathematics. What must their teacher take into account in order to ensure that the instruction is effective? Firstly there must be an awareness of what they already know about mathematics that is necessary to the understanding of the new work. They cannot be taught how to solve simultaneous equations until they can cope with ordinary equations. Successful learning is rather like building a wall - each new topic may only be added if the ones on which it depends for meaning are already in place. Secondly, the new material must be presented at a rate which is slow enough for Jack and Jill to process it. Understanding, whether it be of the meaning of a spoken sentence or following written algebra, takes time and pupils need sufficient opportunity to analyse each new fact and relate it to what they already know.

The basic conditions mentioned so far apply in a similar manner to both Jack and Jill. There are two further ones in which they may be quite dissimilar, and here the instruction will need to be adapted to their particular characteristics. One of these is the manner in which they represent information in memory. Jack finds that he learns best when verbal descriptions are given, while Jill prefers visual presentation of the material in form of graphs, diagrams and pictures. We could call Jack a "verbaliser" and Jill an "imager" in their learning styles. The second way in which pupils may differ in the sensitivity of their learning system. Jack requires material to be clearly structured by the teacher, while Jill can impose her own organisation without difficulty.

If learning is to be effective, all four of these conditions must be adjusted to suit the individual student. In this chapter, methods for ensuring efficient learning will be considered by taking these basic aspects of the process in turn. The four areas may be summarised as follows:

(1) The learning system has an input limit because time is required to analyse the meaning of new information and if insufficient time is available some details will be lost from the system and consequently not actually learned.

(2) The meaningfulness of learning depends on there being in memory the necessary knowledge to make sense of any new material. If this knowledge is not available new learning will either not take place or will be rote in character.

(3) Information can be represented in memory in either verbal or imagery form, or both, and which mode is preferred varies from individual to individual.

(4) People also differ in the sensitivity of their learning system in that some are very analytical and good at discrimination while others are not.

(1) THE INPUT CAPACITY OF THE LEARNING SYSTEM

The learning system can be viewed as consisting of three stages:

    1   Sensory memory
    2   Primary (or short-term) memory
    3   Secondary (or long-term memrory)

Information is received by the eyes and the ears and is stored in sensory memory while it is transferred to primary memory (which is also frequently referred to as short-term memory) where it is analysed before being permanently stored in secondary memory (also known as long-term memory) where it is retained until it is recalled.

The present section will concentrate on the processing capacity of primary memory. Consider the sentence, "The squirrel ran across the grass and bounded up the trunk of the oak tree". As you read these words the pattern of them is transferred to primary memory where their meaning is determined in terms of what is already known. You give meaning to the words by scanning through your knowledge of them stored in secondary memory and then working out the overall sense of the sentence. Since you analyse meaning automatically and quickly you are not consciously aware of the process. Although it is done quickly it does take time, and so there is a physical limitation on the rate at which you can learn. Like all processing systems, the human system has a limited rate of processing. If this rate is exceeded then all of the information will not be completely processed and consequently not properly transferred to secondary memory.

As an example of how the system can be overloaded read these digits: 9 5 2 7 4 1 0 9 8 3. Now close your eyes and see if you can remember the numbers. If you did not cheat you probably got about seven of them. Why not all? Because of the limited processing capacity of your learning system. The limitation only applies to the input system of primary memory and not to the capacity of secondary memory, since much longer lists of items can be learned if sufficient presentations are given.

The evidence for the existence of primary memory is briefly described by Riding (1977, pages 12-16). (For a more comprehensive and technical discussion see Craik and Levy 1976). Here a single typical experiment that has implications for learning will be described. Glanzer, Gianutsos and Dubin (1969). They studied the free recall of word lists by asking student subjects to read a twelve word list aloud and then do an adding task for one, five or ten seconds before recalling the list. They found that the longer the adding task the poorer the recall of the most recently received words. In other words, the longer the task the more information lost from primary memory. The question now arises whether this is due to time alone or to the task. Do items fade from primary memory or are they displaced? They investigated this in a further study by trying different combinations of the size of the task done after reading the list and time for which it was performed. They found that increasing the size of task from reading two additional words to six words reduced recall, but increasing the time in which the task was undertaken from two to four seconds did not. This suggests that words were lost from primary memory by displacement and not by fading.

In the practical situation this will mean that a child listening to a lesson or to instructions given by the teacher must analyse the meaning of a sentence in primary memory before it is displaced by the next sentence. The child who is slow at processing will find that either he analyses the present sentence and neglects the next, or the other way round. In either case he will not get all the information and so the whole sense of the information will not be completely understood and stored in secondary memory.

Now pupils will not be consciously aware of the sentences, or parts of sentences, that have been lost from primary memory, but will simply realise that they do not completely understand what has been said. The consequence will be that they are unable to do some subsequent activity based on the instruction or will lose interest in the lesson. Insufficient time to processs information will probably affect young children differently. With some children in infants school a shortage of processing time will result in the sense of a sentence not being determined, while with older pupils, since they will be more proficient at analysing sentences, the problem will be in relating the new information to the details that preceded it and the knowledge already in secondary memory.

Studies of Presentation Rate

The general effect of reducing the amount of time availble for processing spoken material is to decrease the level of comprehension. Work on the comprehension of time compressed speech indicates that as speech rate is increased from normal speech (approximately 150 wpm) up to 400 wpm, performance decreases fairly linearly (see Foulke 1971). Since comprehension decreases as rate increases, it is likely that performance will increase if presentation rate is reduced. This has been found to be the case. Improved learning performance following a reduction in presentation rate has been found with children over a wide range of age and ability.

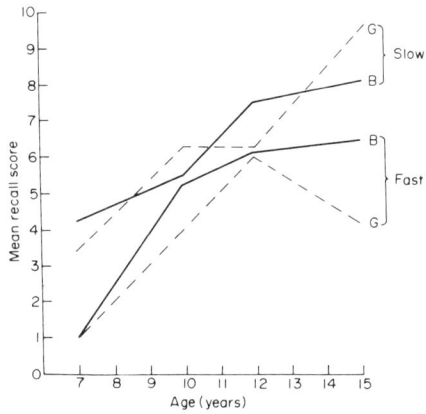

Figure 4.1. Recall at the Speech Rates by the Age Groups

Woodcock and Clark (1968) showed that reducing speech rate to 78 wpm improved comprehension compared with normal rate particularly for children of below average intelligence. Riding and Shore (1974) attempted to facilitate the reception of a story by maladjusted educationally subnormal 14 year old children. Performance on a recall test following normal rate presentation was 28 percent and this improved to 46 percent at 73 wpm. Riding and Vincent (1980) compared comprehension by normal children over the age range 7 to 15 years following fast (198 wpm) and slow (73 wpm) spoken presentation of a prose passage. The results are shown in Figure 4.1 and indicate that, while the slow presentation produces better performance at all ages, the improvement was most marked at 7 and 15 years. This was probably because the level to which

94

information is processed begins to change at about 12 years from a simple analaysis of the words heard to more emphasis on relating the content of the new material to the structure of knowledge in secondary memdory. At 7 years children are still struggling with analysis of the grammatical structure of the sentence, while at 15 they are trying to ensure that the new information is fitted into their store of knowledge about the topic. This distinction will now be considered more fully.

Assimilation and Accommodation

The results of studies of presentation rate on learning performance indicate that the amount of time available to a pupil for analysing new information and storing it in secondary memory has a critical effect on performance. For learning to be effective sufficient time must be given for the learning to be completed. In practical terms, the teacher will enquire what this means, and how the presentation of material to be learned can be adjusted to give peak performance? In order to answer this it is helpful to distinguish between two aspects of the learning process, assimiliation and accommodation. Assimilation is the reception and analysis of the meaning of new information. Accommodation is the relating of this new material to what is already known and this may result in some restructuring of the organisation of secondary memory. The distinction between the two aspects may be illustrated by considering the problems that follow the purchase of a grand piano. First of all you have to get it into the house (assimilation) by carefully manoeuvering the piano through the front door and along the hall and into the lounge. The next task is to position it in the lounge relative to the other items of furniture already there. This will probably mean a rearrangement in order to fit the piano in (accommodation).

Time will be required for both of these activities, and as children grow older accommodation becomes more involved and will require relatively more time than when the pupil is young.Consequently with young children (roughly 5 - 11 years) presentation should be slow enough to allow an analysis of the language used, and careful attention to speaking slowly and clearly will facilitate learning. With older children who have mastered the assimilation skills, the accommodation of information in secondary memory will probably be the principal consumer of time, and sufficient opportunity should be provided for this. As a general comment, since studies of slowing presentation rate have always shown an improvement in performance, it may be said that children learn more slowly than their teachers think they do!

Presentation Rate and Repetition.

Obviously there are at least two ways in which opportunity can be given to pupils to process a detail during learning. The one that has already been considered is to slow presentation rate so that more time is available to analyse each item of the material. The other is to repeat the information in order to give an additional opportunity for the child to process any parts of the topic that were missed on a previous presentation. Since this last method is often used by teachers it deserves examination. A typical situation would be that after explaining a point, the teacher says, "Now, Karen, do you understand that?" At which young Karen looks awkward, and shakes her head, and so the teacher says, "Well, listen carefully, and I will explain it again".

In a study by Riding and Smith (1981), eleven year old boys and girls listened to a tape-recorded account of the birth of the volcanic island of Surtsey. Different groups of the boys and girls heard at either approximately normal speech rate (160 wpm) or at slow rate (80 wpm) the passage once or the same passage twice or the passage followed by a paraphrase. One week later the children were given a 20 question test of the information in the passage. Their mean recall is given in Figure 4.3, which shows that while slowing presentation rate

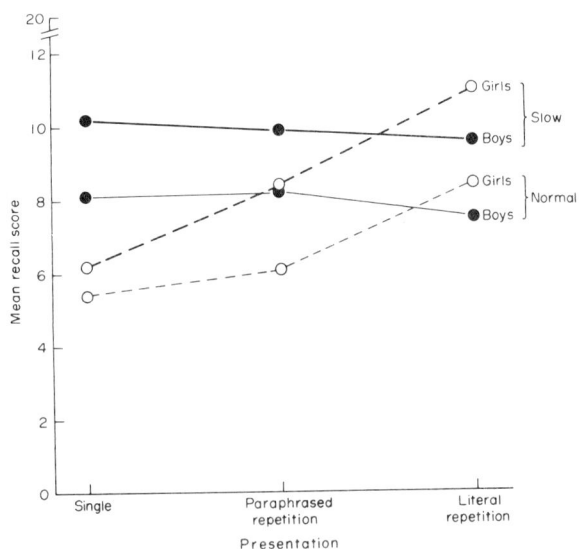

Figure 4.2. Recall for Presentation Conditions

improved learning for both sexes, repetition did not help the boys, but considerably aided the girls, particularly when it was verbatim. The reasons for this difference is not clear at present, but the findings indicate that using the optimum mode of presentaion can greatly improve performance. In the case of the girls, giving two slow presentations more than doubled learning compared to a single one at normal rate.

To conclude, the analysis of information during learning requires time and this limits the rate at which material can be processed.

(2) THE PUPIL'S PRESENT KNOWLEDGE

For new learning to be successful the information must make sense and also be related to the structure of knowledge the pupil already has in secondary memory. To illustrate this, consider the sentence, "The children saw an axolotl near the water". Since you give new information meaning in terms of what is already known, as you read each of the words in the sentence you quickly and automatically search through the lexicon of words in secondary memory to determine the sense of the sentence. This was easy for all words except "axolotl", which you probably did not recognise, so that overall the sentence did not make complete sense.

Suppose now that you are told that an axolotl is an amphibian, which is like a newt and lives in lakes in Mexico, then not only does the sentence have more meaning, but you are able to relate the concept of "axolotl" to information already in secondary memory by relating it to water life, or to Mexico.

For the two stages of analysis to be successfully completed there must obviously be within secondary memory the necessary concepts both to give meaning to the new information and for this new knowledge to be related to. Ausubel (1968) has stressed the importance of the relevant related concepts being readily available in memory before new learning is attempted. If information is presented that is not relatable to existing concepts in secondary memory, then, if it is learning at all, the learning will be rote and the new material will be stored as an isolated package. Rote learning takes longer than meaningful learning, and because the information is poorly organised in memory, retention is also often poor. This has implications for the way in which information should be sequenced to make learning efficient.

Sequencing Instruction

In school, before commencing a topic the teacher needs to assess which concepts are necessary to make it meaningful for the pupils, and then to ensure that they are already known. If they are absent they will need to be taught before embarking on the main topic, so that the new information can be learned.

The teacher should plan the topic so that all new concepts can be attached to those that have preceeded them. Sequencing a topic may be compared to building a wall, where each course of bricks must be laid on the bricks already in position. If any bricks are missing from a course, the next will not only be difficult to lay, but also unstable. The same principle applies to learning a topic. If some concepts are omitted or are not learned, then other ideas that are dependent on them for meaning will be difficult to learn.

The efficiency of the first stage of learning new information, whether it is a matter of sentences or a whole topic, depends very much upon the learner already having the necessary knowledge to give meaning to the new material. At the fairly low level of understanding a single sentence, if the meaning of the words is not known by the child, then the sentence cannot be understood. In the case of the description of a principle, such as the physical one of density, it cannot be fully understood until the pupil comprehends the concepts of mass, volume and inverse relationship upon which the definition of density depends. Similarly, ten year old children who live in an inner city area far away from the country-side, are likely to find difficulties with a topic such as life on an Australian sheep farm that requires pupils to have some experience of sheep and rural life and farms in this country, before they can fully understand the topic.

Now the necessary knowledge to make new learning meaningful may be absent from a pupil's secondary memory for two reasons. Firstly, he may not have learned it on a previous occasion either because it was not taught, or because he did not understand it, or was absent when the topic was considered, or secondly because it has been forgotten. Since learning will involve both additional learning of the various topics in the curriculum and a revision of those previously taught, a typical learning sequence of topics may be represented as follows: learn material A - recall A and learn related material B - recall AB and learn related information C - recall ABC and learn D - and so on. With this sort of sequence in mind Bruner (1960, page 52) has suggested a spiral curriculum in which, periodically, new information is learned and added to a series of basic concepts. Consider three basic concepts or ideas which are denoted by A, B and C. A spiral sequence might be a shown diagrammatically in Figure 4.3, in which developments, or additions, to the basic area are connected by broken lines, and the sequence of presentation is shown by a continuous line. A2, A3 and so on indicate the

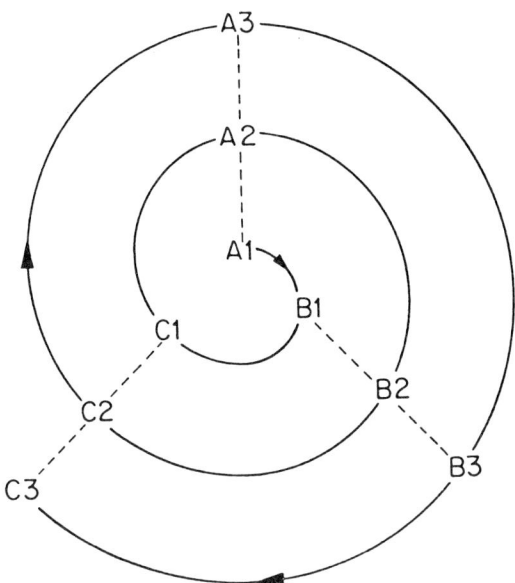

Figure 4.3. Schematic Diagram of a Spiral Curriculum.

additions or extensions of the basic area of subject matter denoted by A1.

As a practical example, A, B and C might represent the three fundamental aspects of number work, the concepts of number, addition and subtraction. A1, 2 and 3 might then be extensions of the basic concept and could deal with counting in tens, hundreds, fractions of whole numbers, decimals and so on. B1, 2 and 3 could be additon, simple multiplication, and long multiplication. C1, 2 and 3 could be subtraction, subtraction of tens and hundreds, and simple division.

A spiral arrangement of the subject matter allows an extension of each topic and also a periodic revision of what has already been taught, so that a structure of knowledge may be built up in the pupil's secondary memory.

The need to allow sufficient time for children to process information during learning and the crucial importance of their having in secondary memory the necessary relevant concepts for new material to be meaningful are basic principles which apply in the same manner to all pupils. The children will only need to be treated differently from one another in that some will be slower than others and some will know less than others prior to the presentation of a new topic, but the application of the rules will still be basically the same for all pupils. The next two sections deal with ways in which children differ not just in amount but in the manner in which they process information during learning.

(3) MODES OF REPRESENTING INFORMATION IN MEMORY

There appears to be individual variation in the manner in which information is represented in memory. Consider the sentence. "The little group of men hurried along the cliff path to where the schooner was lying wrecked on the jagged rocks". As you read the words you automatically analysed their meaning and gave sense to the whole sentence. While this will be so for all readers, the form in which the meaning was represented in memory will vary from person to person. There are two basic modes of representing the meaning of information, verbal and visual. How did you, the reader, code the meaning? Did you do it in verbal form, perhaps in terms of associations, or did you form a picture of a scene? Since you are very used to your own way of representing information and you accomplish it quite automatically you may have to think carefully about what you actually do. It is likely that you used some combination of verbal code and images, although upon reflection one mode will seem to be more dominant than the other.

Discussions about prose comprehension with both adults and children suggest that some people experience pictures or mental imagery much more than others. Indeed, some individuals report that when listening to say, a story, they do not have any images at all. These casual observations suggest a considerable variation in the way in which individuals represent information during learning.

Voluntary and Involuntary Representation

An initial point to make clear is that it is not suggested that some people cannot form images, or cannot represent material in verbal form, if they make the deliberate effort. In fact almost all individuals appear to be able to generate an image of, say, a tree, if they try. The distinction is rather in terms of what people do habitually and automatically during their routine analysis of information when they are attending to, not how they represent the detail, but what the content of the detail is. Now the study of this involuntary mode of representation posed the immmediate problem of how it is to be assessed. Obviously the moment a person is questioned about the presence of images and how vivid they are the automatic process is interupted and the individual begins to make deliberate attempts to generate images. This would not matter if the ability to produce voluntary images reflected the form of representation habitually used, but, if anything the reverse appears to be the case, and the individuals who are good at generating an image at will, probably do not use that mode of representation to a large extent during the routine analysis of material (see Riding and Dyer 1980).

In the practical situation most learning is likely to use the involuntary level of representation where the learner's attention will be on the content of the information rather than on the mode of representation. An individual's learning style is the mode of representation that is habitually used. Those whose preferred mode is predominately verbal will be termed "verbalisers" and those who produce visual representations "imagers".

The Assessment of Verbal-Imagery Learning Style

There have been two general approaches to the determination of learning style. In the first, scores on tests of verbal and spatial ability are taken as indicators of learning style on the assumption that verbal representation will help verbal performance and imagery will facilitate spatial ability. In the second the mode of representation used is monitored during the analysis of short prose passages.

(1) <u>Measurement</u> <u>of</u> <u>Verbal</u> <u>and</u> <u>Spatial</u> <u>Ability.</u> Here verbal performance might be assessed by reading the subject a list of words and then asking for them to be recalled, or by testing verbal fluency. Spatial ability can be measured in terms of how quickly a subject can rearrange a set of coloured blocks to produce a given pattern, or how well a shape or pattern that is given can be found in a series of very similar ones containing the shape, or how well cardboard shapes can be fitted together to form, say, a square.

(2) <u>The</u> <u>Verbal-Imagery</u> <u>Code</u> <u>Test.</u> In the monitoring of the way in which information is represented during the processing of spoken prose the method is rather different. Consider the paragraph, "The afternoon was hot and Jane was tired by the time she reached the bridge over the stream. It wasn't much of a bridge really, just a plank with a handrail on one side. She stopped in the middle and rested her elbows on the rail and stood watching the fast stream flowing towards her. Here and there were stones which the water rushed around. All of sudden a toy boat came into view, swept this way and then that around the rocks before it was taken by the swift water under the bridge". Now suppose a child is asked, "What colour was the boat? If he had formed an image of the scene and added to it the details as they had been presented then he could "read off" the image the colour of the boat very quickly. However if

he had used a verbal coding of the details this would not have been possible and he would have had to search lexical memory for appropriate colours for boats, which will take longer. Now consider an alternative question, "Is the stream the same as a brook?". This time an image is no help in answering the question, but the child who used verbal representation would have aroused the associations of the various items mentioned in the paragraph and would be able to make the judgment about the concepts of "stream" and "brook" very speadily.

The basis of this method of assessing the representation of information in memory is that the time taken to respond to the two types of question will indicate the type of coding used. In practice several paragraphs are used with either a question that can be answered quickly from imagery or from verbal associations after each. A subject's average response time on the verbal questions is then divided by the average time on the imagery questions. This is done because some people are quicker than others at answering generally and so a ratio allows them to be compared with themselves. If a subject is very fast on the verbal questions (say, 2 seconds), but slower on the imagery ones (say, 4 seconds), ratio would be low, (0.5), and the person would be classified as a verbaliser. On the other hand, if the mean verbal time were high (say, 5 seconds) and the imagery time low (say, 2 seconds) then the ratio would be high (2.5), and the person would be designated as an imager. If a subject is equal on both types of question then the ratio is obviously 1.0.

Riding and Dyer (1980) applied this method to 214 12-year-old children from an urban middle school and found a wide variation in ratio which ranged from 0.3 to 4.8 with a mean of 1.2. When the children were grouped according to their ratio there were roughly equal numbers who could be termed extreme verbalisers and imagers, with similar numbers on each side of the central position. The importance of this for the teacher is that in a typical class of children there will be a wide range of learning style with approximately a quarter of the pupils in each section.

Verbal-Imagery Style and Learning Performance

Studies of cognitive performance in which involuntary verbal and imagery performance was likely to feature will now be considered. The first three of these studies only assessed imagery performance. Stewart (1965) divided female subjects into high and low imagers on the basis of their performance on tests of spatial ability and then compared the ease of which they learned lists of pairs of either words or pictures. The high imagery ability subjects were superior on the picture lists, while the low imagery ability ones were best on the word lists. Hollenberg (1970) gave children aged six to nine years a battery of spatial ability tests and found that, while high imagery performance ones did better than those of low imagery on visual aspects of a concept attainment task, the low imagery ability subjects were superior on verbal aspects. Riding and Taylor (1976), used an earlier version of the monitoring test described above which only assessed imagery performance, and found that seven-year-old children who were high on imagery did better on the immediate recall of a concrete prose passage than those of low imagery, while those of low imagery were superior to those of high imagery on an abstract passage whose details were difficult to visualise.

The studies described so far show that subjects who are high on imagery are good on tasks that can be visualised but poor on verbal ones, while for those who are low on imagery the reverse is so. These suggest that those who are low on imagery are good verbally, but verbal performance was not actually assessed. Several investigations since then have assessed both verbal and imagery performance. Delaney (1978) tested subjects for verbal fluency and spatial ability and found that in the learning of lists of foreign word-English word pairs, a verbal strategy for connecting the words improved performance of subjects of high verbal ability, while a visual elaboration strategy was more effective for the low verbal ability subjects. A division of the subjects according to their spatial ability did not show a significant interaction although the means were in the predicted directions.

Riding and Calvey (1981) used the method of monitoring the way in which information is represented in memory that has already been described. Eleven-year-old children listened to four prose passages each of approximately 216 words in length. The content of the passage ranged from being very visually descriptive (concrete) to acoustically and semantically complex (abstract). As an example of a sentence from a concrete passage, "The reindeer were the size of Shetland ponies, and their hair was as white as snowflakes", and from thé most abstract passage, "My name", said the young girl, "is Myagino, and I am the daughter of Tsutsuzi Ga-oka, the son of Emi No-asakee". After hearing each passage the children were given a 15 question test of immediate recall. The children were grouped into five groups according to their verbal-imagery code ratio and their performance on the passages was compared. For the verbalisers recall was highest on the abstract passage and decreased as the passages became more visually descriptive. The reverse was found with the imagers who did best on the concrete passages and who performance decreased as the passages became more acoustically and semantically complex. While verbal-imagery learning style affected performance on each passage, the overall performance of the groups on the two passages added together was roughly the same at all levels of the ratio. That is, overall, neither verbalisers or imagers could be said to be superior, so that one style could not be said to be more "intelligent" than the other.

Verbal-imagery learning style has also been shown to interact with the mode of presentation of information in its effect on learning performance. Riding and Ashmore (1980) grouped 11-year-old children into three divisions according to their verbal-immagery code ratio; verbalisers, intermediate and imagers. Half of the subjects in each division looked for four minutes at a picture from the Macmillan Geography Series depicting a rural canal scene with two barges passing through a lock and showed the lock-keeper at work and some cottages and individuals around the canal and on the barges. The other half of the subjects in each grouping read a page of description (396 words) which described the same scene and gave details of the actions in which the people were involved. Immediately after looking or reading, all children were given a 20 question test of recall. Half of the questions asked about gross details which were main features of the picture or description such as the number of barges, the cottages, and the rural setting while the rest of the questions dealt with fine details such as "What was the date on the plate on the side of the lock?" Generally it was found that verbalisers

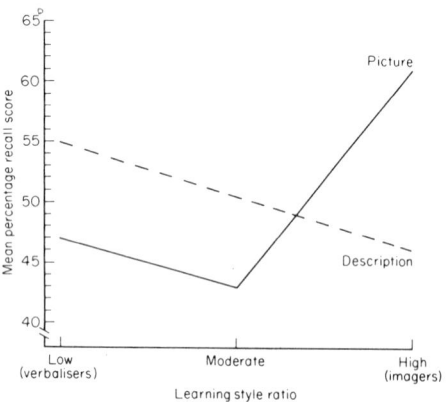

Figure 4.4. Recall of Gross Details by Learning Style Groups.

learned best from the written version of the material while the imagers were superior with the pictorial material. This was particularly so for the gross, or main, details. Figure 4.4 shows the recall for the gross details by the learning style groups.

Inspection of the graph indicates that as the ratio increases and subjects are more imaginal in their style, so their recall after the written presentation decreases, but with the pictorial version, increases. Again the overall performance on the two types of presentation added together is fairly constant for all levels so that no one style could be said to be superior in overall terms.

The evidence presented so far indicated quite a wide variation in verbal-imagery learning style among individuals which is related to the content of the material to be learned, and the way in which it is presented to the pupil. An obvious question concerns the source of the difference in style, particularly whether it is inborn or aquired. This is an important isssue since, if it is the product of experience, pupils could be given training in the mode in which they are less proficient so that they will be more able to cope with a wide range of materials and teaching methods. However, if learning style is inborn and not subject to major change, then the teacher's task will be to encourage the individual to adapt his particular style as best he can to a variety of situations. Unfortunately, the short answer to the question is that the source of learning style is at present unknown, although since it appears to be related to the personality dimension of extraversion, the probability is that it is inborn.

Before considering further the implications of learning style differences, work on extraversion will be discussed.

The Personality Dimension of Introversion-Extraversion

Eysenck and Eysenck (1969) distinguished two basic dimensions of personality, extraversion and neuroticism. The present consideration will be confined to the first of these since it is more directly related to school learning performance. In terms of social behaviour the extravert is typically outgoing, lively, social and impulsive, while the introvert is inward, unsociable and more quiet. However, the relationship between extraversion and behaviour extends far beyond the social situation and affects several aspects of instruction.

In children, the position of an individual on the introversion-extraversion dimension may be determined by means of a questionnaire, the Junior Eysenck Personality Inventory, developed by Sybil Eysenck (1965). The test contains 24 items which assess reaction to social situations, after the style of, "I like playing at other children's homes", or "I am happy when I can be alone to read a book". An extravert is likely to answer "yes" to the first and "no" to the second, while for the introvert the response would be reversed.

Extraversion-introversion is thought to reflect the level of cortical arousal of an individual (see Eysenck 1967, pages 230-231). The higher this level, the more introverted the person. The level affects social behaviour in that persons of low arousal (extraverts) seek stimulation in social situations in order to increase their arousal to a level that produces reasonable performance. Individuals with high arousal choose activities which will not raise their arousal much beyond its already high level, and so tend to be quiet. The level of arousal of a person also affects their cognitive performance, probably by influencing the mode in which they represent information in memory.

It appears likely that both extraversion and verbal-imagery learning style are manifestations of the resting level of arousal of the cortical system. Consequently, extraversion-introversion may be expected to be related to learning performance in a manner similar to that for verbal-imagery learning style, and the studies described in the section that follows are consistent with this view.

Extraversion and Learning Performance

The order of presentation of verbal and visual parts of a learning task has been considered by Riding and Wicks (1978). Eight year old children received learning material which gave details about lions in Africa and consisted of 25 colour-slide photographs each having an associated descriptive and explanatory tape-recorded commentary. The commentaries averaged 33 words and were tape recorded with a ten second silent interval between them. The slides were presented by an automatic projector linked to the tape recorder so that each slide was shown for the silent interval. The children were designated extravert, ambivert or introvert according to their personality score. Half of the children in each personality category received each picture before its associated commentary, while the other half heard the commentary before the slide to which it referred. Immediately after the presentation the subjects were given a 20 question recall test. The mean scores are shown in Table 4,1 where it can be seen that extraverts do best when the commentary comes before its related slide while for introverts the reverse applies.

Table 4.1. Mean Recall recall scores for presentation order

Personality group	Picture first	Commentary first
Extraverts	7.6	10.3
Ambiverts	7.7	9.0
Introverts	11.4	8.1

Again these findings may be explained in terms of the mode of representation of information in memory. Introverts, who perform better in the imagery mode, do less well when the commentary comes first because they are inclined to translate the verbal content into imaginal form. Not only does this take processing time, but the resulting image will probably conflict with the actual picture so that when it is present ed additional processing will be required, or the two versions may interfere with one another in memory. On the other hand, when the picture is first the introverts will be able to represent it as it is and then, from the commentary that follows, add the details on to the image. By contrast, the extraverts will find the picture a hindrance when it comes first because they will tend to represent material in memory in verbal mode. Consequently they will translate the information in the picture into verbal form and again this will take additional time and may conflict with the verbal form of the commentary. When the commentary precedes the picture they will find the processing more suited to their mode representation.

The content of the learning task has been investigated by Riding (1979). Eleven-year-old extraverts, ambiverts and introverts listened to a prose passage which described an American moon trip and later recalled the details. The passage contained six different types of detail which were abstraction, action, time interval, quantity, appearance and direction. Extraverts performed well on abstraction and time intervals, but were weak on quantity and direction. By contrast, the ambiverts are good at quantity and time, and poor on direction, while introverts were best on direction, but relatively poor on the other categories, particularly time interval. The reasons for these differences are consistent with the notion that the preferred mode of representing information in memory varies with arousal. The verbal coding of the extaverts is fairly flexible and may be satisfactorily applied to most categories of detail and so the performance of

107

this group is generally high. With introverts where the imagery mode is used, performance is generally lower than for the other groups because visual representation is often not the most appropriate to code information. The exception to this was the the more spatial category of direction. An interesting finding with the ambiverts was of that they are good at details that involve numerical information.

While further studies are required to clarify the number of representations used and of their nature, it is plausible that just as we may represent information on paper in three forms, verbal, mathematical and pictorial, so in memory there are three possible modes in which material may be coded, and that the one of these which a person is most proficient at is related to their level of arousal. However this may be, there is already sufficient evidence to show that the mode of representation in memory has implications for instruction.

The important practical conclusion is that for the best results, the learning method and material should be chosen to be compatible with the learning style of the pupil. Pupils who are consistently taught with materials or methods that do not suit their style will perform considerably below their possible level.

(4) THE SENSITIVITY OF THE LEARNING SYSTEM

During the 1940's Witkin and his co-workers studied the perception of the vertical and observed that some individuals' judgment was more affected by the surrounding cues than others. Witkin (1962) distinguished between those he described a field-dependent and those who are field-independent. Three general methods have been used to study field-dependence and field-independence. (a) The Body Adjustment Test. In this the subject sits in a tilted chair (22 degrees from the vertical) in a tilted room (56 degrees) and has to instruct the tester to adjust the chair until it is vertical. Performance is taken as a mean of six trials, half with the room and the chair in the same direction and the rest tilted in opposite directions. (b) The Rod and Frame Test. In its simplest form, the subject is seated verticallly in a dark room looks at a luminous square frame with a rod in it. The rod and frame are tilted 28 degrees and the subject rotates the rod until it appears vertical. The mean error over eight trials is converted into a standard score based on age and sex. (c) The Embedded Figures Test. The subject has to locate one of eight simple figures (e.g., a triangle) in each of 12 (or 24) geometrical patterns. The score is the mean solution time per item. There also a group version of this test which is scored as the number correct in a given time.

Field-independent individuals are those who are able to judge the vertical accurately even when the surroundings are distracting and who can see a shape even when it is embedded within a complex pattern. By contrast, field-dependent persons are influenced by the background and find difficulty in isolating a rod or shape from it.

Although the field-dependent independent distinction was first observed in connection with perception it has subsequently become clear that it represents a difference in the way individuals reason about and structure all information. Consequently field-dependence-independence is related to cognitive performance when reasoning and organising are involved.

Field-Dependence-Independence and Learning Performance.

Witkin, Moore, Goodenough and Cox (1977) reviewed studies which compared field-dependence and learning, and argued that field-independence people would be likely to do better than field-dependent ones on tasks in which information was embedded within a context and needed to be extracted. In other words when the learning task required that the student restructures or imposes his own organisation on the material then field-independents do better than field-dependents, but when the material is clearly structured and can be learned as in its presented form there is no difference between them. Witkin et al cite a study (Fleming, 1968) in which subjects were required to free-recall a list of words. When the words were presented with a clear structure by being ordered from superordinate to subordinate (e.g., animal, vertebrate, man) there was no difference in recall between field-independents and dependents, but when the organisation was less obvious with the order being subordinate to ordinate (i.e., man, vertebrate, animal) the field-independent subjects did better.

In learning concepts, Witkin et al suggested that field-independents would use a hypothesis-testing strategy while dependents would employ a spectator approach. Nebelkopf and Dreyer (1973) used a concept-attainment task. They found that field-independents showed little improvement in accuracy from trial to trial for a while and then showed a sudden change in performance as they attained the concept, presumably because they had been testing various hypotheses and then finally come to a conclusion as to the correct one. By contrast the field-dependents showed a gradual improvement from trial to trial, in keeping with a more passive approach to learning. However, the number of trials taken to learn the concepts were similar for both groups, suggesting that they differed in the method employed to learn but not in the amount learned.

Satterly and Telfer (1979) studied the performance of field-dependent and independent 14-year-old children learning about word structure in the school situation. In one condition the pupils received two lessons on the topic while in another different groups were given an additional preliminary lesson as an advance organiser in which the general concepts into which the new material could be fitted was taught, and during the two main lessons reference was made to these general concepts. Learning performance was tested by means of both immediate recall and a transfer test in which information had to be applied to new situations. In simplified form the results are given in Table 4.2.

Table 4.2. Mean Immediate Recall and Transfer Scores

	Mean Scores			
	Recall (max 30)		Transfer (max37)	
	Less. only	Org.+ Less.	Less. only	Org.+Less.
Field-independent	15.3	16.6	13.3	15.0
Field-dependent	12.4	10.3	7.4	9.2

(Adapted from Satterly and Telfer 1979)

For field-independent subjects the use of the organiser and linked instruction resulted in superior performance on both recall and transfer compared to lessons alone, while for dependents not only was overall performance poorer but the use of an organiser resulted in lower recall. While these findings need further investigation it is possible that the field-dependent pupils find difficulty in integrating pieces of related information to form a new whole and so find the use of the organiser interfers with the material in the lesson.

The Nature of Field-independence.

Having seen that field-independence is related to performance on learning tasks, the question naturally arises of how field-independence relates to extraversion. The results of several studies suggest that they are separate dimensions. Fine (1972) reported finding only very low correlations between them in adult male subjects. Satterly (1979) observed a correlation of only 0.04 with 11-year-old children, and Riding and Dyer (1982) obtained a similar result with 12-year-olds.

We have already noted that extraversion is thought to reflect the resting level of arousal of the nervous system and that this affects cognitive performance by influencing the mode in which information is represented in memory. Fine ((1972) has suggested that field-independence represents the "sensitivity" of the system. He has argued (Fine 1973) that "sensitivity" reflects the degree to which the nervous system becomes "differentiated" as the individual develops. That is, how many nerve endings or cells are produced and how complex the neural networks become. He supported this view by demonstrating that field-independents are superior to dependents in discriminating between differences in both colour and weight.

In the school situation it is of interest to consider how extraversion and field-independence may affect learning performance when taken together, since if they are separate dimensions, consideration of their joint effect should result in a clearer picture of how learning materials and methods can most helpfully be adapted to suit the individual pupil. Unfortunately the number of studies available at present is very limited, but they do suggest that this is a worthwhile area for further investigation.

The Joint Effect of Extraversion and Field-Independence.

Riding and Dyer (1981) studied the performance of 12-year-old children on a reasoning task and on prose comprehension. The reasoning task was devised by Peel (1966) and designed to assess the level of the subject's operational thought. The prose recall test consisted of 30 questions which assessed overall performance on the American moon trip passage already referred to. The results which showed that while field-independence improved scores on both tasks, extraversion only significantly affected the prose comprehension.

In a study of art work done by 13-year-old pupils as part of their routine school assessment, field-independence and extraversion interacted in the way in which they were related to different aspects of the quality of the work. When the pictorial art work was marked by their teachers according to their performance on the following categories, pattern, imagery, composition, space,, affect and colour, the scores improved with increasing field-independence most greatly on imagery for introverts, on pattern and colour for ambiverts, and on space and composition for extraverts, (see Riding and

Pearson 1981).

These two studies support the view that extraversion and field-independence are separate dimensions and indicate that they both need to be taken into account in adapting instruction for the learner.

Conclusion

For new learning to be efficient, the student must have sufficient time to process the new information, have the necessary concepts already in memory to give it meaning and structure. Further, the material should be presented in a form that suits the learning style of the student. The two aspects of learning style are the verbal-imagery mode of representation of information in memory, and the sensitivity of the learning system which will affect the amount of structure that the learner will find helpful.

REFERENCES

Ausubel, D.P. Educational Psychology: A Cognitive View (Holt, Rinehart and Winston, New York, 1968)

Bruner, J.S. The Process of Education (Harvard University Press, Cambridge, Mass, 1960)

Craik, F.I.M. & Levy, B.A. "The concept of primary memory". In Estes, W.K., Handbook of Learning and Cognitive Processes: Vol.4, Attention and Memory (Lawrence Erlbaum, Hillsdale, New Jersey, 1976).

Delaney, H.D. Interaction of individual differences with visual and verbal elaboration instructions Journal of Educational Psychology, 1978, 70, 306-318.

Eysenck, H.J. The Biological Basic of Personality (Thomas, Springfield, 1967)

Eysenck, H.J. & Eysenck, S.B.G. Personality Structure and Measurement (Routledge and Kegan Paul, London, 1969).

Eysenck, S.B.G. Manual of the Junior Eysenck Personality Inventory (Hodder and Stoughton, Dunton Green, 1965)

Fine, B.J. Field-dependent introvert and neuroticism: Eysenck and Witkin united Psychological Reports, 1972,31, 939-956

Fine, B.J. Field-dependence-independence as ,sensitivity' of the nervous system: Supportive evidence with color and weight discrimination Perceptual and Motor Skills, 1973, 37, 287-295

Foulke, E. The perception of time compressed speech. In Horton, D.L. & Jenkins, J.J. (Eds.), The Perception of Language (Merrill, Columbus, 1971)

Glanzer, M., Giannutsos, R. & Dubin, S. The removal of items from short-term storage Journal of Verbal Learning and Verbal Behavior.1969, 8, 435-437.

Hollenberg, C.K. Functions of visual imagery in the learning and concept formation of children Child Development, 1970, 41, 1003-1015

Neblekopf, E.B & Dreyer, E.S. Continuous-discontinuous concept attainment as a function of individual differences in cognitive style. Perceptual and Motor Skills, 1973, 36, 655-662

Peel, E.A. A study of differences in the judgment of adolescent pupils British Journal of Educational Psychology, 1966, 36, 77-86.

Riding, R.J. School Learning: Mechanisms and Processes. (Open Books, London, 1977)

Riding, R.J. The effect of extraversion and detail content on the recall of prose by eleven-year-old children British Journal of Educational Psychology, 1979, 49, 296-303

Riding, R.J. & Ashmore, J. Verbaliser-imager learning style and children's recall of information presented in pictorial versus written form Educational Studies, 1980, 6, 141-145

Riding, R.J. & Calvey, I. The assessment of verbal-imagery learning style and their effect on the recall of concrete and abstract prose passages by 11-year-old children British Journal of Psychology, 1981, 72, 59-64

Riding, R.J. & Dyer, V.A. The relationship between extraversion and verbal-imagery learning style in twelve-year-old children Personality and Individual Differences, 1980, 1, 273-279

Riding, R.J. & Dyer, V.A. Extraversion, field-independence and performance on cognitive tasks in twelve-year-old children Research in Education,1982,(in press).

Riding, R.J. & Shore, J.M. A comparison of two methods of improving prose comprehension in educationally subnormal children British Journal of Educational Psychology, 1974, 44, 300-303.

Riding, R.J. & Smith, D.M. The effects of speech rate and repetition on the recall of prose in children Educational Psychology,1981,1,253-260.

Riding, R.J. & Taylor, E.M. Imagery performance and prose comprehension in seven-year-old children. Educational Studies, 1976, 2, 21-27

Riding, R.J. & Vincent, D.J.T. Listening comprehension: the effects of sex, age, passage structure and speech rate. Educational Review, 1980, 32, 259-266

Riding, R.J. & Wicks, B.J. The effect of extraversion and presentation order on learning from picture-commentary sequences by children. Educational Review, 1978, 30, 255-257

Satterly, D.J. Covariation of cognitive styles, intelligence and achievement. British Journal of Educational Psychology. 1979, 49, 179-181

Satterly, D.J. & Telfer, I.G. Cognitive style and advance organisers in learning and retention. British Journal of Educational Psychology. 179, 49, 169-178

Stewart, J.C. "An Experimental Investigation of Imagery" (unpublished PhD thesis, University of Toronto, 1965). (Described in Paivio, A. Imagery and Verbal Processes, pp. 506-510, Holt, Rinehart and Winston, New Yorkk, 1971)

Witkin, H.A. Psychological Differentiation: Studies of Development (Wiley, New York)

Witkin, H.A., Moore, C.A., Gooodenough, D.R. & Cox, P.W. Field-dependent and field-independent cognitive styles of their educational implications. Review of Educational Research, 1977, 47, 1-64

Woodcock, R.M. & Clark, C. Comprehension of a narrative passage by elementary school children as a function of listening rate, retention period and I.Q. Journal of Communication, 1968, 18, 259-271

Chapter 5

THE SOCIAL CONTEXT OF LEARNING IN THE CLASSROOM

Michael Beveridge and Roy Griffiths

This chapter is in two sections. The first considers the mechasnisms by which children's experience of social contexts outside the classroom bear on their thought processes within it. The second explores the decision processes of teachers in classrooms.

(1) THE MECHANICS OF CHILDREN'S THINKING IN A SOCIAL CONTEXT

Bronfenbrenner (1976) has stressed the importance of studying the relations between the characteristics of learners and the environments in which they live. And his "ecological" approach, while in some ways similar to that of Bernstein (1971), has emphasised the psychological mechanisms involved as opposed to the broader sociological issues.

presumably sociological claims that there are important subcultural differences between teachers and pupils imply that what goes on in children's heads in the classoom has some connection with their experience of the outside world. Very little work has been carried out, however, which attempts to map the way these effects occur. In this section we indicate what we think might be relevant ways of looking at this mapping process. We also expose some of the problems inherent in selecting cognitive activities in the classroom and trying to identify their social antecedents. Of the long list of ways in which thinking can be approached we have concentrated on relective thinking especially as used in making sense of teacher's language.

Both Donaldson (1978) and Flavell (1980) have argued that being able to reflect on the meaning of language is a crucial component of children's success in school. Donaldson stresses that children do better if they can identify and reflect on language that they do not fully understand. And that in consequences, differences between children in their ability to reflect on language should contribute to differences in their school attainment.

In Childrens Minds Donaldson discusses research which indicate that children do much better on cognitive tasks if these tasks appear in a context that makes "human sense" to the child. She particularly emphasises the child's ability to place the task in a context where it would become socially meaningful. In a more recent paper (Donaldson 1980) she has examined social and cognitive skills in relation to the development of inferential reasoning. Her suggestion is that it is through the formulation of conflicting purposes that the child experiences the pre-requisite conditions for drawing logical inference. She lists these as being:-

1. Experience of conflicting impulses.

2. The representation of impulses as options.

3. Awareness of non-actualised options.

So, for example, a child who has been told to go upstairs and then remarks "not downstairs" is giving evidence of seeing an alternative option. And through recognition of alternatives the child develops its ability to infer that X implies not (not X).

One of the implications of Donaldson's analysis, which she herself has hinted at, is that if a child has mental access to a context in which the language of the classroom becomes meaningful then he has more chance of understanding the logic conveyed by the language. Donaldson has used the term "Imaginative Embedding" to characterise the process whereby children fit the problem into a possible real world context; and she has emphasised that this process is an important part of making sense of logical problems.

However, the "cognitive" work done by the child while the embedding process takes place is under the influence of the actions and language of the teacher. (Vygotsky 1978; Walkerdine, 1981). What the teacher does and says is a crucial part of the way the child makes sense of what is going on; and this sense is constructed or negotiated by teacher and child together.

An interesting example of this process is given by Walkerdine and Corran (1979), who have examined the ways in which teachers use metaphor to encourage children's understanding of new concepts. For example when teaching place value. teachers often use the term "bundle" to refer to piles of matchsticks. In this instance a "bundle" of ten matches helps the child to see ten "units" make up a new entity, a "ten". The point of using the term "bundle" is that it can help capture for the child the idea that a number of single items can together make-up another single item of a different category. In order to learn place value successfully the child must see the bundles of ten matchsticks as:-

a. made up of individual identical objects each of which is equivalent in all possible ways to the others,

b. complete, but no longer a "bundle" if one or more the matchsticks is removed, and

c. having a precise maximum size which limits the addition of objects to the bundle.

The term "bundle" is selected by the teacher in the hope that it will drive the child to perceive that "tens" in place value have these above qualities.

It is by no means certain, however, that the real-life bundles with which the child has had prior experience will have the above list of properties. In fact many collections of objects in the real world could be correctly termed bundles without having the properties listed above. Not all items in a bundle of washing will be identical and nor will different bundles of washing necessarily contain items in common. And, from a functional point of view, bundles of firewood are not made up of individual sticks, but of smaller, more physically manageable, collections which can be placed on a fire. Also firewood, as with washing, can remain a bundle after one items has been extracted.

When using the term "bundle" in the teaching of place value the teacher is asking the child to work out what kind of bundle is involved. And the child is required to identify a particular type of bundle and to map its properties on to the groups of matchsticks. While the above example is taken from the primary school, the use of metaphors is not restricted to the teaching of young children. For example the way that many teachers introduce such topics such as electricity in secondary school physics or molecular structure in chemicstry require that the child correctly interprets words like "current" and "bond". And both of these terms will be familiar to most children in other contexts, where they express different relationships from those of the natural sciences. And, as a consequence, teachers need to think carefully about the mapping rules which allow the successful use of familiar words in unfamiliar contexts. And, in particular on the role of reflective thinking in making these mappings more effective.

Social Origins of Reflective Thinking

The reflective skills, regarded as so important by Donaldson, could well develop directly out of social exchanges, especially those occuring during instructional sessions. Control of reflective thought may come about through the internalisation of other people's comments during instructional communication (Lloyd and Beveridge, 1981). Children may initially learn how to monitor their own cognitive processes in situations where others do the monitoring for them. And one source of experiences which could facilitate cognitive monitoring in this way is the children's interactions with parents.

Contexts which demand skills similar to those needed in school do occur in the interactions between parents and young children, e.g. resolving cognitive conflict, understanding metaphors and analogies, and identifying mistaken comprehension of reference (Beveridge and Dunn 1980). So it might reasonably be asked whether some parents specifically encourage and help their children to reflect on these problems in ways which prepare them for school.

Beveridge and Dunn outlined the results from two studies which point to the complexity of the relationship between reflective thinking and early communicative experiences and suggest that it may be misleading to map specific home experiences onto directly related school contexts.

The first study examined conversations between two and a half year olds and their mothers (20 lower middle class/working class families observed at home; first born children).

It was found that in families where the complex cognitive use of language is frequent, the mother is also significantly more likely to make explicit to the child her incomprehension, or ambiguities in message, to engage in joint imaginative play, and to discuss and explore intentions, wants or feelings of the child or of others. The point stressed by Beveridge and Dunn is that the child in such families is exposed to the whole range - the whole package. It is therefore inappropriate to link any one feature of the "package" causally to the skills which the child is developing.

Beveridge and Dunn suggest that this kind of mother-child relationship is one in which:-

1) the mother makes explicit features of their relationship - their disagreements, their reasons for feeling and behaving in particular ways, and encourages the child to express his/her confusion, wants, feelings, etc. and to reflect on the

interactions etc. of others

2) mother is child-centred in the sense that she is closely interested in and tuned to the child's wishes, NOT however necessarily permissive (no negative correlation with the proportion of the conversation which is about control etc.)

3) there's a sense in which child and mother are more equal in these families, which is reflected, for example, in their discussions of confrontation , in their joint pretend, in their taking joint responsibility for a sibling. The second study discussed by Beveridge and Dunn which showed evidence for a long-term association between the early mother-child relationship and the developing child's ability to reflect on language, comes from a longitudinal study of mother-child dyads followed from birth through to five and a half years. A number of "communiciation tasks" were given to the children at five and a half (Light 1979). These were "referential communication" games, based on a technique used by Krauss and Glucksberg (1969). In these games the child had to sit on one side of a screen, with an adult on the other; both child and adult had identical sets of pictures. The child, knowing that the adult had identical material, was required to describe one picture specifically, in such a way that the adult could identify the particular picture and was given feedback of the results. The games tested, then, the ability of the child to select the relevant attributes for the listener, and to make them explicit. A story telling game was also played; in this the child looking at a series of three pictures was asked to tell the story; he was also asked about the intentions of the characters. The scoring gave two measures, one of the coherence of the story, one of the attribution of intentionality.

At 14 months of age, these children had been observed at home, and tape recordings made of the family conversation. The speech of the mothers to the children had been categorised according to Katherine Nelson's (1973) categorisation of "acceptance" "direction" and "rejection". When the scores of the children on the communication tasks at five and a half were analysed in relation to the mothers' speech at 14 months the following relationships were found;

Children whose mothers were high on "acceptance" gave a higher proportion of useful information needed, fewer prompts to provide relevant information, and showed a higher degree of sophistication in attributing intentions to characters in a story.

Children whose mothers were high on "rejection", in contrast scored poorly on the communication tasks.

As Beveridge and Dunn indicate, this kind of correlational data leaves the problem of causal inference wide open. But it would seem that:

a) that the categories of "acceptance" and "rejection" are tapping a much broader aspect of the relationship between mother and a 14 month old than simply a characteristic type of verbal response on the mothers' part.

b) that the correlations do show we can find links longitudially between the quality of family relationships well before five and a half years differences in children's communication skills later.

Beveridge and Dunn conclude that it is unlikely that children develop skills in reflectiing a language only by experiencing interactions which specifically take language as the object of reflection. Or at the very least it would be difficult to argue that specific reflective skills are learned in the home and then applied in school. Their view is that there will be differences in the extent to which reflective skills are important across the broad spectrum of the parent-child relationship; and that in some families they will be crucial to the maintenance of this relationship, in others less so.

Understanding versus Pretending to Understand

The family relationships experienced by children may well have other effects on their behaviour in the classroom. For example, children who have been "rejected" might become to those who are so anxious to succeed that they try to avoid giving the teacher any clues that they don't understand.

Some children certainly are skilful at using crucial cues to give the impression that they understand what is going on in the classroom. When the teacher asks the class the question they may verbally shadow the child who responds quickly and with confidence; and in this way they attempt to "hide" in the group, leaving the impression that they knew the answer. Our own studies of nursery children suggest that there are differences between children in their tendency to "hide" in this way. We have focussed on 4 year old children who had just begun to attend nursery school. And after only six weeks of schooling some of them were regularly echoing other children's answers. But when the same questions were given to these children in a one to one teaching context it was revealed that they did not really know the answer. (Beveridge and Hodgkinson, 1980).

The heavy demands on teachers' time preclude extensive one to one teaching and therefore some children may survive for years in the school system by using such social cues. However because teachers need to know what is not being understood before they can remedy the situation, it is important that children do demonstrate their difficulties. By giving the impression of knowing what is going on, a child may be left even further behind. At the very least our work suggests that some very anxious children are so afraid of being thought stupid that they concentrate more on social cues than on what the teacher is saying.

Of course not every child who echoes another child is failing to understand what is going on. Children may be reminded of what they already "know" by the answers given by their peers. And as Hartup (1978) has pointed out, mixed age ability groups can help the less able child to learn. But teachers must be careful to distinguish between what children can do only in a group and what they can do when social cues are unavailable. For example, of the forty children studied by Beveridge and Hodgkinson there were five who generated a high proportion of their "on task" utterances by echoing other children.

The Growth of Awareness

One way to the root of the interpersonal difficulties experienced by children may be to attempt to find out about their own perceptions of the situation. On this point Donaldson (1978) writes "We do not have much hard knowledge as yet about the growth of awareness. Most psychologists have been nervous of the subject for too long. But Piaget, who has opened up so many pathways in the past, has begun also to blaze this trail for us".

Donaldson is here referring to Piaget's (1974) volume "La Prise de Conscience", in which the problem of self awareness is tackled by asking children to describe and talk about their understanding of activities as diverse as walking on all fours and solving complex intellectual tasks. Piaget is here squarely facing up to the problem that children's own perspective of their world is even more elusive than that of their adult counterparts. This elusiveness is due to such factors as the child's lack of sophisticated introspective skills and the tendency of children to give answers which they believe adults expect.

Peevers and Secord (1973) have begun work which is pertinent to this problem. They are concerned with the development and attribution of person concepts and they assume that there is a process by which children construct their view of another person.

Peevers and Secord have identified a developmental trend in the way in which children and adolescents describe other people and themselves. This trend moves from use of specific items, often context bound, e.g. "him, he threw a rock at me" through the use of fairly specific personal characteristics which are less tied to the situation, e.g. "he wants to be a lawyer", to the use of trait descriptions which have implications for behaviour in a wide variety of situations. The main developmental trend in the use of these types of description is that the last two categories increase strongly in occurence when children are between thirteen and seventeen years of age.

A further dimension noted by Peevers and Secord is that of personal involvement. As children get older they move from descriptions that are Self-Oriented, e.g. "He scares me", through Mutual Descriptions, e.g. "We're both the same at sports", to Other Oriented descriptions, e.g. "She's quiet". This latter category increases dramatically as the child moves into his middle teens. It is also at this age that the child begins to use descriptions which qualify personal characteristics as conditional upon certain situational, temporal, or internal states. And it is even later than this that explanations of behaviouur tend to be offered.

These results as a whole suggest that changes are taking place well into adolescence in the kind of interpersonal perceptions that children have. The child's personal concept seems to move from seeing people as a collection of different specific attributes, often related to the child himself, to seeing them as relatively stable objects whose behaviour may be the result of cultural (skin colour) and specific situational (drunkenness) influence. It is worth noting how this change seems to have structural aspects basically similar to cognitive changes which have taken place at a much younger stage. Many of the so-called egocentric activities seen in young children may be a kind of social/developmental analogue of the early understanding of, and relationship to, concrete objects, i.e. that the child's constructs of other persons are expressed (initially) in relation to the child himself and only later seen as properties of an autonomous other.

In the classroom it is, of course, not only the learners who are involved in cognitive activities such as reflective thinking and interpersonal judgements. Teachers are also classroom thinkers.

(2) DECISION PROCESSES OF TEACHERS IN THE CLASSROOM

The study of the nature of teachers' thinking in the social context of the classroom is however a relatively recent development. Compared to the work on children's thinking and its development, very little attention has been given to the use of psychological concepts and research methods in extending our knowledge of the ways in which teachers think. Such studies, however, seem to be becoming increasingly popular, and this section attempts to describe some of the esentially preliminary and tentative findings which have emerged from recent work.

Despite the recency of the upsurge of interest in this area, research has been carried out on quite a wide range of issues. Investigations have been made of how teachers attend to, and make sense of, available information, how information is evaluated and selected, and how it is made use of in solving problems which emerge in the social setting of classrooms. Attempts have been made to identify the processes involved in the thinking of teachers when they are monitoring classroom events, making decisions about appropriate actions, and anticipating consequences. Student teachers, probationer and experienced teachers have been their subject of study.

The Conceptual Framework of Studies

According to Clark (1980) two differennt conceptual frameworks can be identified in recent research on teachers' thinking, one based on a decision making model, the other oriented towards an information processing view. According to the decision making model, teachers' thinking mainly involves assessment of situations, seeking out and processing of relevant information, and deciding on an appropriate course of action to achieve desired goals. The emphasis tends to be placed on the study of the deliberate and rational thinking processes involved in making decisions which guide action. The information processing model, according to Clark, is less clearly focussed on the deliberate decisions that teachers make. Instead, it sees the teacher in the social context of the classroom being faced whith so much complex information that he is unable to process it fully given the limitations of human cognition. The centre of interest is how the teacher uses cognitive processes to help him adapt to and cope with these circumstances.

Clark does accept that the apparent differences may be simply matters of emphasis. Certainly most recent studies attend to both the ways in which teachers process information and the kinds of decisions they make. Perhaps the most significant difference between the two models lies in their hidden assumptions about the teacher. One is tempted to imagine the teacher in the decision making model as the director in charge, making rational moves towards the achievement of educational goals. The teacher in the information processing model is, in contrast, more easily imagined as a participant in a complex social event who is having to use his thinking abilities in order to cope, and seemingly just manages to do so most of the time.

Types of Decisions

Much of the research on teachers' thinking has been carried out in North America. One notable exception is the study carried out at Cambridge University by Sutcliffe and Whitfield (1979). They devised a system to distinguish the different kinds of decisions teachers make in classrooms and used it to study the differences between experienced and inexperienced teachers in terms of the frequency of use of the various types.

Their classification system is based on four dichotomies, the basic one being between immediate and reflective decisions. Reflective decisions concern events and actions in the future, and, therefore, permit contemplation and consideration over time. Immediate decisions are instantaneous responses, usually required in reaction to pupil's interactive behaviours, where the teacher sees no opportunity for reflection. It is these socially contextualized immediate decisions that are the primary concern of the Sutcliffe and Whitfield research. The second dichotomy refers to whether or not the decision manifests itself as an act. Where it does not, for example when it is decided to continue an on-going activity, it is referred to as a null decision. Whether or not the teacher is aware of making a decision is the third dichotomy. The fourth deals with the distinction between composite and simple decisions. Where the decision gives rise to a series of similar acts over time, it is said to be a composite one. Decisions involving no repetitive element or temporal extension are designated as simple ones.

In addition to those categories of types, Sutcliffe and Whitfield also suggest classifications of the classroom stimuli which give rise to decisions and of the content of the decision itself. On the basis of these categories, a research instrument for the analysis of lessons was devised, called LIDOM : Lesson Immediate Decision Observation Matrix.

The research study they report focusses on the frequency with which the various kinds of decisions were made by teachers during their normal classroom teaching. It was also designed to permit comparison between a group of probationer teachers and a group of experienced teachers matched on personality and attitude variables. The results of the comparison are perhaps most clearly seen by describing who did more of what.

The experienced teachers tended to make null decisions more frequently, more often convert potential immediate decisions into reflective ones, and more frequently use composite decisions. They also made relatively more decisions concerning materials and aids, and reported more often being aware of aims and intentions during their lessons. The inexperienced teachers tended to make a greater proportion of immediate decisions, to make decisions more quickly after the occurrence of a stimulus. and to make a higher proportion of decisions in response to classroom management stimuli.

One common theme which seems to emerge from these results is that the experienced teacher somehow manages the time variable in decisions more flexibly. He seems freer to make decisions more slowly and in a more reflective manner, to have time to consider that it is better not to change, and more often makes decisions which have implications for action over longer periods of time. Some possible explanations for these differences may be inferred from the work of Doyle discussed later.

The Selection of Teaching Acts

One of the major centres for American rsearch on teacher decision making is the University of Stanford, where Shavelson and his colleagues have been carrying out a series of experimental studies. Shavelson (1976) sees decision making as the most important teaching skill, and advocates the study of "the process by which teachers consciously make rational decisions with the intention of optimizing student outcomes". He accepts that not all teachers' thinking can readily be seen as rational decision making after complex processing of available information, especially that which occurs in socially interactive situations. Nevertheless, he is enthusiastic about the heuristic value of devising a model of how teachers might decide about which particular act to us, and how they determine when it is appropriate to use it. Shavelson's model assumes that a teacher chooses a teaching act from a set of alternatives having in mind the attempt to reach a goal. The goal is usually educational in nature, comprising learner outcomes of a cognitive, affective or social type. The problem facing the teacher is the selection of a teaching act that is most likely to work given the various states of nature that may exist. These states of nature are environmental conditions not directly under the teachers's control, but which influence the extent to which a particular course of action will be effective. The most important of these states of nature are the cognitive, affective and social states of the learners.

The research approach of the Stanford group has been dominatly experimental to date (Borko et al, 1979). In order to make initial investigations of the hypothesized relationships inherent in their model, they decided to vary systematically different parts of it by stimulating classroom decision making in the laboratory. They achieved this by providing teachers with fictitious descriptions of pupil characteristics and classroom behaviour, and asking the teachers to make various types of decisions related to different teaching tasks.

Four of these studies are discussed by Borko et al (1979). The first of these, also reported in Shavelson et al (1977), looked at the accuracy with which teachers estimated pupil aptitudes, and the influence these estimates had on the teachers' decisions. The results suggested that, in reaching estimates about pupil ability, teachers were sensitive to the differences in reliability and valence of the information given to them. In addition, when given additional information, they revised their initial estimates in the appropriate direction. Moreover, ability estimates were used in deciding the suitable level of materials to be used with a child, and these decisions were also revised when additional relevant information was made available. However, in making interactive decisions, the teachers gave little or no weight to the information provided in the descriptions. This may suggest that teachers discriminate between different kinds of decisions in terms of the type of information relevant to them. The other three studies summarised by Borko et al (1979) investigated selected decision making tasks in reading, mathematics, and classroom management and organization. The results obtained point in the same general direction. The teachers looked at reading scores to estimate the likelihood of pupils attaining certain reading objectives, and, in turn, used these estimates to decide the composition of reading groups. Managerial decisions were based on estimates of disruptiveness formed from information about previous behaviour patterns.

The extent to which these laboratory findings can be generalized to naturalistic settings is open to question, but the studies do provide reasons to remain optimistic about teachers' ability to seek different kinds of information, choose that which is most reliable and relevant to the task in hand, and decide upon a course of action consistent with the results of this information processing. The hypothesis that teachers consciously make rational decisions of a complex kind is certainly not refuted by these data.

Classroom Interactions and Decisions

An account of a more direct study of the kinds of decisions teachers make during classroom interaction has been published by Peterson et al (1978). Twelve experienced teachers were shown brief videotaped episodes from their laboratory classroom teaching, and were asked to report on a range of matters, including how the pupils were responding, what alternative actions they were considering, if any, and whether anything caused them to act differently than they had planned. The results indicated that the teachers used the participation and involvement of the pupils as the most pertinent sign of the success of the lessons. The teachers considered alternative strategies only when the signs were that the lesson was going poorly, and even in these circumstances they rarely deviated from their plan. Instead, interactive decision making seemed to be reserved for fine tuning of the lesson plan, and for adaptation to those aspects of the situation that were in principle unpredictable, such as particular pupil responses.

These results are consistent with the evidence emerging from other research in the area. The vast majority of decisions made during interaction in classroom seem to be concerned with the immediate interaction process itself, and with the implementation of an existing plan in a unique situation. Relatively few decisions are made to include activity not a part of the original plan.

Decision Strategies

As indicated earlier, teachers' thinking can also be seen as an adaptive response to the demands of the classroom environment. If classrooms are not to be complex confusions to the teacher, he must construct classroom knowledge schemas to be used to monitor the social system of the classroom, interpret events, choose appropriate activities and anticipate consequences. The major current advocate of this conceptualization of teachers' thinking is Walter Doyle of North Texas State University.

In order to obtain descriptive records on the relationships between environmental events and teacher thinking, Doyle (1977) carried out an ecological study of the classroom behaviour of student teachers. The observational data obtained pointed to three main classroom demands impinging upon student teachers. Firstly, classroom demands were multidimensional, in that the teachers were faced with pupils with diverse interests, abilities, desires, and patterns of behaviour, were required to cope with a variety of events over time, and had top carry out a multiplicity of tasks which interacted with one another. Secondly, many classroom events occurred simultaneously, and the student teachers were faced with the need to attend to several dimensions of activity at the one time. Thirdly, this simultaneous occurrence of multiple events contributed towards a greater unpredictability in the course of classroom events as perceived by the student teachers. The data also indicated that the magnitude of environmental demands was affected by the nature of the methods and activities being implemented. For example, discussions involving sequences of higher cognitive questions involved more intense levels of multidimensionality, simultaneity and unpredictability than did lectures.

The observational data was then analyzed to identify the cognitive strategies used by the teachers to attempt to adapt to this complexity in the classroom environment. Students judged as less successful on research criteria tried to reduce complexity by attending to one area of the classroom and to one activity at a time, thus ignoring the multiplicity and simultaneity of events. In comparison, the more successful student teachers transformed the complexity of the environment into a conceptual system which they used in interpreting and anticipating events. Doyle suggests that five strategies can be seen to be involved in this mode of adaptation. Three of these are interpretive in nature, involving the ability to group events into units (chunking), the ability to discrimate among these chunks in terms of their immediate and long-term significance (differentiation), and the ability to interpret events quickly (rapid judgement). In addition to these interpretive strategies, two skills were identified which relate to the way in which events were regulated. These are described as the ability to attend to two or more events at once and react to changes in circumstances (overlap), and the ability to monitor and control the duration of events (timing).Tentatively it can be suggested that initial development as a teacher involves learning how to use a set of cognitive strategies to reduce the complex demands of the social environment to manageable proportions.

More recently, Doyle (1979) has focussed attention on the information processing tasks involved in the teacher's continual monitoring of the classroom group for information on pupil cooperation. The basic problem is that, though a wide range of stimuli are nonconsciously or automatically received by the teacher at the physical level, he has limited capacity to process information at a conscious level. In other words,, attention can be focussed only on a selected amount of information, and thus interactive decisions are inevitably based on only a part of the available information, and allocation of focal attention to relevant information is critical.

The problem is not, however, as great as it might appear, as several information processing mechanisms operate which aid efficiency. Incoming information which is not the centre of focal attention seems to build up along nonconscious pathways, and attention can be sifted to relevant parts, thus permitting the teacher to monitor more information than he is aware of at any particular moment. Moreover, though capacity for conscious processing is limited, the speed and accuracy of such processing tends to improve with experience. This is partly ahcieved by learning to tune attention to those cues which provide most relevant information. For example, Doyle suggests that teachers learn the value of shifting processing from strictly individual pupil cues to group phenomena and to those individual cues which are relevant at a group level. He also suggests that experience can produce automaticity. In other words, sequences of behaviour that have been mastered can eventually be initiated and carried out without constant focal attention, thus permitting conscious awareness to be directed elsewhere.

The benefits of fine tuning and automaticity are, however, limited in the context of social interaction in the classroom. They are mechanisms which operate well in stable environments, but classrooms are seen by Doyle as inherently unstable, and thus requiring more regular conscious processing than might otherwise be necessary. Nevertheless, it seems to be possible for teachers to maximize the value of these information processing mechanisms by implementing what Yinger (1980) calls routines. Doyle describes these as recurring classroom activities that function as predictable sequences or "scripts" for teacher and pupil behaviour. Their predictability allows the teacher to use fine tuning and automaticity more often, and thus permit conscious attention to be given to the monitoring of discrepant and anomalous events.

These ideas from Doyle's work stimulate us to consider the contribution made by thinking processes in helping the teacher cope with the complex demands of the social environment of the classroom, and serve to remind us of the importance of the tacit knowledge of the experienced practictioner.

All the research described in this section is at an initial and exploratory stage, and the results must be regarded as tentative. The extent to which they fit experiential knowledge and match our understanding of adult thinking processes in other settings, however, may lead us to be optimistic about their validity and their potential value in helping us to understand a part of the complex business of becoming and being an effective teacher.

In conclusion we would say that in the past, researchers have given much more attention to studying teachers' beliefs and attitudes than they have devoted to the exploration of the cognitive processing activities of teachers in classrooms. In addition, relatively little time has been spent studying children's thinking with an emphasis on social variables. This may, in part, account for the responses of some teachers who find it difficult or recognise the phenomena and processes described in their classrooms. Our approach in this chapter which has discussed the social aspects of children's thinking together with the nature of teachers' thinking in the social context of the classroom has been to emphasise two important ingredients to our understanding of classroom processes.

REFERENCES

Berstein, B. Class, Codes and Control (Vol,1) (Routledge & Kegan Paul, London, 1971).

Beveridge, M. and Dunn, J. Communication and the development of reflective thinking. Paper presented at the Developmetnal Section of the British Psychological Society, University of Edinburgh,1980.

Beveridge, M. and Hogekinson, M. Social cues and understanding in infant-school children. Unpublished manuscript. University of Manchester.

Borko, H., Cone, R., Russo, N.A. & Shavelson, R.J. Teachers' decision making, in Peterson, P.L. & Walberg, H.J. (Editors), Research on Teaching - Concepts, Findings and Implications. (McCutchan Publishing Corporation, 1979).

Bronfenbrenner, V. The experimental ecology of education. Educational Researcher, 1976, 5, 5-15.

Clark, C.M. Choice of a model for research on teacher thinking, Journal of Curriculum Studies, 1980,12, 41-47.

Donaldson, M. Children's Minds. (Fontana, Glasgow, 1978).

Donaldson, M. The origins of inference. Paper presented to the British Association for the Advancement of Science, University of Salford, 1980.

Doyle, W. Learning the classroom environment : an ecological analysis, Journal of Teacher Education, 1977, 28, 51-55.

Doyle, W. Making managerial decisions in classrooms, in Duke, D.L. (Editor) Classroom Management, 78th Yearbook of N.S.S.E., Part 2, (University of Chicago Press, 1979).

Flavell, J. Metacognition and cognitive Monitoring. Monograph (University of Stanford, 1980).

Hartup, W. Peer interaction and socialization. In M. Guralnick (Ed.) Early Interaction, (Wiley, London, 1978).

Krauss, R. & Glucksberg, S. The development of communicative competence as a function of age. Child Development, 1969, 40, 255-266.

Light, P. The Development of Social Sensitivity. (Cambridge Press, 1979).

Lloyd, P. & Beveridge, M. Children Communicating. (Academic Press, London, in press).

McMillan, J. The Social Psychology of School Learning. (Academic Press, London, 1980).

Nelson, K. Structure and Strategy in Learning to Talk, S.R.C.D. monograph 38, 1973.

Peevers, B. & Secord, P. Developmental changes in attribution of descriptive concepts to persons. J. Pers. Soc. Psych. 27, 12 -128.

Peterson, P.L., Marx, R.W. & Clark, C.M. Teacher planning, teacher behaviour, and student achievement, American Educational Research Journal, 1978, 15, 417-432.

Shavelson, R.J. Teachers' decision making, in Gage, N.L., (Editor) The Psychology of Teaching Methods, 75th Yearbook of N.S.S.E., Part 1, (University of Chicago Press, 1976).

Shavelson, R.J., Cadwell, J. & Izu T. Teachers' sensitivity to the reliability of information in making pedagogical decisions, American Educational Research Journal, 1977, 15, 417-432.

Sutcliffe, J. & Whitfield, R. Classroom-based teaching decisions, in Eggleston, J. (Editor), Teacher Decision Making in the Classroom, (Routledge and Kegan Paul, 1979).

Vygotsky, L. Mind in Scoiety, (Harvard University Press, 1978).

Wakerdine, V. & Corran, G. Mathematics learning a cognitive experience. Paper presented to the Developmental Section of the British Psychological Society. University of Southampton, 1979.

Walkerdine, V. From text to context: A psychosemiotic approach to abstract thought. In M. Beveridge (ed) Langauge and the Minds of Children. (Arnold, London, in press).

Yinger, R.J. A study of teacher planning, The Elementary School Journal, 1980, 80, 107-127.

When you look out of a window at a garden, what do you see? A lawn with neat lines on it in shades of green, a border with shrubs behind and flowers in front, a tree set in the lawn with birds in its branches, a sparrow, a starling and a blackbird. You turn to someone in the room and say that the dahlias are doing well and that the pears on the tree are getting larger. You look back at the garden and feel that there is something about the shape, texture and pattern that personally, you find satisfying. You contrast it with the one next door that is informal, a bit overgrown, that somehow you find irritating.

How much there is in that response to the garden that we take for granted. Have you ever stopped to consider the processes involved in such a response and how they developed? Suppose a young baby were held up to survey the scene. What would its response be, and how would it differ from that of the adult? Would it perceive the textures, the pattern, the objects? Would it have the concepts of "tree", "bird" and "flower"? Would it be able to communicate its thoughts in language? Would it have personal tastes about styles and achievements?

No, clearly, the responses of a young baby would be very different from those of an adult, because a lot of development takes place between birth and adulthood. The nature of this development and just how it takes place is important to the teacher. In this section three fundamental areas of this development are considered: thinking, language and personality.

In chapter six, Geoffrey Brown, traces the development of perception from birth onwards and describes how from an initial inability to differentiate between sight and sound, children begin to see an object as being the same, even when it is moved to a different position, and how visual-motor co-ordination are established. The formation of concepts and

133

development of thinking are then considered. Finally, metacognition or thinking about thinking, is discussed.

In the following chapter Ruth Clark explores the question of how children learn to talk. Since almost all children appear to develop language without too much trouble it was taken for granted for many years. It is only relatively recently, over the past twenty years or so, that psychologists have begun to take serious interest in what turns out to be an intriguing topic. the task of explaining how young children acquire language has turned out to be as complex, difficult and time consuming as the young child typically finds it straightforward, simple and rapid to do Such is the complexity of this task that psychologists could be forgiven for flinging up their arms in despair of ever discovering the "truth" (indeed many have) but Ruth Clark shows in her careful analysis of the evidence produced so far that we have made some progress. To take just one example, it has been shown that young children do not grasp language as a result of hearing the babble of adult language which surrounds them. It now appears that one of the keys to language acquisition is the remarkable facility which human beings have for moderating the quality and style of the language they produce so as to mesh with the child's current state of knowledge of language. Even children have shown to adjust their language to an appropriate level when talking to a language learning infant.

This chapter, in short, is particularly valuable because it helps us to see how what appears to be a simple, obvious process is considerably more complicated than we might at first suspect. She emphasises, moreover, that children may arrive at the same developmental end point by means of quite different routes and strategies.

In the final chapter the development of personality is described by David Fontana. An important, and much disputed question, is what influences the sort of people we grow up to be. Is it what we inherit from our parents or is it the environment in which we are brought up? The first section of the Chapter considers the evidence for the relative effects of these influences in some detail since an understanding of them is important for the teacher. The second part describes how differences in personality are likely to show themselves in children of school age and indicates ways in which personality may be assessed. Finally this chapter looks at the relationship between personality and academic achievement and also with styles of learning.

Chapter 6

THE DEVELOPMENT OF THINKING

Geoffrey Brown

This chapter is concerned with the developmental changes which occur in the child's interactions with his environment; changes which denote an increasing ability to comprehend events and to function effectively within the environment.

There are two aspects of this process, perception and cognition. The former refers to the ways in which the child attends to, and makes sense of, information coming in via the sense organs. The latter is concerned with the ways in which knowledge is stored and processed. Clearly the division is an arbitrary one. When a child first experiences a stimulus in his environment, such as a toy, his sense organs transmit messages to the brain indicating its appearance, texture, weight, etc. Yet in the absence of any stored information with which to compare these messages they will probably mean little. Only when the percepts can be related to previous experiences is the child in a position to recognise the toy as familiar, identify its colour, class it as toy, attach a verbal label "toy" to it. So the processes of perception are in many respects the same type of processes as those which would be used if a child was thinking about toys. They are different only in as far as the nature of the incoming signals and the adequacy of the sensory organs are limiting factors governing the data which the child's cognitive processes receive.

PERCEPTION

The Functioning of the Senses

The sensory organs of the body consist of highly specialised cells which, when stimulated by a specific external event, transmit electrical impulses to the brain. When light falls upon the retina of the eye it will cause a pattern of cells to be activated. The pattern will correspond to the pattern of the external source, and the specific cells which "fire" will be those which are sensitive to the wavelengths being received. Similar mechanisms operate for hearing, touch, smell, taste, etc.

This suggests that the messages going to the brain are already analysed, in that they come from specific types of receptors in particular bodily locations, and because they are transmitted to specific specialised sites in the brain. Yet there is some evidence that in the infant this is not so.

It seems that an infant of a few weeks is less likely to react to a change in sensory modality than to a change in position of a stimulus. (Bower, 1977). For instance, if he is presented with lights flashing to left and right of him, he will attend to them, but then quickly lose interest. If the lights are replaced by two clicking sounds his interest is unlikely to be recaptured. But if they are replaced by another two lights in different positions his interest is renewed. So it seems that he is not particularly influenced by the type of receptors being activated, but is influenced by the position of the external source of stimulation.

This lack of differentiation between the senses only lasts for a few weeks. After this time the infant is able to differentiate between sensory modalities, but this does not mean that they will function entirely independently. Although he knows that hearing and sight are different ways of obtaining information, with this differentiated sensory awareness comes an expectation that sensations may be associated in a behavioural way. So when a baby sees or hears something he expects to be able to touch it too, and so the act of looking or listening is accompanied by reaching and grasping behaviour. At an even later stage, around 6 months or so, the infant will have learned that not all visible or audible events are tangible, and the reaching behaviour will become detached.

Object Constancy

It has already been noted that information received by the sense organs needs to be processed and classified in terms of previous experiences if it is to be recognised. Yet is is very probable that the phenomenon being perceived may never have been experienced in quite the same way before. Nevertheless we are able to recognise it. A red car remains a red car, whether seen head-on at dusk, from the side in bright sunlight, or from above in artificial light. We are able to make allowances for variations due to light, position and distance and still recognise the constancy of the object.

The infant must learn that some features of his environment do not change, though perception may suggest otherwise. Earlier we noted that the projection on the retina of the eye indicates the size and position of the object in view. When someone walks away from us we do not believe them to be growing shorter, and it does not seem that the infant believes his mother to periodically shrink either. It is likely that the infant learns of the constancy of objects from very early experience.

By setting up experiments which monitor the eye fixation or heart-rate of young babies it is possible to estimate what they are looking at, where they expect to see things, and how surprised they are at what they see or do not see. When they are very young they seem unable to understand the relationship between identity and motion as we do. That is, they do not recognise that an object is the same one if moved to another place, nor that motion is needed to produce this event.

If an object is placed in the centre of an infant's field of vision, and is then moved off to the right and back to the centre, a baby of about 3 months is able to learn to track back and forth quite efficiently. But if the object is now moved to the left he will tend to sweep his gaze back to the right. This has been interpreted as indicating that the baby thinks he is seeing two objects, one in the centre and one on the right. He does not see that the motion converts the percept, and that only one object is involved.

"One might say that for an 8-12 week-old infant an object·
may exist in a place or an object may move continuously,
but an object cannot move from stationary place to stationary place." (Bower, Broughton and Moore, 1971).

By 20 weeks most babies can co-ordinate place and movement, though the exact reasons for this are still unclear.

The converse of this phenomenon is the concept of the unique object. That is, when do babies begin to realise that Mummy is unique, and that simultaneous viewing of two identical Mummies is disturbing? By setting up an array of mirrors Bower (1974) was able to present multiple images to infants. Again it was at about 20 weeks that they found the display disconcerting. Thus the infant has not only learned of the permanence of objects, but he is beginning to classify them according to their appearances as well as their positions. And he has begun to anticipate concepts which will include multiple instances and those which are unique.

There are many other instances of perceptual organisation in the first year of life. Gibson and Walk (1960) set up a visual cliff apparatus in which part of the floor on which a child is

placed is normal and the rest is glass with a space beneath.
Although the babies could safely crawl over the glass, the
perception of the drop of 3 feet prevented most of them from
doing so, even when encouraged by their mothers. So it seems
that by the age of 12 months most babies can detect depth.
Bower (1974) suggested that distance estimates occur earlier.
He arranged objects of two sizes, one close to the eye and one
some distance away, but such that the angles subtended by the
objects was the same (that is, the retinal image was the same
size). When they were moved towards the face of a young baby
only the near one caused a defensive reaction. So, clearly,
babies are developing estimates of movement and distance quite
early. Whether they learn these, or whether they embellish
some basic inborn capacity, is not known. What is certain is
that enormous strides are being made in the organisation of
perceptual and cognitive processes during the first year of
life.

Perceiving Distinctive Features

We have already seen that by the age of 20 weeks the baby is
not only conceiving of object permanence, but also of the
distinctive features of objects such as mummy's face. Much
interest has been shown in whether there is any particular
type of feature to which human babies are particularly
sensitive.

Fantz (1961) presented pairs of visual displays to babies, and
estimated their preferences by the amount of time they spent
looking at each. The displays consisted of different shaped
cards painted with various patterns in different colours. The
babies spent considerably longer looking at the more complex
patterns, and the author concluded that they preferred them.
However, one needs to be cautious in inferring preference, and
commentators have pointed out that more complex patterns
simply take longer to scrutinise. Whether they actually
preferred the complex patterns is therefore open to doubt, but
we are probably safe in assuming that the babies could
dicriminate between the displays.

Similar work by Ruff and Birch (1974) using complex arrays of
straight and curved lines suggested that 13 week-old babies
had preference for curved, concentric configurations. In this
case all the arrays were complex, though it may still be the
case that the infants took longer to scan some patterns than
others.

In a subsequent experiment (Fantz, 1963) the patterns were
made up of a stylised human face, or the same elements in
scrambled form. They were presented to very young infants,
just 5 days old, but they still spent longer looking at the

face-like display than the others. It is tempting to conclude that the babies had some innate mechanism which reacted to the human face, but the author resisted such an interpretation, suggesting only that patterns which are similar to social objects have particular attraction as stimuli. However, other studies (eg. Koopman and Ames, 1968) failed to find this preference with very young infants.

Active Perceiving

Active engagement in dealing with the environment is thought to be fundamental to an optimal development of perceptual and cognitive processes. A series of experiments related to the object constancy studies already described emphasises this view, but before looking at it we should note a much earlier study by Held and Hein (1963).

Kittens were raised in a darkened environment for ten weeks, so that their visual development was retarded. This retardation resulted in an inability to discriminate the depth of the visual cliff , and a tendency to wander onto the "dangerous" side. They were then placed in a "carousel", which comprised a circular compartment in which one was constrained and the other free to move around at will. By this means both obtained the same visual stimulation, though in one case it was related to action and in the other case it was purely passive. After 30 hours in the apparatus the active kittens showed a marked improvement on the visual cliff, the passive kittens did not. Whilst the visual system of these passive kittens was apparently normal, their passivity in the experiment had led to a failure to link visual perception with action.

About a decade later the relationship of visual perception and action has again been noted in the baby. The notion of object permanence, to which reference has already been made, implies the idea that when an object disappears from sight it does not cease to exist. It is commonly held that this is not so for the infant, that "out-of-sight is out-of-mind", and this is in keeping with the views of Piaget (1954). Piaget argued that if a toy was placed in full view of an infant, and was then occluded by a cloth, he would cease to display interest. This view was initially contested on the grounds that the original experiments had confused a failure to retain the object concept with a motor inability to uncover it. (Bower, 1967). Presentation of eye-movements rather than hand-movements suggested that quite young infants seemed to remember the existence of the object after occlusion. As a result of subsequent experiments it is now suggested that there may be a time-lag between knowledge of object constancy in the visual process and its acquisition in the motor process. That is, the eye may know but not the hand. Subsequent integration of visual perception and motor activity would be needed before search and retrieval could be successfully accomplished.

Recognition of Perceived Objects

We have seen that within the first year of life the infant rapidly develops the ability to classify an object as one with which he is familiar, in terms of its position or movement pattern and in terms of its characteristics. The ability to perform this act is obviously essential if any order is to be made of his environment. If he came to each event in his environment as a novel stimulus there would be no possibility of his benefiting from past experience, there would be no continuity and no development.

The simplest way of expressing this is to imagine that the child forms a "picture" in his memory, and when perception feeds in the same picture again he remembers. Yet there are serious problems with such a naive view. Can memory be a pictorial representation in the brain? If so, who or what is looking at the picture? Furthermore, would the child need a memory "picture" or template for each form in which he may perceive an object? Simply looking at a few examples of printed and hand-written letters will draw attention to the fact that we are capable of discriminating the letter A in a wide variety of forms, including those presented sideways or upside down. To possess a template for each seems most implausible.

An alternative explanation liken the stored image to an Identikit of salient features, so that an incoming pattern would be matched against a checklist, and if sufficient similarities were recorded a positive identification would be made. In the case of a letter A the child might build up identifying elements involving the number of curved and straight lines, basic symmetry, open and closed shapes, etc. Gibson et al (1962) suggested that although young children could match abstract letter-like shapes quite early they did not pay attention to the orientation of the shapes, whereas there was an increasing tendency to do so during the early years of schooling. This may represent one of the crucial features which the child must learn to match before he can learn to read. Whereas a doll or a shoe remains the same upside down or on its side, the same is not true of a letter "d", whether this change represents a maturation of the perceptual or the impact of learning new task-demands is not clear.

COGNITION

Forming Concepts

When an infant recognises the identity of an object, and is
able to discriminate its features, we may say that he has
acquired a concept of that object. But a concept is not a
static thing which he either has or has not. Throughout his
life he will go on modifying his concepts in the light of
experience, and he may go on adding more and more
sophisticated and abstract concepts. The rudimentary concept
of the identity of "Mummy" will later develop by acquiring a
verbal label, and then be related to the abstract concept of
"motherhood" and so on.

An interesting case study was presented by Lewis (1951). He
plotted the emergence and disappearance of verbal labels
during a few months in a child's life, and suggested that they
were indicative of changes in conceptualisation. Figure 6.1
shows a segment of this study. The child introduced the word
"tree" to refer to a cat, and subsequently expanded the
meaning to ecompass a cow and a horse. We cannot be sure that
these verbal labels match the internal mental processes, but
the observation certainly suggests that the child developed a
concept of animal which accommodated all three animals, a
sort of live, furry animal-type concept. Pursuing the same
line of reasoning would lead to the supposition that shortly
after this expansion of meaning the child began to
discriminate between the three objects, and felt a need to
recognise his concepts. This resulted in a contraction of
meaning, as each came to be identified separately by its own
label.

Figure 6.1

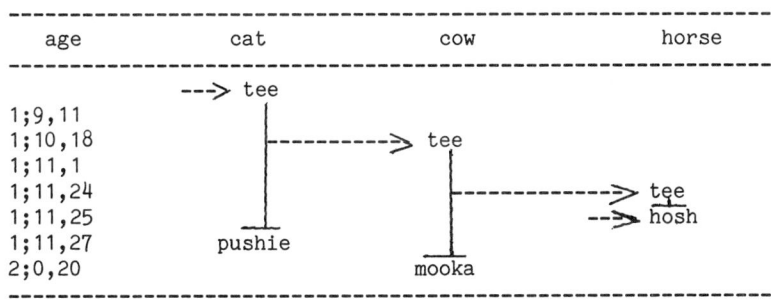

---> first use of word

⌐⌐ word no longer used

(adapted from Lewis, 1951)

141

Objects and events in the environment do not naturally fall into discrete categories. Man has limited mental capacities, and the use of categories is a useful way of subsuming large amounts of information under relatively few headings. By so doing we also limit the information we have available. The concept of fruit subsumes many varieties, the concept of Victoria Plum does not. Under some cirumstances the wider, general concept is of greater utility, for example, in answering the question "What does this shop sell? but is sufficiently precise to answer "What is in this pie?"

Clearly concepts do not have to be related to language, but it is likely that if a particular concept has wide currency in a particular culture there will be a word or phrase to express it. But this is also a circular relationship, for when a culture passes on its information to the next generation it will do so largely through the medium of language. So the world will, to some extent, be pre-categorised for the child by the language he experiences. Thus the Laplander has many different words for snow, depending on its quality, for this is important in his environment. It would be rather extravagant in Britain, although we do find it useful to discriminate snow and sleet.

There are a number of quite celebrated experiments which have investigated the manner in which the individual works out the nature of some concepts which are presented to him. These are concept attainment tasks, in which a pre-determined concept has to be discovered. They should be distinguished from concept formation tasks, in which the individual produces a novel category system to serve his own needs. One set of attainment tasks was conducted by Bruner and his associates in 1956.

Examination of the procedures for identifying the categories into which objects are classed suggested to those authors that there were two basic sorts: identity classes in which various objects are the same (e.g. the girl grows into a woman, but remains the same person), and equivalence classes, in which objects are treated as the same for some specific purpose (e.g. plum and apple are both fruit). The attributes by which we make these judgments vary enormously. Simple classification can be made by colour, and more abstract classification by origin (e.g. born in Africa) or constitution (e.g. made of metal, or man-made). Even the simple colour classification may be complicated, for it has been shown that cultures which name colours differently may classify differently. That is, if there is one word for blues and greens, then they may be classed as equivalent (Brown and Lenneberg, 1954).

Many concepts may also require a combination of attributes.

Thus, a <u>conjunctive</u> concept is one which requires attributes together (e.g. a mammal bears its young live <u>and</u> has real hair). A <u>disjunctive</u> concept is one which is satisfied by the presence of one attribute or another (e.g. a pen must have <u>either</u> a nib, ball point or felt tip). A third possibility is a <u>relational</u> concept, in which attributes must be related one to another (e.g. a shallow dish is one which has an area of cross-section which exceeds its height, irrespective of its actual capacity). The latter were used in a famous experiment by Vygotski, to which we shall turn later.

Bruner and his colleagues employed a set of cards, each bearing either one, two or three identical shapes, surrounded by a border of one, two, or three lines. The shapes were either circles, crosses, or squares, and were printed in black, red, or green. Thus there were 81 cards, comprising 3 shapes x 3 numbers of shapes x 3 colours x 3 borders. A concept was selected by the experimenter and the subject was asked to select cards which he thought exemplified the concept. After each selection he was told whether the selection was correct. By careful recording of the sequence of selections the overall strategy could be deduced.

From the analyses it was possible to determine the success of a subject, in terms of the number of errors made, and the effort and time taken to solve the problem. Whilst the actual procedures adopted were often unconscious, they suggested four ideal strategies:

> <u>Simultaneous Scanning</u>: in which selection is used to determine which hypotheses are confirmed and which disconfirmed for a particular attribute.

> <u>Successive Scanning</u>: in which one hypothesis at a time is tested. Consequently some cards will provide information which will need to be repeated.

Scanning strategies concentrate upon the different attributes as separate elements, they therefore involve considerable mental effort as the subject makes successive modifications to his hypotheses. Focussing strategies, on the other hand, depend upon a guess at the total concept which is then modified in the light of other exemplars.

> <u>Conservative Focussing</u>: involves the changing of one feature of the positive exemplar at a time.

> <u>Focus Gambling</u>: involves risking changing more than one attribute at a time in the hope of shortening the process.

The authors found that about two-thirds of their subjects used focussing strategies, but whichever system was used tended to be used quite consistently, particularly for conjunctive concepts (e.g. has two circles and is green). Disjunctive and relational concepts are much more difficult, for there is no attribute which is present in all exemplars (e.g. circles with borders or crosses without borders; or, having equal numbers of shapes and borders).

Laboratory studies such as this have told us a great deal about the logico-mathematical ideal strategy and the extent to which the human subject can adopt it. Bruner was at pains to point out that in everyday life the concepts we employ may be somewhat different however. Different people may be using a concept label in different ways, there may be no immmediate confirmation or disconfirmation, or there may be no ready-made category to be attained. Given these imponderables it is perhaps surprising that humans manage to communicate and understand each other as well as they do.

Forming concepts and utilizing them is what we usually call thinking, although that term may include many other activities too.

The Process of Thinking

All of us think, but few think about thinking. Consequently description is not easy. We use the term to refer to the musing or day-dreaming which occurs in idle moments. The ideas may be disconnected or illogical, and such thought is sometimes called autistic, or undirected thought. "Thinking" is also used to denote recall (e .g. "I cannot think where I left it") and "imagining" (e.g. "Can you think what that would look like"), or to refer to belief ("I think that there is life after death"). This belief may be a result of careful, logical reasoning based on all available evidence, or slipshod, illogical reasoning based on some evidence, or an emotional response to something which is highly desirable or undesirable. The extent to which children can evaluate evidence and make logical connections between events or ideas is what is intended by the term "thinking" in this chapter. It is that area which has received most attention by psychologists, although it should always be remembered that it may represent only a portion of what is actually "thought".

Piaget's Developmental Psychology

Undoubtedly the greatest influence upon the contemproary views of the development of thinking is that of Jean Piaget, Professor of Experimental Psychology at the University of Geneva. For more than sixty years he has been developing his view of genetic epistemology, that is, the origins of human knowledge and the manner in which it develops. Originally a biologist, Piaget believes that the human mind is governed by basic laws which are analagous to those governing the physical existence of organisms.

An amoeba is a microscopic cell which lives in water. In order to survive it must establish a close relationship with its environment. To feed it must encircle food particles and absorb them into its body. The particles must then be digested by enzymes in order that the nutrients can be utilized by the cell. Thus there are two complimentary aspects to this, the taking-in (or assimilating) and the body's changing-in-order-to-make-the-use-of (or accommodating). This physical model may be used to describe intellectual activity too. Earlier we described of a young child's conceptualisation of animal categories. Although perhaps over-simplifying the process, we might suggest that in the initial stages the child assimilates information about the cat, and accommodates to it by organising his perceptions to form a coherent mental representation of the entity called "tree". Further experiences lead to other perceptions being added, that is taken-in, with re-organisations of the concept, or accommodations, taking place. We have used the term "concept", or more clumsily "coherent mental representation", though Piaget prefers the term "schema". Schemas are seldom static states of mind, for just by using one in a given situation we add to it the knowledge that is has been used, successfully or unsuccessfully, so it is now slightly different.

Piaget describes the structure of a child's knowledge at three different levels of abstraction. At the highest level of abstraction are inherited mechanisms common to the whole species, called functional invariants. One of these is adaptation, comprised of the complementary processes of assimilation and accommodation; the other is organisation. It is axiomatic within this model that the various aspects of intellect are inter-related in an organised way. Whilst these are invariant, the intellectual behaviour of a child is clearly variable. We do not expect the five-year-old to think and act like an eleven-year-old. But at any particular point in his development Piaget believes we may observe that the type of thought process has some high degree of uniformity or structure. That is, the manner in which he may solve mathematical problems, understand schemas, and use his language, will be indicative of some underlying structure, which may be used to describe a particular stage in development. The structure will change with time, giving rise to increasingly sophisticated stages. Irrespective of the child's culture, or the speed with which stages are passed through, the sequence of stages is thought to be invariant for all people.

The most specific of the three levels of Piaget's theory is that relating to content. Although children in different cultures will manifest the same structures in their thinking, the raw material which they experience may be very different, depending upon their geographical location, whether they are in a schooled or unschooled society, etc. Nevertheless, within a relatively homogenous culture such as that in Britain it is reasonable to expect considerable similarity in the experiences of children, but the theory does not require it.

The best known characteristic of Piaget's theory is his description of the stages, and their underlying structures. It is important to remember that this is only the intermediate portion of the overall model, and that, although it is common to relate the stages to specific ages this is meant only as a rough guideline, and no specific age-stage relationship is assumed by Piaget.

Before proceeding to describe the stages there is one other feature of the theory which needs examination. This is the mechanism of change. If Piaget had simply described a succession of stages he would not have provided a truly developmental theory. Only by suggesting the _means_ by which one stage can give way to the next can be to tell us anything about the processes of development. To provide this he introduces the notion of equilibration.

We have already seen that when the child is brought into contact with his environment the two complementary processes of assimilation and accommodation came into play, producing schemas or mental representations of events. The structure underlying his stage of development is a description of the sort of logic he is using in producing these schemas. Yet the type of structure used will have its own particular limitations, so that, as the stage becomes more and more developed, the child will become increasingly aware of its limitations. Thus every stage has, within its developmental pattern, the seeds of its own dissolution. This mental tension and need for reorganisation is described as disequilibrium. Eventually it will lead to fundamental reorientation of structure, and the next stage will be moved into, with the establishment of a relatively stable state of equilibrium for a while. It should be noted that this progression depends upon stimulations from the environment to some extent, but not exclusively. The environmental stimulation only precipitates development when the child's internal representation have been constructed in a way that makes disequilibrium inevitable, and the resulting development is brought about by the active re-construction of schemas by the child. Piaget's theory is immensely complicated, and for a more detailed account the reader should consult more specialised authors (e.g. Flavell, 1963). We shall merely summarise the basic descriptions of the stages.

The Sensory-Motor Stage (0 to about 2 years)

In the early part of this stage the child is restricted to motor activities in his transactions with the environment. He cannot produce an internal representation of an object, but symbolises it in the form of physical action. One of Piaget's best known examples is of his young daughter who, after dropping her rattle, waved her arm furiously in an attempt to reproduce the sound again. The schema of rattling was essentially based upon action. Later this physical action will develop into an ability to think about an object, as when he will reach beneath a cushion to retrieve a hidden object. As the child approaches the second stage of development there is a gradual separation of the act from the thought. This "detached" thought is a pre-operation.

The Pre-Operational Stage (about 2 to 7 years)

With the separation of motor action and thought comes the first change in stage. The pre-operational child is able to represent his environment in symbolic form, and to comprehend the difference between his own body and the surrounding environment. Whilst he makes the distinction, he is not able to understand that other people's experience is different from his. He acts and speaks in an egocentric manner, that is, in the assumption that what he perceives and knows is similarly perceived and known by everyone. Egocentric speech is common in the young child. When telling of an event he makes no allowance for the lack of background information which the audience may have. When viewing a three-dimensional model he is unable to imagine how it will appear to someone in a different position.

Another limitation of this stage is that the child seems to be able to handle only one aspect of a stimulus at a time, and the aspects he focusses upon are usually prominent and very obvious physical attributes. For instance, if five coins and five sweets are laid out in two rows, with a coin against each sweet, the child will readily agree that there are the same number of sweets as coins. But if the coins are now spread out, so that their row extends beyond that of the sweets, the pre-operational child is likely to judge that there are now more coins. Piaget suggests that the child is only able to deal with one dimension, the length of the row, and not to take into account the density of the row. Furthermore, he is n ot aware of the logical necessity for the number to remain the same if nothing is added or substracted. This logical principle will emerge in the structure of the next stage.

There are a number of similar experiments involving estimations of number, length, volume, etc. and in each case it is Piaget's contention that the child's judgment, at the preoperational level, is restricted by a lack of logic and a necessity to focus (or centre) upon one dimension of the stimulus. Towards the end of this stage there will be evidence of disequilibrium. That is, the schemas which have been constructed to deal with these problems will begin to prove inadequate. So, when the child looks at the rows of sweets and coins he may occasionally switch his attention from length to spacing of the coins, and become aware that his hitherto firm response "more coins" is not entirely satisfactory. Disequilibrium has now been caused, and he will need to restructure his thinking to take account of the problems that have arisen.

Concrete Operations (about 7 to 12 years)

When he is able to amalgamate his perceptions of two co-varying attributes (such as the length and density of a row of coins) the child is able to restructure his schemas in a more sophisticated way. As a result of this activity Piaget believes that the first truly logical mental activity arises. So the child establishes a logical reason for the number of coins remaining the same, and that is the Principle of Invariance. This principle affirms that if nothing has been added or subtracted the substance must remain the same. Such orderly, principled thinking is part of a coherent, integrated structure to which Piaget gives the name operation.

In addition to the ability to understand the conservation of number, weight, etc., the concrete operator is less egocentric. He is also able to comprehend quite complex relationships involving inter-related categories. Thus mother and father no longer refer to two people, but to two whole classes of adults who together make up parents. There are also symmetrical relationships such as sister and brother, and a whole series of logical transformations is possible (see Brown and Desforges, 1979). Piaget suggests that these transformations are those which commonly symbolise by plus, minus, multiply, divide, equals, less than, greater than, etc.Although this stage is described as "concrete", it is not the case that the child is limited to thinking which derives from the actual manipulation of concrete objects. But it is suggested that he is limited to a first level of abstraction; that is, he can only think about actual objects which he can imagine. So, whilst he can calculate sums involving ideas of apples and pears, he cannot grasp the second order abstractions of x and y which are used in algebra to represent any entity. This ability emerges in the next and final stage.

Formal Operations (from about 12 years)

In Piaget's model of cognitive development this represents the highest level of human thought. Consequently not everyone will reach this level, and it seems unlikely that many are able to operate consistently in this way. These operations require much more generalised and abstracted thinking and the interplay of real and possible eventualities. Unlike the concrete operational child, the formal operator tackles problems by trying to envisage all possible relations which could obtain for the data. Then, by a combination of experiment and hypothetic deductive reasoning he attempts to determine which hold true.

The classifications which were made possible by concrete operations, and which were themselves a first order of abstraction, are now used as raw data from which even more general, logical relations can be formed.

A typical empirical test of formal operations is the Pendulum Experiment. The child is given a stand, some lengths of thread and assorted weights. He is then asked to determine whether it is the length of the thread, the weight on the end, or the angle of displacement which determines how long it will take to oscillate. Concrete operators attempt to vary the qualities of the pendulum, but do so in an unsystematic way. They seem unable to extract the general feature under investigation from the sensory impact of the actual objects. Consequently they tend to vary a number of attributes at the same time. Adolescents, on the other hand, seem able to dissociate the general issues from the specific objects, and are able to vary them systematically in order to reach a conclusion.

Thus the ultimate goal of human cognitive development is the acquisition of structures which embody a distinctive set of logical processes, and which are implemented by means of hypothetico-deductive reasoning.

Piaget's view is very influential, and has been the guiding principle on which many contemporary studies have been based in most areas of developmental psychology. However, it is not without its critics. Siegel and Brainerd (1978) and Brown and Desforges (1979) have pointed out that the presumption of a logical structure in the form proposed by Piaget has led observers into believing that the validity of the theory has been tested when it has not. That is, data which is consonant with the theory is not proof of its validity unless it can be shown that the data is either not consonant with any other theory, or is only consonant with others which we have good grounds for rejecting. When the theory is put to the test in this way (e.g. Bryant, 1974; Donaldson, 1978; Harris, 1975) the results are sometimes ambiguous and sometimes disconfirmatory. There is evidence of very considerable heterogeneity in the stage structures of a child's performances at any one time, and even of evidence very like that expected at much later stages. In Harris' work with young children of 5 to 7 years he reported that they were able to infer attributes from class membership, i.e., "if this is a red drink it cannot be milk". Whilst this may seem unsurprising, the author points out that the inference is probably of the form :

$$\begin{array}{ll} \text{if milk, then } \underline{\text{white}}, & p.q \\ \underline{\text{not}} \text{ white} & \overline{q} \\ \text{therefore } \underline{\text{not}} \text{ milk} & \overline{p} \end{array}$$

and that this logical structure is part of the cognitive process of formal operations.

Bryant's work on transitive inference is in similar vein. Piaget described an experiment in which he showed a child two sticks, Stick A being longer than Stick B. He removed Stick A and then showed Stick B to be longer than another Stick C. He observed that the child could not make the inference that A was greater than C until around the age of eight years. This inability, he concluded, was because the child's mental structures, which were heavily dominated by the perceptual cues of the experiment.

Bryant articulated the crucial implications of such a belief. It would be impossible for a child to learn to use a ruler to compare the lengths of two objects, as each would have to be compared through their common relations with it. But whilst Piaget's findings were consonant with his theory, there were alternate possible explanations.

The first of these was that the children simply forgot the size of A once it was removed. So he arranged his apparatus to eliminate this possibility. The second was to ensure that children who made the correct response were not simply "parroting" the fomula "A is bigger than", because A had only ever been seen in a "bigger than" situation. To accomplish this Bryant extended the sequence to include five sticks A,B,C,D,E (in ascending order of size). By now using sticks B and D he could choose two which had been seen in both "bigger than" and "smaller than" positions. In these conditions he found that even children of 4 years of age produced a success rate of 82%.

There are now many similar empirical findings, and these coupled with a number of important theoretical reservations (see Brown and Desforges, 1979) mean that Piaget's views must be treated with caution. In particular it may be interpreted by educators as a justification for not encouraging the learner to attempt activities which are "beyond his stage of attainments". This is not to deny the prodigious breadth of Piaget's theory and the wealth of research it has stimulated. Yet it is a complex theory, not readily amenable to simple prescriptions for the teacher.

Problem Solving

Problem solving refers to the activity involved in attempting to achieve a goal in a situation for which one does not have a ready-made procedure. So, although we may refer to $\underline{a2 + 16 = 65}$ as an algebra "problem", it is not so within the present context, for we have a standard procedure for solving it. Wickelgren (1979) identifies a problem as having three components: <u>givens</u>, the facts, materials and propositions, which the problem contains; <u>operations</u>, which are the procedural knowledge used; and the <u>goal</u> which is in some way to be conflated with the <u>givens</u> by means of the <u>operations</u>. This pattern is quite easily identified in mathematical problem, and it is these that Wickelgren often uses as his examples. So in the problem:

> "John is twice as old as Harry was five years ago. Nineteen years from now Harry will be twice as old as John is now. How old is John now?"

the <u>givens</u> are the statements relating the ages of John and Harry, plus all the problem solvers knowledge of numbers and ages. The <u>operations</u> required involve converting sentences to algebraic equations, and all the procedures for solving equations (which, as we have seen above, are not themselves genuine problems). The <u>goal</u> is to find the age of John. As the author admits, this probem may, in its entirety, be rather misleading as many mathematics students have a standard set of procedures for this very familiar task. It should also be noted that we have taken quite a lot of activity for granted. For instance, the interpretation of the sentences themselves requires effort, so it would be possible to break down the task even further. We could also include the routines of finding pencil and paper, and recording the task in some appropriate symbolic form; and at this level it also becomes apparent that the sequence of activities may be important. That is, it is probably better to find the pencil and paper before trying to convert the first sentence into $J = 2 (H - 5)$.

Miller, Galanter and Pribram (1960) demonstrated how a highly ordered sequence of actions and checks could be mapped out as a plan for the task of hammering in a nail. The scheme is know as a TOTE (Test-Operate-Test-EXit).

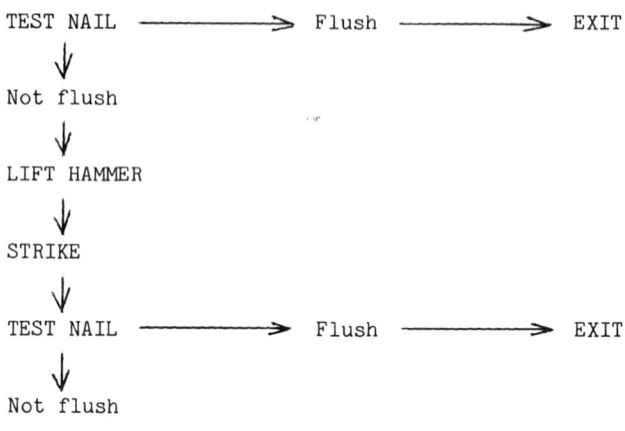

Figure 6.2. (adapted from Miller et al, 1960)

Anyone who has ever bent a nail in anger will realise that this is only part of the picture. A total plan would need to encompass the lifting of the hammer from different positions, the testing and correction of nail not entering the surface horizontally, etc.

What emerges from both of these examples is a representation of a highly complex organisation of sub-routines which are applied to a given situation.

Wickelgren's analysis is perhaps misleading in its simplicity. Whilst it can readily be applied to mathematics it can not so readily be applied to everyday problems. The mathematics problem usually has a known goal (e.g. prove that, if X = 7....), and the operations available are the acknowledged computational procedures. When a managing director is faced with the problem "how can we stop losing money on our brand of dog food?" the model is not so apt. Certainly the goal is still clearly defined, but the givens may include facts ("we lost 2,000 pounds last month") and hunches ("perhaps the advertising is wrong"); and the permissible operations are even more problematic, for they may need to be unique to succeed.

Thus, in addition to the rather precise systematic models of the mathematician and the computer programmer, there is another approach to problem solving which we may call the "applied approach". This term is meant to encompass a wide variety of practical attempts to facilitate the creative aspects of problem solving in industry and commerce. It includes such activities as "brainstorming". "Brainstorming" is typical of these methods in that its crucial feature seems to be the fostering of psychological security within a group, so that ideas can be tried out, no matter how wild, without fear of censure. Davis (1973) refers to this as "the principle of deferred judgement". Other techniques couple this principle with deliberate attempts to seek analogies between the problem to be solved and situations in remote disciplines.

The Development of Problem Solving Abilities

The critic of Piaget's theory have argued that the relatively sophisticated forms of thinking characteristic of formal operations can be found in much younger children. However, they not imply that there is no difference to be found between the thinking and problem solving of the five year-old and the teenager. They argue that the difference is more one of degree than of absolute quality. That is, the young child is highly unlikely to deploy logical inference in as many problem situations as the old child. As experience widens, so more complex cognitive operations are utilised. Even university undergraduates may fail on relatively straight-forward logical tasks if they are presented in contexts which are very unfamiliar (Wason and Johnson-Laird, 1972).

In addition to increasing experience there appear to be progressive increases in the child's ability to think abstractly and to generalise across situations. There have been suggestions that language has a fundamental effect upon the child's capacities, transforming trial-and-error behaviour into more systematised, conceptually based action (Kendler and Kendler, 1961), but this may not be the reason. More tasks are likely to be outside the experiences of the pre-linguistic child than the linguistic child; and trial-and-error seems to be characteristic of many people, irrespective of age, if they are in terra incognita.

Two aspects of Piaget's stage-theory may have particular relevance in the area of problem solving. Indeed, they are aspects of the same phenomenon. The first is the notion of egocentricity. Young children are described as constrained by their own view of the world. They are unable to perceive how a situation may appear to others. The gradual dimination in egocentricity is probably an early stage in a growing ability to decenter, that is, to take into account more than one aspect of a situation. Clearly, if a child is only able to concetrate his attention upon one prominent feature of a problem array, he will be unable to handle variables which inter-act. The gradual evolution of increasing facility to decenter, that is, to take into account additional variables, is considered by some neo-Piagetians to be a crucial factor in the expansion of problem solving abilities (see Pascual-Leone, 1970).

Cognitive Development - The Rise of Metacognition

In an earlier section it was pointed out that the term "thinking" needed some clarification, because although everyone seemed to do it to some degree, very few actually thought about the process. In the last section we also saw that problem solving seemed to involve the implementation of "plans or "sub-routines", such that erstwhile problem areas could be relegated to pseudo-problems when their configuration was sufficiently familiar to enable some well-tried "plans" to be put into operation directly. Recently there has been considerable interest in the extent to which children know what they know, and know that they have techniques for memorising, thinking or problem solving; i.e. "the nature and development of metacognition and of cognitive monitoring/regulation" (Flavell, 1979).

Flavell's thesis is that, in addition to an increasing store of experiences, the child develops new methods of gaining experiences and new ways of using those experiences when they are acquired. He further suggested a tentative analysis of the different aspects of metacognition which may be summarised in terms of metacognitive knowledge and experience and their effects upon goals and actions.

Metacognitive Knowledge consists of knowledge or beliefs about individuals (including oneself), about the success of different strategies, and about the requirements of specific tasks. In this respect it is difficult to distinguish from any other form of knowledge, for it seems to replicate what has already been said about the conceptualisation of a problem area, the activation of plans and the delineation of a goal. If there are differences they may reside in the suggestion that metacognitive processes are often unconscious, and that they may lead to success or failure independently of the factual knowledge and cognitive strategies which the individual can deploy.

Metacognitive Experiences are a form of metacognitive knowledge specifically assigned to assessment of how a task is progressing. It is claimed that the feeling of futility or imminent success can give rise to changing or revising goals and/or strategies.

It is suggested that children lack this ability to monitor their cognitive processes, and evidence seems to support this view. Flavell demonstrated that when a memory task was given to pre-school children they said they were ready to be tested long before they had adequately retained the information. Elementary school children did not make this mistake. Campione and Brown (1978) demonstrated that when retarded children were given training which enabled them to monitor their own success rates they not only retained this ability over the next year, but were able to transfer it to quite dissimilar tasks.

It is noticeable that few secondary schools seem to train their pupils to revise, yet all expect them to do so. Perhaps some of those who fail and protest that they did revise are lacking the metacognitive skills for the job. Campione and Brown recommend that the choice of skills to be presented should be according to these criteria: a) wide application across situations, b) obviously reasonable and productive in the child's eyes, c) have counter-parts in real-life experiences, and d) well understood in terms of the processes comprising the technique. Brown and Deloache (1978) go so far as to suggest that the changes which occur in the development of memory are actually changes in metamemory; "an increasingly conscious control over an early emerging process". The same may be true of other cognitive processes, that is, the basic competence exists, but the ability to deploy it must wait on metacognitive awakening. However, this does not solve many puzzles, but simply changes them. We still do not know how cognition, or metacognition, develops; although we know quite a few of the milestones which show that it is developing.

REFERENCES

Bower, T.G.R. The development of object permanence: Some studies of existence constancy. Perceptual Psychophysics,2, 1967, 2, 411-18.

Bower, T.G.R. Development in Infancy. (Freeman, San Francisco, 1974).

Bower, T.G.R. A Primer of Infant Development. (Freeman, San Francisco, 1977).

Bower, T.G.R., Broughton, J. and Moore M.K. The development of the object concept as manifested in changes in the tracking behaviour of infants between 7 and 20 weeks of age. Journal of Experimental Child Psychology, 1971, 2, 182-93.

Brown, A.L. & Deloache, J.S. Skills, Plans, and Self-Regulation. In R.S. Siegler (Ed) Children's Thinking: What Develops?, (Erlbaum, Hillside, N.J, 1978).

Brown, G. & Desforges, C. Piaget's Theory: A Psychological Critique. (Routledge & Kegan Paul, London, 1979).

Brown, R. & Lenneberg, E.H. A Study in Language and Cognition. Journal of Abnormal and Social Psychology, 1954, 49, 454-62.

Bruner, J.S., Goodnow, J.J. & Austin, G.A. A Study of Thinking. (Wiley, New York, 1956).

Bryant, P.E. Perception and Understanding in Young Children. (Methuen, London, 1974).

Campione, J.C. & Brown, A.L. Training General Metacognitive Skills in Retarded Children. In M.M. Gruneberg, P.E. Morris & R.N. Sykes (Eds) Practical Aspects of Memory. (Academic Press, London, 1978).

Davis, G.A. Psychology of Problem Solving: Theory and Practice. (Basic Books, New York, 1973).

Donaldson, M. Children's Minds. (Fontana, London, 1978).

Fantz, R.L. The origin of form perception. Scientific American, 1961, 204, 66-72.

Fantz, R.L. Pattern vision in new-born infants. Science, 1963, 146, 668-70.

Flavell, J.H. The Developmental Psychology of Jean Piaget. (Van Nostrand, New York, 1963).

Flavell, J.H. Metacognition and cognitive monitoring. Americal Psychologist, 1979, 34, 906-911.

Gibson, E.J., Gibson, J.J., Pick, A.D., & Osser, H. A developmental study of the discrimination of letter-like forms. Journal of Comparative and Physiological Psychology, 1962, 55, 897-906.

Gibson, E.J. & Walk, R.D. The "Visual Cliff". Scientific American, 1960, 202, 64-71.

Harris, P.L. Inferences and semantic development. Journal of Child Language,, 1975, 2, 143-52.

Held, R. & Hein, A. Movement produced stimulation in the development of visually guided behaviour. Journal of

Comparative Physiological Psychology, 1963, 56, 872-76.

Kendler, H.H. & Kendler, T.S. Effects of verbalisation on reversal shifts in children. Science, 1961, 134, 1619-20.

Koopman, P.R. & Ames, E.W. Infants' preferences for facial arrangements: A failure to replicate. Child Development, 1968, 39, 481-7.

Lewis, M.M. Infant Speech (Routledge & Kegan Paul, London, 1951).

Miller, G.A., Galanter, E. & Pribram, K.H. Plans and the Structure of Behaviour. (Holt, Rinehart & Winston, New York, 1960).

Pascual-Leone, J. A mathematical model for the transition rule in Piaget's developmental stages. Acta Psychologoca,, 1970, 32, 301-45.

Piaget, J. The Construction of Reality in the Child. (Basic Books, New York, 1954).

Ruff, H.A. & Birch, H.G. Infant visual fixation: The effect of concentricity, curvilinearity, and number of directions. Journal of Experimental Child Psychology, 1974, 17, 460-73.

Siegel, L.S., & Brainerd, C.J. (Eds.) Alternatives to Piaget: Critical Essays on the Theory. (Academic Press, New York, 1978).

Wason, P.C. & Johnson-Laird, P.N. Psychology of Reasoning: Structure and Content. (Batsford, London, 1972).

Wickellgren, W.A. Cognitive Psychology. (Prentice-Hall, Englewood Cliffs, N.J., 1979).

CHAPTER 7

HOW DO CHILDREN LEARN TO TALK?

Ruth Clark

Let me begin with some examples of child speech:

1   Alison at 14 months, had looked at the moon on several walks with her babysitter, Mimi. One evening, on a walk with her mother, she had been fascinated by the fact that the moon seemed to stop when her push chair stopped. That night at the dinner table she reported the events of the walk to her father, and she used the words 'moon', 'Mimi', and 'Mama' several times. After some minutes she said, quite clearly, "moon stop". (Bloom, 1973, p 97).

2   When Laura was 19 months old her mother tested her responses to questions beginning "Who likes?" "Who likes ice cream?", "Who likes dirt?", "Who likes Peanuts (the cat)?", "Who likes wugs?", "Who likes slugs?", "Who likes Dee Dee (Joanna)?" each evoked the response "Me". (Braunwald and Brislin, 1979).

3   Theo, at about 20 months, followed a visitor around the house, arm and finger rigidly outstretched, chanting insistently and monotonously "What's that? What's that? What's that?....." allowing no time for a reply, nor showing any interest in one. (Personal observation).

4   At 22 months James' mother threatened, in fun, to kick his bottom. "It's not a football" said he, and went off to fetch the football for her. (Mother's report).

5   When my elder son, Adam, was 28 months old the roof of our motor caravan blew off in a storm, and I fixed it back on. On first getting into the van with the newly repaired roof, Adam said "Mummy roof moff", which seems to have meant "Mummy has dealt with the roof that came off." ('Off' and 'on' were always 'moff' and 'mon' at this age. Apparently, Adam had misperceived the word boundaries in utterances such as "It's come off" and "Come on"). (Clark, 1980).

6 Here is a conversation recorded towards bedtime when Adam
   was 4 years 9 months old, and his younger brother, Ivan was
   30 months old:

   Me: "I'm trying to get all the things out, love,"
            removing clothes that Ivan had put in the dining
            room cupboard.

   Ivan: "I'm trying to get all the things in."
   Adam: (Immediately after the above) "Have you fixed it
            all up?"

   Ivan: "I'm tidying all up in."

   Father: "Yes, tidy little chap. Hm! I'm not sure it all
            goes there."

   Adam: "So am I." (I think he meant "So am I tidying
            up.")

   Ivan: "It goes so am I." (Clark, 1981).

Here are a number of reports of things that children have
said. We can enjoy the richness and humour of the episodes,
and relish the quaintness of the expressions, but of what help
can these observations be in answering the question "How do
children learn to talk?". In my view they help by cautioning
us against making our answer too simple. Too simple a model
of language learning could obscure the wealth of inventiveness
and ingenuity that is displayed in these children's efforts to
master the form and meaning of their language.

But linguists and psychologists, like any other theorists,
like to simplify. They like to make complex reality conform
to simple generalisations. Unfortunately, such
generalisations can sometimes cause researchers to ignore, or
miss the significance of episodes that do not fit their
simplified picture.

Each of the above episodes challenges some simplifying
assumption or procedure frequently adopted in child language
research. Alison's description of the moon, for example,
conflicts with claims that young children only talk about
events that are immediately visible, in the 'here and now'.
Laura's response to the 'Who likes?' question suggests that
she has no full understanding of what is being asked. Yet
some researchers use the assumption that children understand
what their mothers are saying to help them to interpret
children's short utterances (Greenfield and Smith, 1976; Dore,
1979). Theo's repetitive chanting "What's that?" highlights

the disadvantages of taking child speech at its face value, and assuming that the words mean what they seem to mean: yet that is a fairly routine procedure in research. James' joke about the football reveals an understanding of his world, and of interactions with other people, that goes far beyond what is typically captured in researchers' descriptions of child speech and child thought. Adam's compression of a sequence of events into a simple utterance belies the common claim that children's speech progresses only gradually from simple statements to more complex combinations of statements (e.g. Brown, Cazden and Bellugi, 1968). The conversation featuring Ivan plays havoc with the routine expectations of researchers that utterance will follow utterance in an orderly sequence, and that adult speech will be simple in form and clear in meaning. The way in which the form of Ivan's utterances is influenced by the adjacent speech shows how ill advised it is to abstract children's speech from the conversations in which it occurs and study its forms without reference to the surrounding speech. Yet study after study of child language has abstracted the speech from its context in just that way. And how much subtler and more complex is this episode, drawn at random from daily life, than the typical stereotype we have of a simple context in which language can be learned.

You may be wondering how we can ever make a start on studying children's speech if we have to take account of all these complexities. I have said that the child may not mean the same by the words he uses as we do, that he may express complex ideas in simple language, that he has knowledge that we cannot begin to characterise formally, and much more! If reality is as complex as this, you may be thinking,, then it is not surprising that linguists and psychologists find it necessary to adopt a simplified view of it to assist their research.

We should now be beginning to understand what theories about language development are. They are simplified models of the process that help us to make some sense of it. In simplifying we make certain assumptions that help us to begin to examine reality systematically. As knowledge advances we may gradually need to dispense with these assumptions, in order to make our picture of reality correspond more nearly to the real thing.

In this chapter I shall introduce three major theoretical pictures that have been painted of the language learning process and explore their strengths and weaknesses. I shall end up by offering a slightly more complicated picture, which, whilst still only a simplified representation, may lie somewhere between the three classical simplifications and reality itself.

SOME APPROACHES TO EXPLAINING LANGUAGE ACQUISITION

Each of the three pictures of language learning that I shall be considering places the main emphasis on a different aspect of the process. The first picture, or model, is concerned with the role of the mother as a teacher. The second model is concerned with the child's inborn knowledge of language, and his inborn capacity to process speech and formulate linguistic rules. The third model focuses primarily on the child's developing understanding of his everyday world.

I shall discuss the models in the order mentioned, tracing how each has developed partly as a reaction against the limitations of the previous model. In the second major section of the chapter, 'A range of strategies', I shall point out which features of each approach should be retained, to contribute to a fuller picture of language learning, and which features should be discarded as simplifications that have outgrown their usefulness.

Mother as Teacher

Until the early sixties, behaviourist principles dominated explanations by psychologists of how children learn to talk (e.g. Carrol, 1964). The behaviourists saw language learning, and every other kind of learning, as conditioning. The major mechanism of learning was reinforcement. (See Clark, 1975 for a fuller account.) The child would produce speech, or respond to speech, and if the behaviour was appropriate, his mother would reward his efforts. If the behaviour was inappropriate, the mother would ignore it, or perhaps punish the child. These would most often be verbal rewards and punishments, praise and censure. The theory, with its associationist basis, could easily explain how phrases like "good girl" or "bad boy" acquired their capacity to function as rewards by association with more material rewards and punishments. The mother, then, had a major role to play in such a model of language acquisition. It was for her to select from the child's utterances and reactions those that were acceptable, and to encourage the child to repeat them, whilst discouraging the unacceptable utterances and reactions. In this way the child's language behaviour would gradually be moulded towards its adult shape.

Will this theory do? Do children learn the right way to speak as a result of their mother's rewarding or punishing their attempts? Research seems to contradict this claim. For example, Brown and Hanlon (1970) report a study of the conversations of Adam, Eve and Sarah with their mothers. (Note: this is a different Adam to the one mentioned in episode 5 of the prologue.) They found that approval and disapproval of the children's speech was mainly related to the content rather than the form of what the children were saying. For example, Eve's mother responded "Um hmm" to Eve's statement "Her curl my hair" despite the grammatical error, since she was curling Eve's hair. On the other hand, when Adam produced the grammatically correct statement "And Walt Disney comes on Tuesday", his mother replied "No, he does not" (Brown and Hanlon, 1970, p.49). If the feedback children are getting about their speech is rarely based upon its formal qualities it cannot be the main mechanism for improving their language skills. Reward and punishment may be encouraging children to use utterances that are more appropriate to their context, but the child will need some other means of eliminating grammatical errors, such as the misuse of the pronoun in Eve's utterance about her hair.

Another major problem for this theory is that for utterances to be selectively reinforced by reward they have to occur in the first place. Behaviourists appealed to simple imitation of adult speech as the source of the child's repertoire, but imitation is not a simple mechanical process. It is an active construction, partly dependent on what the child knows already (Piaget, 1962; Clark, 1975). Some go so far as to claim that the child can only imitate what he is already capable of producing (Rodd and Braine, 1979; Slobin, 1973). Many critics have argued that a repertoire of imitated sequences of words could never add up to a language. Without an awareness of the internal structure of sequences the child would never be able to construct or interpret novel sequences, and this, they argue, is the essence of language use (Miller, Galanter and Pribram, 1970). Attempts by behaviourists to account for novel constructions are clumsy and unconvincing (Clark, 1975). Furthermore, if feedback were the means whereby the child could develop linguistic structure, he would need to understand in what respects his performance was faulty to be able to make use of it (Clark, 1975).

In short, what is left out of this perspective is the role of the child. Mother is treated as the only agent in this process, whilst the child responds passively to manipulation. But there can be no teaching without learning! The negotiation of perspectives that is required for the adjustment of the child's view of the world and his way of talking about the world is a two way process. It can never be achieved merely by one partner moulding the overt behaviour of the other.

In the light of these and related arguments Slobin, in 1972, went so far as to conclude "that parental speech doesn't seem to make much difference at all" (p 205). I shall be returning to this issue later. Meanwhile, this discussion has set the scene for a consideration of two other major approaches. The dominant feature that both share is an emphasis on the child's activity and the child's perspective. We shall need to assess at a later stage whether their corresponding almost total neglect of the role of mother's speech is entirely justified.

The first of the two other approaches that I shall be considering treats the child as a 'little linguist'.

The Little Linguist

This approach places the initiative for language learning in the hands of the child. Or perhaps it would be more accurate to say in the brain of the child. Impressed by the complexity of the structure of language and the apparently unsystematic and error ridden character of the adult speech to which the child is exposed, theorists have argued that a child could not achieve adult competence at a language if he were not equipped at birth with mechanisms for discovering linguistic structure within a haphazard speech input, and perhaps also with prior knowledge of the concepts that languages encode (Chomsky, 1965; McNeill, 1966a; Lenneberg, 1964). These arguments gained strength from considerations mentioned earlier that adult competence could never be achieved by the mere accumulation of a store of sentences. The powerful concept of a 'language acquisition device' was born, and was to exert a very strong influence on language acquisition research.

People working within this framework were also very much struck by the fact that children produce many novel structures of their own creation - "allgone outside" when a door was shut is an oft quoted example. In a formative paper Brown and Bellugi (1964) examined three processes in the acquisition of syntax. Two of them were related to imitation and to mothers' feedback to their children about speech, and hence could fit happily into the framework established by the behaviourists for viewing child speech. But Brown and Bellugi felt that there must be another process at work which gave rise to novel utterances that could not be the product of imitation of adult models, since adults never produce such utterances. Among their examples were "My Cromer suitcase" and "cowboy did fighting me". The child, they argued, must be "processing the speech to which he is exposed so as to induce latent structure" (p 151).

These observations led Brown and Bellugi to support the claims of Chomsky and his associates that the task of the child is to construct hypotheses, with the help of his inherited knowledge and equipment, about the rules underlying his native language. Erroneous forms could be regarded as "mistakes which externalise the child's search for the regularities of English syntax" (Brown and Bellugi, 1964, p 150). Correspondingly, the task of the researcher was to discover what rules the child was working with at any particular stage in his development.

And this is where the problems begin! How is one to discover what rules a child has formulated? Early attempts by Braine (1963), Ervin (1964), and Brown and Fraser (1963) focussed on observed regularities in the recorded utterances of the children they studied. Later researchers criticised this approach for not paying enough attention to meaning. But these researchers then had the problem of identifying the meanings of the children's utterances. I shall look in a little more detail at these successive approaches to the discovery of rules.

The early attempts to formulate rules on the basis of observed regularities came to a head in McNeill's (1966a) treatment. Drawing on the work of Braine, Ervin and Brown and Fraser, mentioned above, he identified two classes of words in early utterances. These classes were defined purely in terms of the positions of words in utterances. He named them 'pivot' and 'open' classes. Any given pivot word always occurred in the same position in an utterance, some pivots in first and some in second position. The class of pivot words was small, and increased only very gradually. On the other hand, children could acquire new open class words very rapidly. Open class words could appear before a pivot word in one utterance, and after a different pivot word in another utterance. For example "more milk", with the pivot word 'more' in first position, and "milk there" with the pivot word 'there' in second position.

Different children used different pivot words. They could be articles (a, the), deictics (here, there), adjectives (pretty), verbs (go) etc. But in general, neither the pivot class nor the open class correponded to any class within adult grammar. McNeill reasoned that if the child was ultimately to arrive at the classes of adult grammar he would need to have built into his language acquisition device a programme for the successive splitting off of sub-categories from within his open and pivot class categories.

Unfortunately for McNeill, the next child he looked at, learning Japanese, appeared to use adjectives as both pivots and open class words (1966 b). Accordingly, he abandoned this conception of the language acquisition device in favour of quite another hypothesis.

Quite apart from conflicting empirical evidence, this procedure of formulating rules to describe a child's corpus on

164

the basis of information about the distribution of words came under energetic attacks on theoretical grounds. One such atack was from Bloom.

Just as the utterance "allgone outside" served as a rallying call for researchers emphasising creativity in children's speech, so did the sequence "mommy sock" function in Bloom's approach which emphasised underlying meanings. In Bloom's records of Kathryn's speech (Bloom, 1970), "mommy sock" appeared twice. On one occasion Kathryn was picking up her mother's sock. On the other occasion, her mother was putting Kathryn's sock on the child's foot. Bloom's claim is simple, but devastating for the positional approach. A pivot open description of these sequences would totally fail to reflect that in one incident 'mommy' was referred to as the possessor of the sock, whilst in the other incident it was her role as agent of an action that the child was drawing attention to.

With this stress on the crucial importance of the underlying meanings of children's utterances, Bloom brought to the fore a vital issue, still unresolved, about child language research, which is how do we arrive at an interpretation as a representation of what the child intended by the utterance. This is legitimate even though the intention may not be made fully explicit by, for example 's' as in "mommy's sock", or by a verb to describe the action as in "mommy put sock". In formulating interpretations of children's utterances that went beyond what the child had actualy made explicit in an utterance, Bloom did make certain provisos. More than one word had to be combined in a sequence, programmed as one unit, within one intonation contour. The sequence also had to follow the appropriate adult word order. If these criteria were satisfied, Bloom would attribute to the child knowledge of a linguistic rule for combining words to express meanings.

Bloom had moved from basing grammatical description on the objective, observable, distributional facts of the earlier work towards description based on meanings attributed to the child by an adult interpreter, on the basis of information about the context of the utterance. Other investigators have been prepared to take inferences from context, and from adjacent adult utterances even further than Bloom. Greenfield and Smith (1976) for example, are willing to attribute unexpressed meanings to children even when the child only utters one word.

Bloom was critical of McNeill, but her own approach, and that of Greenfield and Smith have not themselves escaped criticism. Of one-word utterances Ryan (1974) states "We cannot assume when a child starts to produce one-word utterances, that the possible meanings of her utterances are as clearly delimited for her as they are for the adults who interpret them." Howe (1976) suggests that we learn from adults' interpretations of children's two-word utterances something about how adults interpret, rather than something about what children intend. Macrae (1979) provides a valuable critical review of these issues.

There is a feature shared by all the procedures for discovering rules that I have considered so far. McNeill, Bloom, and Greenfield and Smith all assume that the child means at least as much as he says. This implies that before the child uses verbal expressions he discovers their meanings through studying them in other people's speech. Each form is used with full understanding of its function. This is consistent with the Chomskian view, described earlier, that mechanical imitation of adult speech is a dead end so far as growth towards adult competence in a language is concerned. Most researchers engaged in the task of describing 'the little linguist' hold to the view that children do process the speech that they hear and discover aspects of language structure within it before they use this knowledge to express themselves in speech. Indeed, it would be difficult for them to engage in the activity of writing rules to describe output unless they made this assumption. If some of the child's speech means what it seems to mean and some does not, on what basis can generalisations be made?

However, not all studies with a linguistic focus share this frame of reference. Work by Bowerman (forthcoming) on the speech of her two daughters led her to conclude that they were using forms in their speech without full grasp of their meanings. For example, at an early stage, the children had word pairs like 'bring' and 'come', 'drop' and 'fall', 'kill' and 'die' in their repertoires. At that time they showed no signs of understanding the relationships between the words in the pairs: that 'bring' can be construed as 'cause to come', 'kill' as 'cause to die' and 'drop' as 'cause to fall'. In other words, they were using words in a causal sense, and using them appropriately, without any full grasp of the notion of 'cause'. From using words like 'walk' as in "I am _walking_ the dog" (causing the dog to walk), the child can come to infer that a verb can acquire a causal meaning without any necessary change in form. The child may then over-extend the use of this linguistic device by applying it innappropriately to fresh words, e.g.

"I need to _round_ this circle very much"
Christy at 5 years 1 month.

"You just _cried_ me" (i.e. made me cry)
Eve at 3 years 2 months.

According to Bowerman, it is only when this mistaken over-extension occurs that we have evidence that the child has decomposed the component meanings of the causal verbs in her speech. In other words, Bowerman is acknowledging that forms can be used by the child in spontaneous speech, and used appropriately, without their full force being understood. She also suggests that the child abstracts the component of meaning 'cause' by a scrutiny of the partially understood forms already in her own speech repertoire. For Bowerman it is the mistakes arising from application of the rule to new instances that show that a rule has been abstracted. The mere production of a number of verbs regarded as causative in adult speech is not in itself evidence that the child perceives them in that way. This is a departure from the orthodox approach of researchers in the linguistically oriented school which typically pictures the child learning language structure through scrutiny of the input, comprehension being superior to production and the imitation and subsequent use of forms without full comprehension being ruled out.

We have considered a variety of devices for discovering the linguistic rules that a child has command of. They range through analysis of the distribution of words in utterances, and interpretation of the child's intentions with the help of the context, to mistaken overapplications of rules. It has become clear that theorists within any broad framework, such as a linguistic orientation, will differ considerably among themselves, and that structuring the field of language acquisition into, for example, mother's role, linguistic and conceptual orientations, in order to provide foci for discussion, is a bit like building fences on the bed of a lake to contain the water within certain bounds. Inevitably, the categories are in some measure arbitrary. But for me the theories I have discussed under the heading 'the little linguist' have a family resemblance, though not every member of the family shares all the family features. Let me now look at some of these features in turn and comment on each.

A very valuable emphasis of linguistic approaches has been, it seems to me, the recognition that mistakes have a positive aspect to them, and may reflect the child's progress in developing his linguistic skills, rather than the reverse. As we have seen, not all theorists share this emphasis. Whilst the earliest exponents of the language acquisition device stressed the creative production of unorthodox forms as evidence that children were using rules, later researchers in this tradition, such as Bloom, only attributed to the child awareness of the meanings implicit in his speech if he produced the words in the correct adult word order. In Bowerman's more recent discussion we see a return to an emphasis on mistakes as evidence for understanding.

A less favourable feature of linguistic treatments, I feel, is that, with their stress on children's rule systems, they tend to look at a corpus of the child's utterances, divorced from the conversations in which they arose. I have continually met in my own children's speech errors in usage that seem to be built in systematic ways on the immediately previous adult utterance (Clark, 1977). Even at 9 years 1 month Ivan engages in interactions such as this:

Mother: "That wouldn't be any use to you."

Ivan: "That would be use to me."

Adam, now eleven years of age, can still respond to "You must" with "I mustn't", instead of "I needn't". To take child utterances out of context and formulate explanations for their structure could be very misleading in the light of such dependencies within conversations.

A further disadvantage of the approach, in my view, is that the quest for a language acquisition device predisposes linguists to expect homogeneity among their child subjects. All children are supposed to be discovering linguistic structure in the speech of their community with the help of a common, inborn mechanism which is characteristic of the human species. Sometimes observed differences between children are interpreted as surface ripples, liable to distract the careless observer from a common underlying process (e.g. Brown, 1968). One early account of the development of questions in Adam, Eve and Sarah's speech was based on utterances pooled across the three children (Klima and Bellugi, 1966). The researchers were studying one mechanism which happened to be functioning in three different heads, or one computer programme with three different terminals. If we build in the assumption of uniformity across children it has the consequence that elaborate theories can be overturned by evidence from one further subject, as happened in the case of McNeill's proposals regarding pivot-open constructions. I believe that theories about language development will have to make considerable allowance for individual variation, going deeper than mere ripples on the surface, and I shall return to this issue later.

Another predisposition of a linguistic approach is to see a grasp of linguistic structure as more necessary to effective communication than perhaps it is. As a result, the child may be accredited with the maximum linguistic knowledge consistent with his speech and response to other people's speech, rather than the minimum. But language is a tool for representing

168

reality, and a knowledge of reality can help a listener to interpret a message even when that message is insufficiently explicit, or the listener lacks the syntactic knowledge to decipher some aspects of the meaning encoded in the message. Mothers and children have a resource of shared experience and everyday rituals that may be very necessary for learning to talk.

We have been preoccupied in this section with the problem of identifying the linguistic knowledge underlying child speech. However, in tracing changing approaches to this problem, we have noted a shifting emphasis towards the meanings underlying speech, and away from a sole preoccupation with language forms. McNeill's pivot and open categories were defined in terms of formal criteria, but Bloom wanted to distinguish in the utterance "Mommy sock" between 'Mommy' as possessor and 'Mommy' as agent of an action. This shift of emphasis in the study of child language was paralleled by a shift of emphasis in the study of adult language by linguists. From a preoccupation with the formal arrangements of words in sentences, linguists were increasingly transferring their interest to the relationships between words in terms of underlying meanings.

The task of explaining language development ceased to be a matter of accounting for children's rapid grasp of complex language structures, and became rather a matter of accounting for their understanding of relationships between entities in the environment. The need to believe that the child had some complex inborn mechanism for discovering structures was therefore alleviated. Since the meanings researchers were concerned with had to do with characteristics of objects and actions in the physical world, and relationships between them (including 'possessor', 'agent' and 'action' that I have just mentioned), there seemed to be no need to credit the child with inborn knowledge of cncepts any more than an inborn structuring capacity. It became plausible to view language learning in terms of the child's conceptual grasp derived from his experience.

We now need to explore the second major alternative to behaviourism, by examining research into children's ideas and concepts.

The Child with Ideas

The focal point of this framework is children's conceptual development. Researchers look to cognitive development for an explanation of language acquisition, usually drawing on Piaget's theory. The child is seen as discovering concepts spontaneously, without adult aid, through active exploration of his environment.

Researchers working within this framework often adopt the 'cognition hypothesis' (Cromer, 1974). They typically conceive of progress in terms of the child acquiring a concept, such as 'possessor', 'agent', 'instrument' or 'cause'. The acquisition of the concept motivates the child to search the input speech for a linguistic device for communicating that concept. Like the linguistically oriented approach, this approach is child centred, in that the motivating force for development is seen as originating in the child's own activity, fuelled from within.

In order to test the 'cognition hypothesis' we need to have some way of identifying the concepts available to the child. If the theme of the last section was "how do we identify the rules that children use in their speech?", then the theme of this section is "how do we identify the meanings that children understand?". I shall be exploring a wide variety of methods that researchers have used to study children's grasp of concepts. My purpose will be to highlight the difficulties of interpretation, and the discrepancies between approaches. On the basis of this exploration of methods I shall attempt to evluate the 'cognition hypothesis', and to assess whether it is appropriate to regard language development as a neat, step by step progression from concept to language form, concept to language form, until each concept is grasped, and each form discovered to match it. The issue of whether concepts do, in fact, arise through the child's spontaneous activity, or are assisted by maternal guidance, will be returned to in a later section.

One distinction that can be made between different approaches to the discovery of meanings in child speech is that some researchers attribute understanding of concepts to children without their having marked that understanding by any verbal label; other researchers require evidence in some aspect of children's speech before they will believe that the children have grasped particular concepts.

Among the first group of researchers is Greenfield (1978). She studied the early activities of children, and their exploration of the environment. She saw in these experiences the source of the child's discovery of meanings that would later subserve his language learning. For example, if a child bangs a hammer on a table during play, he is discovering, acording to Greenfield, that he as an _agent_ can perform an _action_ on an _object_ with an _instrument_. This understanding forms the basis for learning to describe such episodes grammatically in a sentence such as 'I (agent) am hitting (action) the table (object) with a hammer (instrument)'. This sentence organises the words referring to aspects of episodes appropriately, according to the role each plays in the total meaning.

But there are problems with this approach, as Lock (1979) points out. How do you decide on the basis of behaviour alone whether a child has a mental grasp of the meaning relations between elements of his activity that are implicit in the activity itself? What is to distinguish the behaviour of a mute animal, who acts effectively on his environment, from that of a young child. The child may have the potential to express himself in speech later on. But does that promise justify us in treating the present behaviour of child and animal differently?

Greenfield and Smith (1976), whose work I have already mentioned, have outlined another method for attributing a grasp of meanings to the child before he expresses them explicitly in speech. They attribute to one word utterances fuller meanings than are contained in that single word, basing their inferences on the conversational setting, the situation in which the utterance occurs, and perhaps a gesture on the part of the child. For example:

(a) "If a child whines, points to a fan that is turned off, and says on, the expansion I want the fan on relates all these elements" (p 44).

(b) "Mathew's mother asks him 'Where did Ismenia go'? and he answers 'byebye'." (p 43). Greenfield and Smith infer that the child meant to say that Ismenia had gone bye bye.

This approach shares with Greenfield's treatment of actions the problem of setting limits on the scope of such inferences. If this principle of interpretation is accepted, how far back can we take it? Should the gurgles punctuating mothers' comments to their infants in the pram be imbued with meaning inferred from their position in the dialogue, from gestures and from features of the situation?

I shall move now to a consideration of some of the criteria applied by researchers who demand some explicit marker in the child's speech before they will attribute grasp of the relevant concept to the child. A researcher who relies partly on explicit markers is Bloom. I have already discussed aspects of her work in the previous section. We saw that Bloom requires that the child programme two words as a single unit, without pause, in his speech, and produce them in the appropriate word order, before she will credit him with the knowledge of a linguistic rule for expressing a relationship.

171

But she also exlored a stage in development prior to this, and
proposed criteria for judging when meanings emerge. Before
producing well-formed sequences of words, according to the
adult pattern, her child, Alison, went through a stage where
she produced sequences of single words, linked by the same
context. There were some sequences in which each single word
utterance was linked separately to some element in the context
('chained' successive utterances) and there were some
sequences in which the successive one-word utterances were all
produced in advance of an event, as if programmed as a package
('holistic' successive utterances). An example of a 'chained'
successive one-word utterance is when Alison picks up a cow,
saying "cow", then tries to put it on a chair, saying "chair".
An example of a 'holistic' successive one-word utterance is
when Alison hands her mother a doll saying
"Mommy"....."wiping", evidently requiring her mother to wipe
the dolly's bottom with a nappy, just as Alison has been
wiping her own. Bloom takes the 'holistic' type of successive
one-word utterance as evidence that the child has a total
mental representation of the situation.

In this analysis Bloom is using information about the context
in which the utterance occurs to distinguish between 'chained'
and 'holistic' expressions. But she is also relying on a
verbal cue. Understanding is not attributed to the child
unless two one-word utterances are produced in succession.

Halliday (1975) adopts a slightly different approach. He too
requires some overt vocal marker of intention, but this need
not be a conventional form adopted from adult speech.

Halliday accepts primitive, regular observable markers of
intention that may be the invention of the child himself. At
nine months, Halldiay's son Nigel had a repertoire of five
elements, which Halliday regarded as a language. These
comprised two intonation patterns and three gestures used
consistently, each in a distinct, identifiable function, e.g.
to comment on something moving; to request someone to repeat
an action.

Older children, too, who already have many conventional words
in their repertoires, may combine these in idiosyncratic ways
to express new meanings which they canot yet formulate in
conventional language. For example, David at 2 years, 3
months was sitting in the back of the car with his mother and
baby sister, Alison, waiting for their father to come out of
the house. I leaned in the window to have a chat, and said to
him "Where's Mummy?". Apparently he wanted to tell me that
his mother usually sat at the front. She happened to be at
the back that day because Alison's car seat was broken, and
she had to be held. It was well beyond David's linguistic

capacity to express this in conventional terms, but he managed to make his meaning extremely clear with "Mummy there" (pointing). "Mummy do at front". Thus it is tempting to attribute concepts on the basis of verbal evidence of intention to communicate, when clues in the situation help us to identify what the child means to say.

In the contrast between Bloom's and Halliday's procedures we see the revival of an issue that arose in the last section. Is it the use of speech incorporating some of the correct elements of the equivalent adult sentences, with no distortion, that gives us the best clue to a child's progress, as Bloom believes? Or is it some deviation from the adult model, whether misapplication of a rule, as Bowerman claims? Or the use of an idiosyncratic expression, as Halliday presupposes, and as I have assumed in interpreting David's utterance?

Implicit in Bowerman's argument was the view that correct forms of causal verbs may be copied from adult speech without full understanding of their import, and therefore a rule for making a verb express cause cannot be inferred until the child shows, by some error in his speech, that he is actively processing the words in a search for grammatical rules. Karmiloff-Smith (1979) uses the same reasoning in a study of children's growing grasp of the concepts expressed in French by adjectives, and by the words 'un', 'une', 'mon', 'ma' and 'meme'.

There is a stage at which children use these words correctly. Later they make mistakes, but these mistakes show that they have begun to unparcel aspects of the meaning that they gave no evidence of grasping before. For example, they will continue to use the correct phrase 'la meme voiture' (the same car) if it is the identical car, but coin their own phrase 'la meme de voiture' if they are speaking of another car of the same type. The use of different forms to express different shades of meaning apparently helps the children to consolidate their grasp of the distinctions in meaning. In a third phase of development they will return to correct usage in all contexts, but at a different level of understanding to their initial correct usage.

Another device for exploring children's grasp of concepts is to examine the range of situations in which a given word or phrase is used, but here again, we meet with different attitudes to what correct and incorrect usage tell us about the child's level of understanding. Brown (1973) noted that Adam, Eve and Sarah used the basic forms of verbs in a variety of contexts, e.g. 'eat' might be a command to someone to eat; a comment that someone is eating; an observation that someone has been eating, but is no longer doing so; or an expression of an intention to eat. Brown took the use of the verb in this range of contexts as evidence that a child understood the full range of meanings. Unexpressed meanings were credited on the basis of situational cues, as in Greenfield and Smith's approach.

Eve Clark (1973) on the other hand takes overextension of a word to novel contexts as evidence of an inadequate grasp of a concept. She would claim that a child using the word 'Daddy' to refer to all adult males has a limited meaning attached to that word, having acquired only two aspects of its meaning - 'maleness' and 'adulthood', without the idea of daddy's family relationship to himself.

In Brown's case the extended range of contexts is invoked to justify an enriched conception of the child's cognitive grasp, and in Clark's case to justify an impoverished conception.

Another dimension for exloring children's grasp of meaning is the developmental dimension. A number of researchers have studied the growth of concepts by tracing the forms from their earliest restricted use through an increasing range of uses. For example, Nelson (1973), in a study of the first 50 words of 18 children found that frequent early words typically referred to objects with salient properties, such as movement or noise. Bowerman (1976) noted that the earliest uses of 'up' and 'down' in her two daughters' speech related to their own activity, and were not comments on the movement of other people, or objects.

Studies of children's speech can sometimes show that they are using a particular linguistic form for their own chosen purpose, rather than for the purpose it fulfils in adult speech. Bronckart and Sinclair (1973), for example, showed that French children used changes in tense not to locate events in time, but rather to describe characteristics of actions. When asked to describe events enacted in front of them, 5-6 year olds used the present perfect to describe brief actions and the present tense for prolonged actions. Older children used different tenses to distinguish repetitive actions from continuous actions.

It can always be argued that a child using a form inappropriately may nevertheless be aware that it is the wrong form. He may be using it deliberately to refer to things for which he has no exact words, in the knowledge that its true meaning is more limited.

In an attempt to clarify this issue, researchers have examined children's understanding in other people's speech of forms that they are failing to use, or misusing, themselves. Unfortunately, the findings are not clear cut. On the one hand Huttenlocher (1975) has shown that children choose the appropriate object when a word is named, even when offered objects that they call by the same name inappropriately in their speech. On the other hand, in a study of the misuse of 'down' by my elder son Adam (Clark, Hutcheson and Van Buren, 1974), we found that his overextended use in contexts where 'up' would be appropriate was paralleled by an overextended interpretation in comprehension tasks.

Similarly, Sachs and Truswell (1978) found that children failing to combine two words in their own speech could nevertheless construct interpretations that required them to relate two words presented to them by an adult. On the other hand, we found that Adam could utter more complex sequences than he could make sense of in other people's speech (Clark, Hutcheson and Van Buren, 1974).

This rich variety of studies tells us that there is a need for clarification of the procedures for discovering unexpressed concepts, and for discerning the meanings of forms already in use. Would we wish to rule out the possibility of concepts being there without the child having any formal means for expressing them? Can we rely on the presence of correct forms as evidence for grasp of meaning? It may be that questions about the relationship between form and intention can never be fully answered.

What these explorations into meaning do tell us is that there is no uniform progression from understanding of a concept, through interpretation and subsequent decoding of input utterances, to encoding of that concept verbally in speech. Concepts that are understood may be expressed in entirely idiosyncratic ways, whilst conventional forms may reflect various degrees of understanding.

It is also clear that the expectation that some researchers have had that the increasing mastery of language structure would be explained by appeal to conceptual growth, has not been fulfilled. Concepts and forms fail to march in step, but rather swirl around in relative independence, like skating partners on an ice rink, meeting periodically, with a frequency that will vary with the style of the particular couple. Furthermore, children's concepts are not always coextensive with the forms that are available in the adult language. To compare a child's repertoire of concepts with that of an adult could be like superimposing two alternative plans for the building of a house, drawn at differrent stages, as the architect's conception evolved. There would be a broad similarity, but boundaries between rooms and other details would not match perfectly.

We do, of course, need to know about children's concepts in order to understand the process of language development. But if forms do not necessarily follow in an orderly manner on the emergence of concepts, we will also need to know more about the manner in which the child does come by verbal forms. This will be one of our main concerns in the next section.

A RANGE OF STRATEGIES

I began this chapter with an anthology of examples of child speech. My purpose was to illustrate the variety of phenomena that occur in conversations with young children. I then went on to examine three broad approaches to explaining how children learn language. I have attempted to show some of the strengths and limitations of these approaches. I should now like to ask you to get to know a little bit more about the language development of eight children: Minh, Brenda, Christy, Eva, Adam, Ivan, Abe and Dusty. With their help I intend to pursue the evaluation of the theories a little bit further.

1   Peters (1977) reports her study of the development of speech by Minh, a boy with a Vietnamese mother and a Caucasian father, living in the United States. From 11 months, and for some time thereafter, Minh had two distinct types of speech. On the one hand he produced clear renderings of single adult words that came to resemble their targets increasingly as time went on. On the other hand, he produced approximations to complete adult sentences. These were rendered at first as mere melodies, reproducing the intonation patterns of the originals. Later they incorporated renderings of some of the sounds from the target sentences. Examples are "a lar ri gu mu nyai" interpreted by Peters as "I like to read Good Moon Night" (a poem); "sili, ini?", apparently "Silly, isn't it". Peters calls the single word type of speech 'analytic' and the approximations to sentences 'gestalt'. The gestalt utterances went unnoticed for some time, partly because theories about child language had not led her to expect such utterances, and partly because of the very debased quality of the child's attempts to render complete adult sentences.

2   Scollon (1979) describes his study of speech development by a girl called Brenda. Observation of Brenda's speech caused him to question the procedure of taking one child utterance at a time and studying the meaning expressed within it. We have seen that Bloom explored a stage in Alison's speech before she was producing two-word

176

utterances in which chained and holistic one-word utterances occurred. Scollon identifies as many as four different types of successive utterances, differing in degrees of cohesion between the words. He sees these as gradual steps leading to syntax. Suncratic constructions he calls 'horizontal', since the words are arranged horizontally across the page. The successive utterances are 'vertical' constructions, each utterance one below the other on a page of transcribed speech, is in constructions with an utterance above or below it. Examples are: 1 "finger" "touch"; 2 "cook" "say", then an adult utterance "What'd the cook say?" "something".

When Brenda graduated to 'horizontal' utterances, according to Scollon, she was merely programming, as one unit, word sequences that would previously have been in relationship, but a 'vertical' relationship. At points within this developmental process Brenda enlisted adult help in constructing more elaborate vertical utterances as in example 2 above.

3   We have already met with Bowerman's work on the development of verbs in the speech of her two daughters, Christy and Eva. She also has a great deal to tell us about other developments in the girls' speech. When they were bringing nouns into construction with other words that modified their meaning, the two girls appeared to use different learning strategies to one another. Eva seemed to learn the position of only one noun modifier at a time (Bowerman 1976), introducing new constructions with nouns into her speech piecemeal. Christy, on the other hand, began all in one go to produce nouns linked to a variety of modifiers in the same position. Constructions like "that wet", "daddy hot" and "bottle allgone" all emerged within days of each other. During the same week Christy began to make naming statements, like "that airplane". Bowerman concludes "Whatever the nature of the similarity in Christy's mind, it seems clear that her production of these utterances was delayed until she had organized the structural information governing them at a fairly abstract level" (p 159).

4   I have described a variety of strategies used by my own sons, Adam and Ivan (Clark, 1974, 1977, 1980; Clark, Hutcheson and Van Buren, 1974). These include 'plagiarism', 'person shift', 'coupling' and 'discourse coupling'. Here are some examples:

Plagiarism: "That's upside down," I said, as Adam tried to put on a garment. He snatched it from me saying "I want to upside down."

In plagiarism the child pads out his own utterance by borrowing undigested sequences from the preceding adult utterance.

Person shift: Adam's father asked him "Shall I carry you?" Adam reached up saying "I carry you." He continued for some time to use this phrase as a request to be carried.

In person shift, the child reproduces elements of an adult utterance without fully interpreting them and uses them himself without adapting them to change of speaker.

Coupling: Ivan learned to say "That's mine" and after using this phrase for some time began to add nouns to it, leading to such sequences as "That's mine jam".

In coupling the child constructs longer sequences by combining sequences already in his repertoire. This may result in grammatical inconsistencies, as in the above example.

Discourse: Over the course of a few days, Adam requested "Adam turn e light on," when he was having his nappy changed. I repeated "Soon". Eventually Adam began to formulate his request as "Adam turn e light on soon."

In discourse coupling the child builds longer utterance by joining two successive contributions to a conversation.

5 Kuczaj and Maratsos (1975) compared imitation with spontaneous speech. The child they studied, whom they call Abe, showed in his imitations that he was a step ahead in applying his grammatical knowledge to imitating utterances spoken to him than in using it to produce utterances of his own. For example, he was able to repeat sentences containing the words 'can' and 'will' before he produced these in his own speech. Furthermore, he would correct utterances in which 'can' and 'will' were misplaced, e.g. "A nice cow eat will the good hay" was imitated as "A nice cow will eat the good hay". However, if the words were contained in questions he did not reproduce them. Later he began to include 'can' and 'will' in some, but not all of his utterances. The utterance types containing 'can' and 'will' that he could produce were precisely the ones that he had been able to imitate, or reformulate correctly at the earlier stage. This implies that his processing of model utterances for imitation was active and not mechanical.

6 Blank (1975) describes her study with Allen of the efforts
of a girl called Dusty to come to grips with the meaning of
the word 'why'. Dusty went through three stages in her
handling of the word. At first she would respond with the
single word 'why?' to adult utterances, e.g. "That's a nice
fire" "Why?". Later she woud append it to phrases, e.g.
"Why green?" "Why the garage door?". Later again, she
prefixed it to a total sentence that an adult had just used
to describe an action, e.g. "He's climbing out of bed."
"Why he climbing out of bed?" Blank interprets these uses
of the word, whose meaning she clearly does not understand,
as the means the child uses to try and elicit information
from an adult that will help her to discover its meaning.
The meaning of a word like 'why', Blank points out, is
particularly elusive, since there is nothing concrete one
can point to in the environment, or any way in which its
meaning can readily be illustrated without the child
grappling with abstractions.

SOME RECURRING THEMES RECONSIDERED

The ages of the children who engaged in the speech activity
just described have not been given. This was deliberate. In
the search for an explanation of language acquisition,
researchers have been tempted to produce a single
developmental outline to account for the way children
gradually achieve mastery of language. But the range of
strategies and procedures described in the above selection
makes it clear that there is no common pattern for all
children. Ages have been left out to discourage the reader
from seeing these glimpses of learning on the part of eight
children as eight stages in a uniform process.

The danger of approaching the study of language acquisition
with the expectation that there will be one pattern is that
conflicting evidence will be ignored. Peters (1980) speaks of
the 'trash heap' of discarded data in language development
studies. A study choosing clear speakers would fail to
uncover Minh's strategy. Studies neglecting single word
utterances, discarding repetitions, or viewing each child
utterance in isolation from those preceding it, would miss all
that Brenda can tell us about language learning. Studies
omitting imitations from an analysis or divorcing a child's
utterances from the maternal speech surrounding them would
overlook Adam and Ivan's devices for communicating. Yet all
these dismissive procedures have been widely used by
researchers into language development. Ochs (1979) in a
chapter entitled 'Transcription as theory', gives a
penetrating account of the way conventional research methods
channel and limit investigations.

At the outset of this chapter I argued that one function of a theory is to help us to make complex reality intelligible to ourselves. If we allow for individual variation between children, how can we achieve a coherent picture of the language learning process as a whole? I must warn you that I do not have a very clear answer to that question. However, in this section I shall try to suggest the character of an adequate theory of language development by exposing the simplifications that it needs to avoid.

To help me in this task, I shall begin by describing a view of language development, whose claims are fairly widely shared. This view attributes to the child some of the characteristics of the 'little linguist' and some of the characterists of the 'child with ideas'. I shall then examine the claims it makes with the help of the illustrations of child speech provided by Minh, Brenda, Christy and Eva, Adam and Ivan, Dusty and other children who have been mentioned in the course of this chapter.

The child, by this viewpoint, begins a piece of language learning with understanding of a concept. He may have inborn knowledge of this concept, wired into his language acquisition device, or he may have evolved the concept in the course of his early interactions with the physical and social environment. Having the concept he searches the input speech for a means to express it. When he utters some form in his speech, equivalent to an adult form, we can take it, according to this viewpoint, that the meaning of that form for the child at least approximates the meaning that it has for us. Furthermore the speech manifests rules for forming words and forming sentences out of combinations of words. Simplified rules, no doubt, reflecting the level of abstraction of structure from the input that the child is currently capable of achieving.

Such a child does not imitate stretches of adult speech mechanically, without comprehension. Such a child does not harbour in his speech packages of adult language that he has not yet unpacked. He progresses not by unravelling the meanings of items already in his speech repertoire, but by returning to the input as a resource for further refining his notions about language structure. Developments in his control of language structure are spontaneous. He is not under the tutelage of his mother.

To frame the viewpoint in terms of three enduring issues about language development, the child projected by this viewpoint is not helped by imitation, or substantially by mother's speech, and his comprehension of language is in advance of his production of language. To put the latter more precisely, he both grasps concepts before he finds forms to express them, and he can interpret adult speech which is more complex than the speech he is currently producing.

Let us now examine the claims embodied in this view with the help of the children with whose speech we have become a little acquainted.

Does the process begin with the understanding of a concept? For the most part we may assume that children have some understanding that they seek to express when they speak. Meaningless utterances are rare. But have they gone from having a concept to scrutinising the input for an appropriate linguistic device with which to express it? To be sure Christy studied a range of sentence types and abstracted a common pattern before beginning to produce them. On the other hand, Halliday's Nigel invented his own means of expression. Adam used more or less conventional words, learned from the input, but combined them in idiosyncratic ways. David adapted his limited verbal system to express recurrent activity in an entirely original way. Ivan extended his own linguistic resources through coupling units already in his repertoire.

If children have examined the input and tried to abstract from it rules for structuring meanings, then we are justified in treating their own output as a reflection of their developing rule system. In the case of Christy and Abe, we can see a justification for regarding aspects of their speech as rule-governed. In the case of Minh and Adam, on the other hand, there seems to be no such justification.

Although some children, like Abe, decoded enough of the input to reject negatives for imitation, in other cases it is clear that segments of adult speech are being adopted into the child's repertoire without full decoding of the elements. These include Adam's 'plagiarisms' and 'person shifts' and Minh's 'gestalt' utterances. Nevertheless, some crude global interpretation of the material copied must take place. There are children, then, who copy and otherwise manipulate adult speech whose meaning they scarcely begin to grasp. These manipulations of input speech have implications for how we view error. You will remember that Bloom looked for conventional forms as evidence of the child's grasp of linguistic material. Bowerman and Karmiloff-Smith saw error as the only adequate evidence for growing mastery of linguistic concepts. Adam and Ivan teach us that standard word order can arise without grammatical analysis of input, through, for example, discourse coupling, and that errors are not incontrovertible evidence for understanding, since they may arise through person shift, or coupling, or a wide variety of other procedures, perhaps as yet undiscovered, for producing speech without full understanding. It would appear, then that neither correctness of a speech form nor error in a speech form can be used as a reliable guide in all circumstances to a child's understanding.

The view that children's speech reflects prior analysis of the input has been the dominant view in child language research of recent years. It follows that little attention has been directed to ways in which the child might make discoveries about linguistic structure through becoming more aware of implicit meanings in the speech items already in his repertoire. Some researchers, whilst willing to admit that children may acquire unanalysed sequences from adult speech, nevertheless deny that this contributes to their language learning. They regard them as 'frozen forms' that will never yield up their implicit meanings (Brown and Hanlon, 1970). Some investigators, on the other hand, have started to explore how children might unravel structure from a repertoire of stored fragments of speech already in use. Peters (1980), for example, suggests that children can identify recurring parts in speech formulae that they are using, and thus discover features of grammatical structure. In this discussion, Peters makes extensive use of the unpublished work of Fillmore and Iwamura on children learning second languges. The findings of these researchers suggest that such processes for learning structure may be fairly widespread. An accident that occurred at bathtime when Ivan was nearly three is also suggestive. The chance occurrence of two alternative ways of saying the same thing led to the child's restructuring an erroneous sequence that had been the product of coupling. As I was running the bath he said "You want to have a bath?". This was apparently an incomplete imitation of "Do you want to have a bath?". A moment later he picked up his teddy bear and said "I want teddy - have a bath", apparently a coupling. He subseqently modified this, presumably under the influence of the previous imitated utterance, to "I want teddy to have a bath".

Lock (1979) believes that the process of becoming consciously aware of linguistic structure depends on the verbal material being actively used. Only in this way can it become an object of reflection, and help the child to achieve an abstract grasp of relationships that are already implicit in his activity in the physical and social world (see discussion of Greenfield's approach).

But what of the claim embodied in the widely shared image of language learning about the negligible role of the parent in this process. The work of Bowerman on the verb system of her daughters, Christy and Eva, and of Karmiloff-Smith on the development of French words such as 'même' shows us that children can unravel implicit meanings of the words they are already using, independently of aid from an adult. On the other hand, generous allowance needs to be made for individual variation in the age and manner of achieving such illumination. For example, at 9 years, 5 weeks and 4 days Ivan failed to make explicit an awareness of the components of meaning in causal verbs of the type that Christy and Eva had come to terms with at a much younger age. When Adam complained that he could not find his pullover because Mrs Quinn had "disappeared it", Ivan said to me "You can't disappear a pullover, can you?". On being asked "What do you do?" he replied "Put it on ...burn it?". I said "What should you say if you don't say 'disappear it'?". To this his response was "I don't know". Quite conceivably, because of hereditary factors the daughters of linguists go about acquiring language rather differently to the sons of psychologists.

Furthermore, our examples show us that the elaboration of structure is not always achieved without adult assistance. For example, Scollon's study of Brenda shows that she was helped by adult interaction to move from crude approximations to English words to fluent, intelligible sequences. Maternal props to her own structures within conversations supported her as she moved from primitive to more polished exchanges. Shugar (1978) makes similar points about the 'scaffolding' mothers provide when constructing discourse with a child. In the case of Adam's discourse coupling, too, the construction of linguistic form was a collaborative process.

Mothers appear to have a role also in helping the child to clarify the meaning of verbal items. Dusty, for example, enlisted her mother's help in her search for the meaning of the word 'why'. She attempted to elicit clear information from her mother that would help her to link this elusive word to something in her concrete experience. But the role of mothers in sustaining the discovery of meaning begins much earlier, according to many researchers. Minh was helped by the fact that his mother treated his 'gestalt' approximations to sentences as genuine attempts to communicate. Peters (1977) noted that Minh resented her own inability to make sense of his speech. After a while he began to produce, apparently as a protest, a form of 'mush speech' in her presence, which was genuine nonsense, rather than barely intelligible, bona fide attempts to communicate, as were his 'gestalt' tunes. Peters speculates that if Minh's mother had failed to respond to his 'gestalt' utterances he might have ceased to pursue this preferred strategy for language development, and thus been forced to progress more slowly by some other avenue.

183

Many researchers have stressed the value of mothers treating children's gestures and vocalisations as meaningful, even before they truly become so (e.g. Snow, 1976; Newson, 1978). Mothers also go to great lengths to make their own speech meaningful to their children, reformulating utterances again and again to make them more intelligible (Bridges, 1979). Cross (1978) identifies the mother's ability to make her speech meaningful to the child as the most important factor in facilitating development.

But it is possible to trace the role of the mother back even beyond the emergence of speech. Not all researchers into child language believe, with Chomsky, that children come into the world with preformed concepts nor do they believe with Piaget that they discover concepts through their own independent exploration of the physical environment. A great deal of interest is now taken in interactions between mothers and their children in the period prior to the onset of speech. Some researchers believe that through these interactions mothers are laying, with their children, the foundations of language development. For example, Ratner and Bruner (1978) claim that simple repetitive games provide children with frameworks whose familiarity and predictability make it possible for the children to master basic meanings essential to subsequent language learning.

The importance of familiarity as children begin to be verbal is convincingly argued by Ferrier (1978). She reminds us of the highly stereotyped nature f a great deal of adult speech, that recurs time and time again in exactly the same form and in exactly the same everyday contexts. The repetitive nature of a great deal of early speech to children may be an invaluable aid to them in their mastery of language.

One author in her autobiography has ventured to say 'maybe that's all understanding is, "a terrific familiarity"' (Agnelli, 1977). Agnelli was talking about understanding of people and their feelings and actions, but her statement could well apply to understanding of linguistic structure. Maybe familiarity on its own is not enough, but for some children it is undoubtedly a necessary basis for the eventual growth of understanding.

The suggestion that mothers' contribution may not be as negligible as has been claimed, should not be taken as a claim that there is a mystical bond of understanding between mothers and children. We cannot assume in any given situation that the mother's and the child's perspective will coincide. A given object, place or event can be described accurately in words in a number of ways (Macrae, 1977). The speaker may be thinking one thing about a situation and the hearer another. In such circumstances language can be misconstrued. Evelyn Waugh (1964) illustrates this with an anecdote about a traveller who asked his guide the name of a nearby village. "Laiku" came the reply, and 'Laiku' became the name by which the village was known, and the name that referrd to it on maps. What the traveller was unaware of was that "Laiku" meant "I don't know". When we say "ta" to a child meaning "Say thank you" when we give children things we need not be surprised when the child begins to use "ta" himself when he is giving things to other people, rather than when he receives them. When we regularly say "phew!", as Ferrier (1978) did in reaction to the smell of a soiled nappy when she entered her daughter's room each morning, we need not be surprised if the child comes to use "phew!" as a form of greeting.

Even if concepts are shared, forms may be misconstrued, as in the case of Adam's perception of prepositions as 'mof' and 'mon'. Adam's bias towards the last word in an input utterance led him to learn to call an elephant an 'intit' because someone said to him "That's an elephant, isn't it," when they were looking at a picture book together. Ferrier (1978) gives many more, fascinating examples of similar misinterpretations by her daughter. Mothers' responses to children's utterances may unwittingly mislead the children about linguistic form as Cazden (1968) pointed out. Consider, for example, the following exchange:

Child: "Because I caught..."
Mother: "What did you catch?"
Child: "I catch my bicycle." (p 231).

Let me try to capture the variety of approaches I have been discussing here by an analogy. Suppose we conceive of the conceptual containers waiting to accommodate forms as shopping baskets, waiting to receive merchandise. The linguists believing in the language acqustion device see the shopping baskets as available at birth. Piagetians focussing on cognitive development believe the child weaves the baskets from his own early experience in the environment. The researchers concerned with early interactions between mothers and children believe the basket weaving is a joint exercise with the child being the mother's apprentice. Mismatch of forms and concepts, due to the wrong form presenting itself at the moment of learning, can be likened to the wrong merchandise getting put into the baskets because it is too eye catching, or nearer to hand on the shelves.

But we also have to make allowances for individual shopping styles. We have the careful shoppers who plan their purchases thoroughly in advance, and the shoppers who get to know more about the goods they have purchased rather rashly when they get them home and unpack them at their leisure.

CONCLUDING COMMENTS

Of the three broad approaches to language acquisition that I
reviewed above the first, in its simplest formulation, seems
to have underestimated the child's own contribution to the
process, whereas the other two seem to have minimised the role
of the mother. We appear to need an interactive model,
incorporating insights from the subtler aproaches to mother's
role that we explored in the last section. In short, we need
a conception of interaction that takes account of the impact
of maternal teaching styles on individual children's language
learning strategies.

The contexts in which language is acquired are communication
contexts, and it is a characteristic of communication that two
or more people interact, each approaching the dialogue from
his or her own perspective. When a mother and child are
communicating there needs to be a negotiation of very
disparate perspectives.

In the earliest stages, the mother is far better equipped than
the child to sustain communication, or it might be the
illusion of communication, in the face of a broad gap in
knowledge of both language and the world. It may be that
there is an emotional need on the part of a mother to feel
that communication is taking place. At any rate, she has far
more resources at her command.

As the child progresses communication need not necessarily
improve, since if the child adopts forms that are mismatched
with his concepts, in one or other of the ways that we have
been observing, this might serve to reveal communication
failure where it was previously obscured. What it is
important to recognise is that utterances that young children
produce cannot be taken at their face value. What the child
intends may not be what the words seem to say. But what is
also important is that this does not matter. A child carrying
verbal material which is ill-formed, or mismatched with
concepts, will not cease to learn until he has tangled the
strands within it.

Furthermore, communication can take place without perfect
linguistic expression, since a great deal of meaning is
sustained by contexts, and many children seem to have quite a
sophisticated grasp of social relations and the significance
of everyday events which goes far beyond the sophistication of
their speech. Remember James and his football, for example.
Communication is a far broader phenomenon than merely the
exchange of words. There is a wide range of other channels of

meaning on non-verbal planes whose significance for language learning is worthy of much fuller research. Imagine the child's engagement in interactions in terms of a parachute with several strings. Even if a number of strings are absent there may still be enough to keep him airborne.

It is easy to get the impression from reading some discussions of language acquisition that the discovery of the system of linguistic rules underlying speech is the sole object of the child's engagement in conversations, and that the sole object of the mother's engagement is to assist him in this process. This is far from the truth. Even the child's interest in verbal forms is not purely a linguistic interest. Consider the motives of a child for gleefully and repetitively chanting "man in a van, man in a van", and another chortling as he points to his mother and says "you". The mother, if she is functioning as a teacher at all, is teaching far more than language structure. She is transmitting to the child cultural patterns of non-verbal communication (Miller, 1973), and cultural attitudes to silence (Basso, 1972). She may well be suppressing intrinsic responses by the child to information from non-verbal sources and narrowing his attention to the verbal channel that our culture values more (Ornstein, 1973). Such narrowing, if it does occur, will probably continue in educational contexts, and we would do well to find out more about it. The mother, too, through her use of language is highlighting for the child the social significance of certain of his actions, and playing down others (Shotter ad Gregory, 1976). She is modelling for the child social attitudes, for example attitudes to siblings (Dunn, in press). In some cultures she uses verbal formulations from birth onwards to provide the child with scripted utterances that help him play his role in social situations in accordance with adult expectations (Schieffelin, 1979).

Mothers and children are negotiating a common reality in the course of conversations, and more broadly, in the course of development. The negotiation process may be more effective if initial demands are not too stringent. Wells, Barnes and Satterly (1980) and Nelson (1973) have found that others who are most successful in enhancing their children's development of language are those who adapt to the child's perspective. Hubbel (1977) argues that testing and training procedures that restrict children's scope for responding too narrowly inhibit rather than encourage communication. Children need freedom to grow. Furthermore, the process of negotiation needs to be sufficiently rewarding for the children to feel that their own efforts of adjustment are worth making.

Anyone who wonders what justifies us in making children adjust their perspective so radically in the course of development to accommodate to ours should take comfort in the thought that if the communication is genuinely a two way process, our own perspectives should be enriched by accommodating to each child.

REFERENCES

Agnelli, S. We Always Wore Sailor Suits. (Corgi, London, 1977)

Basso, K.H. To give up on words: silence in Apache culture. In Giglioli P.P. (ed.), Language and Social Context. (Penguin, Harmondsworth, 1972).

Blank, M. Mastering the intangible through language. Annals of the New York Academy of Sciences, 1975, 263, 44-58.

Bloom, L. Language Development: Form and Function in Emerging Grammars. (M.I.T. Press, Cambridge, Mass., 1970).

Bloom, L. One Word at a Time. (Mouton, The Hague, 1973).

Bowerman, M. Semantic factors in the acquisition of rules for word use and sentence construction. In Morehead, D.M. and Morehead, A.E., (eds.), Normal and Deficient Child Language, (University Park Press, Baltimore, 1976).

Bowerman, M. Starting to talk worse: clues to language acquisition from children's late speech errors. In Strauss, S. (ed.), U-Shaped Behavioural Growth. (Academic Press, New York, forthcoming).

Braine, M. The ontogeny of English phrase structure: the first phase. Language, 1963, 39, 1-13.

Braunwald, S.R. and Brislin, R.W. The diary method updated. In Ochs, E. and Schieffelin, B.B., (eds.), Developmental Pragmatics. (Academic Press, New York, 1979).

Bridges, A. Directing two year olds' attention: some clues to understanding. Journal of Child Language, 1979, 6, 211-226.

Bronckart, J.P. and Sinclair, H. Time, tense and aspect. Cognition, 1973, 2, 107-130.

Brown, R. The development of wh questions in child speech. Journal of Verbal Learning and Verbal Behaviour, 1968, 7, 279-290.

Brown, R. A First Language: the Early Stages. Harvard

University Press, Cambridge, Mass, 1973).

Brown, R. and Bellugi, U. Three processes in the child's acquisition of syntax. In Lenneberg, E.H., (ed.), New Directions in the Study of Language. (M.I.T. Press, Cambridge, Mass., 1964).

Brown, R., Cazden, C. and Bellugi, U. The child's grammar from I - III. In Hill, J.P. (ed.), Minnesota Symposia in Child Psychology II. (University of Minnesota Press, Minneapolis, 1968).

Brown, R. and Fraser, C. The acquisition of syntax. In Cofer, C.N. and Musgrave, B., (eds.), Verbal Behaviour and Learning. (McGraw-Hill, New York, 1963).

Brown, R. and Hanlon, C. Derivational complexity and order of acquisition in child speech. In Hayes, J.R., (ed.), Cognition and the Development of Language. (Wiley, New York, 1970).

Carroll, J.B. Language and Thought. (Prentice-Hall, Englewood Cliffs, 1964).

Cazden, C. The acquisition of noun and verb inflections. Child Development, 1968, 39, 433-8.

Chomsky, N. Aspects of a Theory of Syntax. (M.I.T. Press, Cambridge, Mass., 1975).

Clark, E.V. What's in a word? On the child's acquisition of semantics in his first language. In Moore, T.E. (ed.), Cognitive Development and the Acquisition of Language. (Academic Press, New York, 1973).

Clark, R. Performing without competence. Journal of Child Language, 1974, 1, 1-10.

Clark, R. Adult theories, child strategies and their implications for the language teacher. In Allen, J.P.B. and Corder, S.P. (eds.), Edinburgh Course in Applied Linguistics, 2. (Oxford University Press, London, 1975).

Clark, R. What's the use of imitation? Journal of Child Language, 1977, 4, 341-58.

Clark, R. Assessing language in the home. In Davies, A. (ed.), Language and Learning in the Home and the School. (Heinemann, London, 1981).

Clark, R., Hutcheson, S. and Van Buren, P. Comprehension and production in language acquisition. Journal of Linguistics, 1974, 10, 39-54.

Cromer, R.F. The development of language and cognition: the cognition hypothesis. In Foss, B. (ed.), New Perspectives in Child Development. (Penguin, Harmondsworth, 1974).

Cross, T.G. Mothers' speech and its association with rate of linguistic development in young children. In Waterson, N. and Snow, C. (eds.), The Development of Communication. (Wiley, New York, 1978).

Dore, J. Conversational acts and the acquisition of language. In Ochs, E. and Schieffelin, B.B. (eds.), Developmental Pragmatics. (Academic Press, New York, 1979).

Dunn, J. The speech of two and three year olds to infant siblings: baby talk and the context of communication. Journal of Child Language, (in press).

Ervin, S.M. Imitation and structural change in children's language. In Lenneberg, E.H. (ed.), New Directions in the Study of Language. (M.I.T. Press, Cambridge, Mass., 1964).

Ferrier, J.L. Some observations of error in context. In Waterson, N. and Snow, C. (eds.), The Development of Communication. (Wiley, London, 1978).

Greenfield, P.M. Structural parallels between language and action in development. In Lock, A. (ed.), Action, Gesture and Symbol. (Academic Press, New York, 1978).

Greenfield, P.M. and Smith, J.H. The Structure of Communication in Early Language Development. (Academic Press, New York, 1976).

Halliday, M.A.K. Learning How to Mean. Explorations in the Development of Language. (Edward Arnold, London, 1975).

Howe, C. The meanings of two-word utterances in the speech of young children. Journal of Child Language, 1976, 3, 29-47.

Hubbell, R.D. On facilitating spontaneous talking in young children. Journal of Speech and Hearing Disorders, 1977, 42, 216-31.

Huttenlocher, J. The origin of language comprehension. In Solso, R.L. (ed.), Theories in Cognitive Psychology. (Lawrence Erlbaum, Hillsdale, New Jersey, 1975).

190

Karmiloff-Smith, A. Language as a formal problem-space for children. Paper presented to the MPG/NIAS conference, Beyond Description in Child Language. (Nijmegen, Holland, 1979).

Klima, E.S. and Bellugi, U. Syntactic regularities in the speech of children. In Lyons, J. and Wales, R.J. (eds.), Psycholinguistics Papers. (Edinburgh University Press, Edinburgh, 1966).

Kuczaj, S.A. and Maratsos, M.P. What children can say before they will. Merrill Palmer Quarterly, 1975, 21, 89-111.

Lenneberg, E.H. A biological perspective of language. In Lenneberg, E.H. (ed.), New Directions in the Study of Language. (M.I.T. Press, Cambridge, Mass., 1964).

Lock, A. The early stages of communicative and linguistic development. Underlying process. Paper presented to the NIAS Conference, Knowledge and Representation. (Wassenar, Holland, 1979).

McNeill, D. Developmental psycholinguistics. In Smith, F. and Miller, G.A. (eds.), The Genesis of Language. A Psycholinguistic Approach. (M.I.T. Press, Cambridge, Mass., 1966 (a)).

McNeill, D. The creation of language by children. In Lyons, J. and Wales, R.J. (eds.), Psycholinguistics Papers. (Edinburgh University Press, Cambridge, 1966(b)).

Macrae, A. Combining meanings in early language. In Fletcher, P. and Garman, M. (eds.), Language Acquisition: Studies in First Language Development. (Cambridge University Press, Cambridge, 1979).

Miller, G. Non-verbal communication. In Miller, G. (ed.), Communication, Language, and Meaning: Psychological Perspectives. (Oxford University Press, London, 1973).

Miller, G.A., Galanter, E. and Pribram, K.H. Plans and the Structure of Behaviour. (Holt, Rinehart and Winston, London, 1970).

Nelson, K. Structure and strategy in learning to talk. Monograph for the Society for Research in Child Development, 1973, No. 149, Vol. 38, Nos.1 & 2.

Newson, J. Dialogue and development. In Lock, A. (ed.), Action, Gesture and Symbol, (Academic Press, London, 1978).

Ochs, E. Transcription as theory. In Ochs, E. and Schieffelin, B.B. (eds.), Developmental Pragmatics. (Academic Press, New York, 1979).

Ornstein, R.E. (ed.), The Nature of Human Consciousness. A Book of Readings. (W. H. Freeman, San Fransicso, 1973).

Peters, A.M. Language learning strategies: does the whole equalthe sum of the parts? Language, 1977, 53, 560-73.

Peters, A.M. The units of language acquisition. Working Papers in Linguistics, 12 No 1, 1980, Department of Linguistics, University of Hawaii at Manoa.

Piaget, J. Play, Dreams and Imitation in Childhood. (W.W. Norton, New York, 1962).

Ratner, N. and Bruner, J. Games, social exchange and the acquisition of language. Journal of Child Language, 1978, 5, 391-401.

Rodd, L.J. and Braine, M.D.S. Children's imitations of syntactic constructions as a measure of linguistic competence. Journal of Verbal Learning and Verbal Behaviour, 10, 430-43.

Ryan, J. Early language development: towards a communicational analysis. In Richards, P.M. (ed.), The Integration of a child into a Social World. (Cambridge University Press, Cambridge).

Sachs, J. and Truswell, L. Comprehension of two word instructions by children in the one word stage. Journal of Child Language, 1978, 5, 17-24.

Schieffelin, B. Getting it together: an ethnographic approach to the study of the development of communicative competence. In Ochs, E. and Schieffelin, B.B. (eds.), Developmental Pragmatics. (Academic Press, New York, 1979).

Shotter, J. and Gregory, S. On first gaining the idea of oneself as a person. In Harre, R. (ed.), Life Sentences: Aspects of the Social Role of Language. (Wiley, London, 1976).

Shugar, G.W. Text analysis as an approach to the study of early linguistic operations. In Waterson, N. and Snow, C. (eds.), The Development of Communication. (Wiley, London, 1978).

Slobin, D.I. Seven questions about language development. In Dodwell, P.C. (ed.), New Horizons in Psychology. (Penguin, Harmondsworth, 1972).

Slobin, D.I. Cognitive prerequisites for the development of grammar. In Ferguson, C. and Slobin, D. (eds.), Studies in Child Language Development. (Holt, Rinehart and Winston, 1973).

Snow, C. The language of the mother-child relationship. In Rogers, S. (ed.), They Don't Speak Our Language. (Edward Arnold, London, 1976).

Wells, G., Barnes, S. and Satterly, D. Effects of adjustment in adults' speech to children. Paper delivered at the Child Language Seminar, University of Manchester, April, 1980.

Chapter 8

PERSONALITY AND DEVELOPMENT

David Fontana

The term 'personality' is a complex one, and it is doubtful if
there is any single definition of it which is likely to be
acceptable to all psychologists. The problem lies in deciding
where personality ends and other aspects of the psychological
life of the individual begin. Does personality include
intelligence, for example, and creativity, and the
individual's characteristic patterns of behaviour, and his
attitudes, opinions, beliefs and so on? Certainly when we
think about personality we often take these things into the
reckoning. When we say that a particular child is 'bright',
we often imply not only something about the way in which he
tackles academic problems but something about the way in which
he responds to life generally. We do the same when we say
another is 'slow' or 'unoriginal' or 'irrational'. However,
if we do include all these attributes in what we mean by
personality we end up with a definition so broad that, as
Allport (1961) pointed out, it includes practically everything
that interests us about people. By its very breadth, it
becomes of little value to us, since it serves merely as a
synonym to the term 'human personality' itself.

In an attempt to introduce some precision, psychologists
generally suggest that personality should be taken to include
only affective and conative traits, that is traits to do with
emotionality and with willing and desiring, and should not
cover cognitive traits like intelligence and creativity,
though inevitably it will interact with them at a number of
points. Such a definition is somewhat arbitrary, but it is
useful, nevertheless, in helping us to focus and formalise our
thinking. What it does not attempt to do, however, is to
indicate where personality comes from. Is it something we
largely inherit, or something which we acquire through
interaction with the environment? Such a question is of
particular interest to the teacher since the answer to it
helps indicate the limits of the influence that education can
have upon children. If personality is largely inherited, then

194

this influence will obviously be less than it would be if personality is largely acquired.

THE ORIGINS OF PERSONALITY

Heredity

Nature (inheritance) and nurture (environment) interact with each other from the early days of life onwards, and it is virtually impossible to separate out their relative contributions with any real precision. One of the best ways of attempting to do so, however, is to take a group of very young babies, at a time when environment has had, as yet, little time to influence behaviour, and observe whether there are consistent identifiable differences between them of a kind that might in some way be associated with personality. The babies can then be followed through into childhood and eventually into adult life to see if these differences appear to persist. Just such a study has been attempted by the American paediatricians Thomas, Chess, and Birch (e.g. 1970) with a sample that consisted initially of 141 children at eight to twelve weeks. Results showed that on such measures as activity levels, regularity of bodily functions (e.g. feeding, sleeping, excreting), adaptability to new situations and changes in routine, sensitivity to stimuli (i.e. reactions to minor discomforts, loud noises and the like) and disposition (cheerful, cranky etc.), there were indeed significant identifiable differences between the children. These differences allowed 65 per cent of the children to be allocated to one or other of the following three broad categories:

The <u>easy</u> <u>group</u>:   characterised by regularity, by adaptability, by a positive approach to new experiences, by low sensitivity to unpleasant stimuli, and by cheerfulness of disposition (40 per cent of sample).

The <u>difficult</u> <u>group</u>:   characterised by irregularity, by low adaptability, by a negative response to new experiences, and by a general crankiness of mood (10 per cent of sample).

The <u>slow</u> <u>to</u> <u>warm-up</u> <u>group</u>:   characterised by low activity and adaptability, by withdrawal in the face of new experiences, by mild response to stimuli, and by a slight negativity of mood (15 per cent of sample).

When followed through into adolescence it was found that, although methods of assessment had naturally to be altered in tune with age, the children's membership of the three groups remained remarkably constant. This prompted the researchers to conclude that what we can perhaps best term temperament (the raw material of personality) is apparent in the early weeks of life, and therefore would appear to be linked to genetic factors. This does not mean, of course, that the child's subsequent environmental experiences are unimportant. The members of the Thomas, Chess, and Birch sample were all drawn from homes with an apparently good standard of parental care, and it may well be that, as we shall see in the next section, an adverse environment would turn even the easiest of children into a serious behaviour problem. Environment also seems to be important in determining the success or otherwise with which 'difficult children' adapt to their temperaments. Thomas, Chess and Birch found, for example, that without extra careful handling from patient, consistent, and understanding parents these children tended to become even more negative and awkward, and by adolescence 70 per cent of those assigned to this group (as opposed to only 18 per cent of the 'easy' children) had developed specific personality problems. In other words these children seemed to be by nature intense, spirited individuals, who felt disappointments and frustrations keenly, and who needed parents who could give them clear and sympathetic guidance if they were to come to terms with themselves and learn to relate sensibly to others.

Somewhat less dramatically, the 'slow to warm-up' children in the Thomas, Chess, and Birch sample also appeared to benefit from parents with an above average amount of patience and understanding. These children needed plenty of stimuli to arouse and interest them, but at the same time tended to withdraw if forced too abruptly into new experiences, and flourished best with parents who were able to maintain the correct balance. The 'easy' children, on the other hand, seemed able to cope pretty well with a wide range of parental behaviours. They adapted to both permissive and authoritarian approaches, and developed generally into outgoing and sociable children who took readily to school when the time arrived, joined in enthusiastically, and became well-liked and popular. Doubtless they benefited particularly from parents who took a special interest in their doings, and encouraged and supported them within the context of a loving and consistent relationship, but the point was that these children apeared temperamentally more resilient than those in the other two groups, and better able to adjust to the problems of daily life.

Knowledge of the apparent importance of heredity in personality comes from a number of other studies into temperament in young babies (e.g. Berger and Passingham 1973) and also from so-called twin studies. Fundamentally such studies involve studying pairs of identical and fraternal twins to establish whether there are greater similarities between the behaviour of the former than of the latter. Identical twins (monozygotic or MZ for short) are formed from a single ovum and a single sperm and therefore share a virtually identical genetic pattern, whereas fraternal twins (dizygotic or DZ for short) are formed from separate ovums and sperms and are therefore no more alike genetically than any other two siblings. Clearly, if we assume that each twin in a given pair receives a similar environment (not always a valid assumption as MZ twins are often treated more alike than are DZ), then any tendency of MZ twins to resemble each other psychologically more closely than DZ twins is likely to be the consequence of heredity. A more elaborate approach still is to examine pairs of MZ and DZ twins who have been separated at birth and subsequently reared apart. In both cases environmental influences are now no longer similar, and if the personalities of MZ twins persist in resembling each other more closely than do those of DZ twins, then again we have significant evidence for the workings of heredity.

Since it is difficult to locate and test large samples of twins, and in particular large samples of twins reared apart, twin studies are less extensive and conclusive than one might expect. An early study by Newman, Freeman and Holzinger (1937) concluded that the personalities of MZ twins do indeed resemble each other more closely than do those of DZ, while Shields (1962) found that on Eysenck's personality measures of extraversion and neuroticism (which we discuss in more detail later in this chapter) the resemblance between MZ twins reared apart was still so marked that it was greater even than that of DZ twins reared together. Doubt has since been cast (see Kamin, 1974) on whether some of the MZ twins in Shield's sample could really be said to have been reared 'apart'. Sometimes they were brought up by related pairs of aunts, and even on occasions played and went to school together. The evidence generally is strong enough for Eysenck, at least, to conclude (Eysenck and Eysenck, 1969) that, on his own dimensions of extraversion and neuroticism, the balance in favour of heredity may be as high as three to one (that is 75 per cent of the measurable differences between people on these dimensions may be due to heredity and only 25 per cent due to environment).

Such a conclusion should not be taken to mean, of course, that heredity is more important than environment in all aspects of personality. There is more to personality than scores on the paper and pencil tests devised by Eysenck and other psychologists working within the field of personality measurement. Nobody would pretend that identical scores on extraversion and neuroticism tests mean that two people share identical personalities. Nevertheless the general evidence on the part played by heredity in personality has important implications. In particular it suggests that those responsible for young children should not demand behaviours from them that appear incompatible with basic temperament. To make an active, lively child conform to strict rules of silence, to force a quiet and withdrawn child to be outgoing and sociable, to insist that an intense nervous child makes light of his anxieties, may lead to frustration and confusion in the short term and to more enduring personality problems in the long-term. The role of the adult would appear to be to help the child's development within the boundaries laid down by inheritance, rather than to expect him to conform to some theoretical notion of what personality in children ought ideally to be.

Environment

What we are in effect saying is that the idea that by manipulating the environment we can produce any kind of personality we want in children does not seem to be tenable. What we are also saying, however, is that an adverse environment can prevent a child from fulfilling his temperamental potential, just as it can prevent him from fulfilling his intellectual or his physical potential. We have already seen the apparent importance of patient and sympathetic child-rearing practices in the case of so-called 'difficult' and 'slow to warm-up' children, but we also made reference to the fact that a thoroughly unsatisfactory environment would probably turn even the easiest of children into a behaviour problem. What do we mean by such an assertion, and in particular what do we mean by an unsatisfactory environment in this context?

One approach to the question is deliberately to deprive the young of various aspects of what might be called their normal environment, and study the results upon their behaviour. Since it is obviously unthinkable to conduct such research with children, studies of this kind have employed animal subjects instead, and have then made cautious extrapolations as to what their findings may mean for human beings. One of the best known investigators in this field is Harry Harlow at the University of Wisconsin in the USA. In a programme of work stretching back over two decades, he has shown that rhesus monkeys raised in social isolation during the first six months of life, appear to suffer permanent damage to their subsequent behaviour patterns. Not only do they manifest extreme withdrawal and anxiety in infancy, they appear unable to relate satisfactorily to their own kind, either socially or sexually, in later life. The damage inflicted upon them by their early isolation appears, in other words, adversely to affect their 'personalities' in a number of identifiable and important ways. Not only does this early neglect prevent them from enjoying satisfactory relationships with their peers in adult life, subsequent research also shows, that in the instances where females are successfully (though very reluctantly) caught and mated by normal males, they appear unable to fulfill their social functions as mothers, either neglecting their offspring altogether or abusing them cruelly. This last finding is particularly important in that it appears to indicate that even patterns of behaviour that cannot emerge until adult life, like maternal care, can be influenced by the experiences of early childhood (Harlow and Harlow, 1966).

Mercifully no human infant, even in the least satisfactory of homes, is likely to suffer the kind of extreme social isolation experienced by Harlow's monkeys. Nevertheless his findings led Harlow to suggest that extreme deprivation during the first two years of a child's life (and by extreme deprivation he meant essentially deprivation of any affectionate and solicitous adult care) may lead to some permanent damage to the child's ability to relate socially to others. Later findings have led him to modify this claim somewhat since, given appropriate remedial conditions, some at least of the harm done to experimental monkeys by early neglect seems reversible (Novak and Harlow, 1975). But we are still left with the conclusion that, in the absence of such appropriate and adequate later care, early neglect can profoundly influence subsequent behaviour patterns in animals and, presumably, in man. Such a conclusion is of help to us in understanding a number of aspects of personality, not least of course in understanding the personality of the neglectful parent him or herself. Neglectful parents it seems, and parents who abuse and mistreat their children, may be those who were not fortunate enough to learn the lessons of loving baċk in their own early childhood.

Further evidence of the importance of the early years in personality development, this time from work with human subjects, comes from studies of children brought up in institutions where, however dedicated the standard of care, there is less scope for close personal contact between adult and child. In an influential study carried out some years ago, Goldfarb (1955) showed that at adolescence children who had been institutionalised for the first two years of life and then fostered were less able to relate warmly to others and showed more personality problems than childrn who had been fostered soon after birth. These findings have been supported

PERSONALITY AT SCHOOL AGE

If the child is fortunate enough to receive nursery education, then his acquisition of autonomy will take place in part within the supportive social context of school life. But whether he does or not, by the time he is four years old and ready to move into the infant school he is on the brink of the next task, that of learning initiative. He now has the emotional security that comes from trust in others, and a developing sense of independence within a framework of realistic self-control and a growing respect for the rights of others, and is ready to build on these by learning increasingly to think for himself and to manifest originality. Initiative of this kind enables the child to make choices between possible alternatives, to take decisions, to assume increasing responsibility for his own doings, and to form appropriate links between thought and action. One of the arguments against too formal and rigid a school environment is that it hinders the growth of initiative by preventing the child from taking the lead in any aspect of his work. An inflexible, teacher-centred classroom leaves the child with little choice but to refer all important aspects of his behaviour to the teacher's authority. We are not suggesting, of course, that all the child's attempts to show initiative are equally appropriate, and naturally there will be numerous occasions when the teacher will need to provide both guidance before a child carries out an activity and evaluatory comments after he has done so. But such guidance should be part of a clear attempt to work with the child rather than against him, and should be seen as a necessary part of teaching the child the increased responsibilities that go with initiative.

Having mastered the basic task of initiative, which frees the child to do things, he is next faced with the task of learning to do them well, that is of learning the task of competence. In a sense this task persists throughout life, but Erikson stresses its particular importance in the primary school years when the child is laying the foundations for more advanced skills, and is absorbing important lessons on how he measures up, as a person, to other individuals of his age. If the child finds he is able to tackle successfully the problems, both social and academic, presented to him during these years then he develops a picture of himself as someone able to control his environment satisfactorily and to do the things expected of him. If, on the other hand, he finds himself to be consistently falling behind his contemporaries, or failing to measure up to the standards expected of him, or, in other ways, is made to doubt his worth as a person, then he will inevitably develop strong feelings of inferiority. If he gives way to these feelings then he acquiesces, at this early age, to the notion that he is a failure, and must learn to be

202

content with second or third best in all he does. If on the other hand (and in addition to temperamental factors there will be social factors at work here, as we shall see shortly) he fights against his feelings of inferiority, then he may well become a behaviour problem in the classroom by vying noisily for the teacher's attention for example, or by trying to disrupt or belittle the work of his more successful classmates, or by aggressively rejecting school and everything to do with it (i.e. by in effect saying that my lack of competence is not due to any failure in me but to the 'boring' or 'unfair' nature of school itself).

It is clear from this that one potent source of personality problems in children is the lesson learned during these years that they do not really seem to count much as people. Because those around them undervalue them they come to undervalue themselves. One of the most important pieces of research carried out into such undervaluation is that of the American psychologist Stanley Coopersmith (e.g. 1968). Working with a sample of boys of primary school age, Coopersmith found that on a series of tests (and on teacher recommendations) they could be divided into three groups, which he labelled respectively 'high self-esteem', 'medium self-esteem' and 'low self-esteem'. High self-esteem boys had a confident approach to their work and to personal relationships, showed a realistic appraisal of their own abilities, an independent approach to problems and a tendency to aim high. They were not unduly wounded by criticism, and in the event of initial failure showed an eagerness to try again. Low self-esteem boys, on the other hand, showed the consistent tendency to under-rate themselves, to which we have already made reference, were easily wounded by criticism, showed undue reliance upon the opinions of others, and because of their extreme fear of failure set themselves artificially low goals to decrease the risk of having to encounter it. Medium self-esteem boys fell somewhere between these two extremes.

Coopersmith found that the levels of self-esteem in his sample did not appear to correlate with intelligence, with physical appearance, or with economic background (all the samples came from middle class homes). They did correlate, however, with parental attitude. Parents of high esteem boys were revealed as showing by word and deed that they prized their children as people. They were interested in their activities, knew the names of their friends, showed physical affection towards them, listened to their opinions, and behaved consistently towards them. Although they eschewed the use of corporal punishment and encouraged a sense of domestic democracy, they nevertheless set high standards and expected the children to do their best, and the children responded with confidence and determination. Importantly, the boys praised their parents' fairness, and seemed to enjoy a secure and affectionate relationship with them. Low self-esteem boys, on the other hand, came from homes where standards were inconsistent and veered between over-permissiveness and over-authoritarianism. Their parents seemed to take little real and sustained interest in their pursuits, showed little signs of wishing to encourage democracy, and generally gave little sign that they had much faith in their offspring. The boys tended to rate their parents as unfair.

Coopersmith has since followed his sample through into early adult life, and has found that high self-esteem boys have, not surprisingly, generally met with significantly greater success than their low self-esteem peers. Since, as we have seen, there did not appear to be any marked difference between the boys in terms of fundamental ability, this success seems to be due in large measure to the positive self-concepts which they developed in childhood. The low self-esteem boys, by contrast, learned in childhood to think of themselves negatively, and became in Coopersmith's words 'a sad little group', isolated, fearful, self-conscious, doubting their ability to meet and cope with any real challenge. Note, however, that we have said Coopersmith's sample was a middle class one. As such it consisted of boys who tended to respect authority, and to conclude that if those in authority did not appear to think well of them, then it must be they themselves who were to blame. Had the sample come from working class homes, where there is traditionally less respect for authority and more emphasis upon toughness and self-assertion, it is possible that they might have shown the alternative response to failure that we mentioned above, namely that they might have rejected not only the implied opinion their parents had of them, but also the standards and values of other controlling agencies such as school. There is evidence, for example, that delinquents tend to be low in self-esteem (Rosenberg, 1965), and this seems to suggest that their delinquent activities are in part a way of trying to bolster and protect the concepts they have about themselves. The same is true of children who show less extreme forms of disruptive behaviour, both inside the classroom and outside.

The research findings of Coopersmith are based upon a sample of boys, but there is no reason to suppose that the general pattern would be markedly different for girls, except that it is known that girls as a sex tend to be lower in self-esteem than boys. This may be because girls, from an early age, are allowed less independence than boys (Lewis 1972), and are more anxious generally for parental approval (Davie, Butler and Goldstein, 1972). They may thus fail to master the task of autonomy as thoroughly as boys, and although they tend to be ahead of boys in reading and verbal skills at least during the early primary school years (Davie et al, 1972), they may nevertheless tend to conceive of themselves as inferior when it comes to the acquisition of competence. The situation is made worse by the fact that the girl is bombarded by lessons (from the media, from social encounters, even from school) to the effect that there are all sorts of exciting and important things that are open to boys and men but which are barred to her because of her sex. By the time she is old enough to realise the inequity of this, the harm has been done and she has taken over a role model of the female sex based upon inferiority and under-privilege.

The implications of the points we have been making in this section so far for the teacher are clear. Just as the child apears to need the overt esteem of his parents if he is to value himself adequately, so does he need the esteem of the teacher. It is the task of the teacher to provide opportunities for children to develop proficiency at the skills which go to make up school life, and to shield them from the damaging effects of avoidable failure by setting them tasks appropriate to their abilities, that is tasks that challenge without deterring, that excite without frightening. A golden rule for the remedial teacher is that if children are to be helped to overcome the damaging effects of previous failures they must be allowed to experience success at <u>however low a level</u>, so that they can build up confidence and be encouraged to go on to tasks more appropriate to their abilities. In a modified form this rule holds good for the general class teacher, in that it emphasises that success breeds success, just as failure breeds failure. As a child finds he can meet challenge, and as he is encouraged and reassured by the faith his teacher has in him, so he is emboldened to set his sights increasingly high, while all the time he is learning to reappraise the picture he has of himself. The lesson of competence, it seems clear, is learned as importantly in the school as in the home.

The final childhood task in Erikson's list is the learning of identity (Erikson, 1968), which comes with the advent of adolescence. The child has learned what kind of child he or she is, and now, on the threshold of adult life has to learn what kind of man or woman he or she is about to become. To Erikson, many of the storms and problems of adolescence are caused by this need to establish identity, to move from the world of the child to the, in many ways quite different, world of the adult. If the child has come successfully through the personality learning tasks already outlined, and if he is blessed with parents and teachers who understand that their relationship with him must now be allowed to change and develop towards one of eventual equality, then he should have few real problems with the task of identity, and should move confidently forward into adult life.

PERSONALITY MEASUREMENT

Since an individual's personality does not normally fluctuate
wildly from day to day, it ought to be possible to devise some
way of measuring at least certain aspects of it and obtain
results which yield reasonably reliable results (i.e. the
scores obtained by a given individual on the test or tests
should not vary much at least in the short term). Numerous
attempts have, in fact, been made over the years to do just
this, and though we have, as yet, no single measure (and
probably never will have) that purports to cover all of
personality at one fell swoop, we nevertheless have a range of
devices that each have their specific uses. One of the best
known of these is the Eysenck Personality Inventory (Eysenck
and Eysenck, 1964), which measures people along two <u>dimensions</u>
of personality, namely <u>extraversion-introversion</u> and
<u>neuroticism-stability</u>. These dimensions were arrived at by
Eysenck after inviting large and varied samples of people to
respond to a number of questions about themselves, and then
submitting the results to factor analysis. Factor analysis is
a statisticl technique that looks for relationships amongst a
large number of measures on the assumption that such
correlations are due to some common underlying element. For
example, suppose the measures concerned were questions about
people's individual likes and dislikes, and suppose we found
that a significant number of people who said they liked rowdy
parties also said they liked bold colours and also said they
found long-term planning boring. We might then reasonably
suppose that the inter-correlations between responses to these
three items were due to a common factor of personality which
for the moment we will call factor x.

Our next step would be to look for all the other questions
where people's replies also showed a significant inter-
correlation with our first three items, and we would say that
these as well showed the influence of factor x. We could then
draw all these questions together into a single test and claim
that it measured this factor. Of course it would then be up
to us to decide what factor x actually was. If all our
questions seemed to refer to whether someone gets on well with
other people we might decide to label this factor <u>sociability</u>.
If on the other hand they all seemed to do with the amount of
control an individual feels he wishes to assert over his
fellows we might call this factor <u>authoritarianism</u> and so on.
Obviously low scores on these measures would indicate that the
individual has relatively little of the quality concerned, or
may even be high on a quality diametrically opposed to it
(e.g. tender-minded as opposed to tough-minded, timid as
opposed to brave).

In Eysenck's case, research has suggested that many of the similarities and differences between people in terms of personality are accounted for by the two factors already mentioned in connection with his name, i.e. extraversion-introversion and neuroticism-stability. The typical extravert is someone who is orientated towards the outer world of people and experiences, who is fond of physical activity, likes change and variety in his life, makes social contacts easily, is quickly aroused emotionally (though usually not very deeply), and tends to be materialistic, toughminded, and relatively free from social inhibition. The typical introvert is the opposite of these things, and is generally much more orientated towards the inner world of his own thoughts and feelings. The typical neurotic, as measured by Eysenck's second factor, is timid and fearful, prone to extreme anxiety and doubt, while the stable person is quite simply the opposite of these things. Although extremes on either of the two dimensions are relatively rare, we all of us find our places somehere on both of them, with our position on each being independent of our position on the other (i.e. the fact that one is, say, an introvert tells us nothing about whether one is neurotic or stable).

Eysenck does not claim, of course, that these two dimensions account for the whole personality, and he is actively at work attempting to isolate others (one of these, psychoticism, has already been incorporated into the latest version of his personality test, but has as yet received little attention within education). Nor is Eysenck the only psychologist to adopt this psychometric (i.e. the application of measurement and mathematics to psychology) approach to personality. Using the same factor analytical technique Cattell (1965) claims to have isolated no fewer than sixteen factors (fourteen in children) of personality, while other tests such as the Sandler-Hazari Obsessionality Inventory (Sandler and Hazari 1960) and the F Scale (devised by Adorno in 1950 to measure authoritarianism) concentrate upon more specific aspects of the subject. Many personality tests have versions developed specially for use with young children, and work with these tests has given us considerable insight into the relationship between personality variables and educational achievement, and it is to this work that we now turn our attention.

PERSONALITY AND EDUCATIONAL ACHIEVEMENT

The link between cognitive factors and educational achievement is generally accepted within schools as being an important one, and a great deal is known about the way in which it operates. Until recently, much less attention has been focussed, however, upon the link between personality and such achievement, and the precise nature of this link is still by no means clear. Research studies for the most part have concentrated upon administering personality tests to children and then seeking correlations between test results and various measures of academic attainment (e.g. teacher ratings, 11+ success, standardised attainment test scores), and the evidence is fully reviewed by Entwistle (1972) and by Elliott (1972). The personality test most frequently employed in this research, in Britain at least, is the Junior Eysenck Personality Inventory (i.e. the children's version of the Eysenck Personality Inventory), and results show an interesting if not entirely conclusive pattern. As proposed by Elliott, this pattern indicates that as we move up the estimated mean attainment age from top infants (mean age 7.9 years) to university students (mean age 18 years) we find an initial <u>positive</u> significant correlation between extraversion and scholastic attainment of .19 turning gradually into a significant <u>negative</u> correlation of -.55.

Since Elliott is merely pooling the results of a number of other peoples' investigations, and is not dealing with a properly constituted stratified sample (i.e. a sample in which the individual groups vary only on age and are matched on all other relevant attributes), we must treat this pattern with caution. Nevertheless, it does suggest a link between extraversion and attainment in the primary school which becomes transmuted into a link between introversion and attainment by the time higher education is reached. The obvious explanation for this apparent state of affairs is that the scholastic environment in the primary school tends to favour the outgoing, sociable child, whereas in the upper secondary school and in higher education, where the emphasis is upon private study and individual work, the introvert comes into his own. This seems to suggest that the extravert gets off to the best start in the primary school but gradually falls behind the introvert as he grows older, but this interpretation may be too simple since there is strong evidence that most people tend to become more introverted as the years go by. Mean extraversion scores peak at approximately age 14, then decline throughout life, and it may therefore be possible that children who are precocious intellectually also peak early in extraversion, and become more intoverted than their peers by the time they reach late adolescence. Thus, they may be more extraverted than the norm in the primary school, and more introverted than the norm by the time they go up to university. The issue will only be settled when we have longitudinal studies which follow children throughout their school careers, keeping careful records of personality growth and development alongside records of attainment in a range of academic subjects.

Turning to Eysenck's neuroticism dimension, we find that the picture is also a little unclear. Many years ago the American psychologists Yerkes and Dodson propounded what has become known as the 'Yerkes-Dodson Law', namely that <u>moderate</u> levels of anxiety act as motivators and improve performance whereas <u>high</u> levels lead to inhibition and a deterioration in performance, particularly where the task is a difficult one. This complex relationship between anxiety and performance makes it hard to arrive at firm conclusions when simply seeking significant correlations between scores on a neuroticism test such as Eysenck's and school attainment. For example, children with high N scores (i.e. high neuroticism scores), which indicate that they have a <u>general</u> tendency towards high levels of anxiety, may nevertheless cope well with even very difficult learning tasks when in the presence of a sympathetic and supportive teacher, while children with low N scores might do less well simply because the teacher's gentle manner is insufficient to put them on their toes. Conversely, in a demanding environment, the latter children might clearly outstrip the former. The importance of teacher style in influencing children's learning is, in fact, amply demonstrated by Bennett (1976) who, in a major investigation, found, for example, that motivated stable extroverts substantially <u>overachieved</u> in a formal classroom environment (where presumably the pressures were more intense), but <u>under-achieved</u> in an informal environment (where presumably their motivational levels were less fully aroused).

Lest it be thought that this means that high N pupils will do better in informal environments, Bennett showed that they too appeared to achieve more in a formal context. In the informal classroom they spent only half as much time on work activity as did those with a lower neuroticism score, whereas there was no apparent difference between the two groups in a formal environment. In the absence of firm evidence we cannot be sure of the reason for this but it seems possible that in the informal environment the high N pupils find they are able to avoid the anxiety-provoking challenge which work activities inevitably imply. They appear to do best, therefore, in a more structured environment where they are more fully aware of what is expected of them, and where guidelines and standards are generally clearer.

Overall, Bennet's work indicates the extent and the subtlety with which teacher styles and pupil personalities interact with each other, and the difficulty of studying the one in isolation from the other. It is probable, also, that we need to take the nature of the academic subject studied by the child or the student into account. High N scores may be less of a disadvantage in arts subjects, for example, where more emphasis is laid upon subjective judgements than in science subjects where the stress is upon a more objective approach. To take a further example, we know that high anxiety levels have an inhibiting effect upon the recall of detailed material, and in consequence the over-anxious student may face greater problems in courses assessed by examination that demands detailed recall of facts than in dealing with work that invites analytical and critical appraisals.

Another important factor linked both to personality and school achievement is sex. We know (e.g. Davie et al, 1972) that girls in the early school years tend to be more verbal than boys, to read earlier, and to experience fewer general learning and behaviour problems, while boys tend to be more successful at solving spatial and mechanical tasks. What is not clear is the extent to which these differences are due to genetic factors and the extent to which they are due to acquired characteristics associated with personality, and complicated further by teacher styles. We have already made reference to the fact that girls appear to be lower in self esteem than boys, and more dependent upon parents and upon parental approval, but we also know (Lynn, 1971) that females tend to score more highly on neuroticism throughout their years of formal education than do males, and it could be that this higher anxiety level acts as a motivator, particularly in the early years of schooling when girls have still not learned that society apparently expects them not to out-perform boys. However, lest we load the balance too strongly against the male sex, there is now some evidence to the effect that in their early years in school, when they are taught almost exclusively by women, boys come to associate school with feminine values, and therefore show less interest in it than girls. When boys are taught by men in the early years, then these sex-related differences in performance tend to disappear (Shinedling and Pederson, 1970).

PERSONALITY AND COGNITIVE FACTORS

We said at the beginning of this chapter that although personality is not normally taken to include cognitive factors such as intelligence and creativity, it nevertheless interacts with them at a number of points. What does this interaction entail and what relevance does it have to education? Again the answer is by no means a simple one. Intelligence, in particular, seems to influence some areas of personality more strongly than others. It will be recalled that in our definition of personality we suggested that the term covers emotionality and conative traits such as willing and desiring, and it is with these latter traits rather than with emotionality itself that intelligence appears to interact most significantly. Put another way, intelligence appears to have little influence upon how emotional we are (though it might help us hide our emotions or learn when displays of emotion are inappropriate), but it does seem to affect our willing and desiring. Our beliefs and values, for example, may sometimes be directly linked to our ability to see the force of an argument or to reason things out for ourselves, and our goals and ambitions may also be tied to some extent to our ability to think and plan realistically and analytically.

Conversely, the use we make of our cognitive abilities may be influenced by the kind of personalities we happen to possess. We have already looked at one aspect of this in our discussion of personality and educational achievement, but it may be that even such things as our measured intelligence itself may be affected by personality traits. Research at the Fels Institute in the USA (Kagan et al, 1958) into a sample of children who between the ages of six and ten manifested either a marked increase or a marked decline in IQ scores showed that children in the increase group were more independent, more competitive, and more verbally aggressive than those in the decline group. They were also readier to work hard, showed a stronger desire to master intellectual problems, and were less likely to withdraw in the face of challenge (this links in interestingly with the work of Coopersmith on self-esteem which we described earlier in the chapter). In one of the most ambitious studies of its kind ever attempted Terman and Oden (1947) showed that high IQ children were more likely to make use of their potential as they matured through adolescence and into adult life if they were high on self-confidence, on perseverance, on work interest, and had well integrated life goals (i.e. life goals that were realistic and single-minded). Terman and Oden's study is of further interest to us in that it lends no support to the notion that genius goes with odd, withdrawn, eccentric behaviour. Their most successful children, all with IQs of 140 plus, showed themselves generally better adjusted and more socially balanced than the less successful children in the sample, and more likely to go on to make successful marriages and to achieve satisfaction in their personal and professional lives.

More generally McCandless (1969) suggests research indicates that high IQ children tend to be taller, better looking, physically stronger, and more popular than children at the opposite end of the normal ability range. They also seem better judges of other people (particularly strangers) and, not surprisingly, tend to be more self-confident and less anxious. This prompts us to ask whether it is the high intelligence that leads to the development of the desirable personality traits, or whether it is the other way round? Or could it be that both sets of abilities tend to be inherited, at least potentially, together? The answer is probably that all three of the suggestions implicit in these questions are partially correct. We have already reviewed evidence that suggests some part of personality appears to be inherited, and there is at least equal evidence that inheritance also has a role to play in intelligence (see e.g. Vernon, 1979 for a review). So it could be that there is some kind of complex link at the genetic level. Less speculatively it is also clear that high intelligence prompts certain kinds of personality development while certain kinds of personality assist the growth of intelligence. The high IQ child finds in the main that people react favourably to him. He has the ability to develop the skills prized by our society, and thus to complete satisfactorily the tasks of initiative and competence that we discussed earlier in the chapter in connection with Erikson's work, and which we said appear to be important if the personality is to develop satisfactorily. Conversely, the child endowed temperamentally with high potential for determination and perseverance, the child with a friendly outgoing nature, the child with high levels of adaptability, will all find that they have enhanced opportunities for the kind of experiences important to intellectual growth.

There is also evidence, albeit less extensive, that another cognitive ability, namely creativity, interacts with personality. This is not the place to enter into a discussion of whether or not creativity is an ability distinct from intelligence, or whether creativity is as essential in the sciences as it is in the arts. Suffice it to say that creative people appear to be more autonomous, self-sufficient, self-assertive, and resourceful than average, and also more introverted, more aware of their impulses, and more open to the irrational in themselves, (Taylor and Holland, 1964). They also have a high tolerance for ambiguity (i.e. do not demand that things should always be cut and dried and issues always made clear), and enjoy engaging in abstract thought. Some of these point may come as a surprise to the teacher. We are all of us reasonably able at encouraging the qualities that appear to go with intelligence in children, but those that go with creativity may at times make the child a rather uncomfortable member of the class. Since the class is a rather large social unit which has to go about its business with maximum efficiency, there is often something of an emphasis upon conformity in attitude and behaviour, and the child who exhibits a degree of openness to the irrational and a tolerance (even a liking) for ambiguity, for example, may appear to complicate the teacher's task. (There is, indeed, evidence that teachers tend to perceive highly creative children more negatively than highly intelligent children - see Getzels and Jackson, 1966).

In a general examination of the problem Jerome Bruner (e.g.

Bruner et al, 1956) speaks of holistic (creative) thinking and algorithmic (rational) thinking, and considers that in education we lay stress upon the latter at the expense of the former. That is we expect children for the most part to think like the teacher and come to the same conclusions that he does. Sometimes such an approach is right and proper, but sometimes the particular problem faced by the child demands an holistic rather than an algorithmic approach, and by insisting upon the latter we may handicap his problem solving behaviour. The essence of creative thinking is that it is spontaneous and open-ended, concerned with possibilities and insights rather than with certainty and precision, and Bruner suggests that often guessing is evidence of creative effort and as such should not automatically be discounted by the teacher. Bruner goes further and suggests that there are other forms of thinking behaviour that influence both the way in which an individual tackles a specific problem and his general approach to life. This behaviour is usually given the title cognitive style, and in recent years a number of attempts have been made by researchers to identify different types of cognitive style, and to suggest their implications for the teacher.

Cognitive style theorists start from the accepted fact that we are bombarded by data from our environment every moment of our waking lives, and develop characteristic ways of deciding what to attend to and what to ignore, and also of coding and categorising the former (that is of making sense of it in the light of previous experience, of current emotional reactions and so on). The teacher is well aware of this characteristic behaviour when he says that one child always tends to rush things, that another always seems to miss the point, that another is disorganised or that another is precise and methodical. The characteristics represented by these labels are evidenced not only in problem solving but also in social behaviour and the depth of consideration given to life goals, and the next step of the cognitive style theorist is to attempt to develop some way of testing them. Bruner himself claims to have identified a dimension of cognitive style which he labels focussing-scanning. Children who exhibit a focussing style characteristically appear to delay hypothesis making when faced with a problem until they have sufficient evidence to go on, while children with a scanning style form an hypothesis quickly and on slim evidence, and usually have to go back and start all over again when this hypothesis is eventually seen to be untenable.

The relevance of this for the teacher is that children who focus may sometimes delay too long over forming an hypothesis and therefore, be handicapped in work that demands rapid responses, while children who scan may be at a disadvantage in mentally presented problems where they are unable to go back and check earlier clues as this becomes necessary. In social terms, the scanner may also make his mind up quickly (and perhaps inacurately) about other people, while the focusser may take longer to make friends though his friendships may be more durable. Another interesting dimension of cognitive style is that identified by Witkin (e.g. Witkin 1959), and called originally field dependence-independence (since changed to global-articulated). The individual with a global style tends to respond to the overall picture presented in any given situation, whereas someone with an articulated style is able to distinguish the relevant factors and reject those that are more peripheral. For example, in an early series of experiments, Witkin found that some people with global styles are unable to tell whether the chair in which they are sitting is upright or not if they are made to look at visual stimuli which are also being tilted. In other words, they were unable to separate the relevant stimulus (the subjective feeling of whether the body is being tilted or not) from the irrelevant one (the visual stimuli at which they were looking).

Witkin has since shown that global individuals seem less able to remember the details in a given situation when attempting recall tests, seem less perceptive, and apear to be more easily influenced by their fellows. They also tend to do less well on analytical items in IQ tests than do articulated individuals, though there is no difference on verbal items. Witkin suggests (1965) that this low analytical ability may in consequence sometimes be masked by high verbal skills, and that the teacher may in consequence be unaware of the real reasons for the difficulties a child may experience with certain kinds of learning tasks. He therefore suggests that cognitive style tests are of even more use to the teacher than IQ tests, and should indeed replace the latter since they are more comprehensive and "recognise the rooting of intellectual functioning in personality".

Space does not allow us to deal here with other aspects of cognitive style, and the reader who wishes to explore the subject further is referred to chapter 4. The essential point that we are making is that personality not only influences school learning by virture of its impact upon emotional adjustment, general social behaviour and general motivational orientation, but also by its effect upon the way in which children go about the actual business of thinking. This area offers a particularly fruitful field for possible future research and there is every reason to suggest that it should attract as much attention as do the more socially orientated dimensions of personality isolated by Eysenck and his colleagues.

CONCLUSION

Personality is such a vast subject that it is impossible in one short chapter to touch on more than a few selected aspects of it. We have not looked, for example, at personality theories, that is at theories that speculate on _why_ the individual responds as he does to environmental influences. The reader may already know that some of these theories are in sharp contradiction to each other, and we could only have done justice to them within the context of a much more extended survey than the one here attempted. In any case, these theories are of less immediate practical use to the teacher than the points which we have covered, and those who wish to read further are referred to the suggested reading at the end of the chapter. Nor have we had time to look at aspects of social psychology that link closely with personality such as the study of attitudes and opinions, but here also there is guidance provided in the suggested reading for those who wish to go into these matters.

The final thought with which we would leave the reader is that, as a teacher, he should attempt to study his own personality as well as to study the personalities of his children. We have already indicated in our discussion of Bennett's work that teacher styles interact importantly with pupil personalities, and the same is true of the other personal characteristics that the teacher brings with him into the classroom. The extraverted teacher, for example, may find that he responds best to the extraverted child, and tends to censure the introvert for being too quiet and withdrawn. Conversely, the intraverted teacher may see the extraverted child as being too lively and boisterous. In these and in all other similar instances, self-knowledge will help the teacher to resist being unfair to some members of his class just because they are unlike him in general social and emotional orientation, and will assist him in establishing the kind of relationship with individuals that best enables them to cope successfully with the personal and academic problems of school life.

REFERENCES

Adorno, T.W., Frenkel-Brunswick, E., Levinson, D.J., and Sanford, R.N. The Authoritarian Personality. (Harper and Row, New York, 1950).

Allport, G.W. Pattern and Growth in Personality. (Holt, Rinehart & Winston, London, 1961).

Bennett, N. (1976). Teaching Styles and Pupil Progress. (Open Books, London, 1976).

Berger, M. and Passingham, R.E. Early experience and other environmental factors: an overview. In Eysenck, H.J. (ed.), Handbook of Abnormal Psychology, (second edition). (Pitmans Medical Press, London,1973).

Bruner, J., Goodnow, J., and Austin, G. A Study of Thinking. (Wiley, New York, 1956).

Cattell, R.B. The Scientific Analysis of Personality. Penguin, Harmondsworth, 1965).

Clarke, A.M. and Clarke, A.D.B. Early Experience: Myth and Evidence. (Open Books, London, 1976).

Coopersmith, S. Studies in self-esteem. Scientific American, 1968, February).

Davie, R., Butler, N., and Goldstein, H. From Birth to Seven. (Longmans, London, 1972).

Elliott, C.D. Personality factors and scholastic attainment. British Journal of Educational Psychology, 1972, 42, 23-32.

Entwistle, N.J. Personality and academic achievement. British Journal of Educational Psychology, 1972, 42, 23-32.

Erikson, E.H. Growth and crisis in the healthy personality. Psychological Issues, 1959, 1, 50-100.

Erikson, E.H. Identity: Youth and Crisis. (Norton, New York, 1968).

Eysenck, H.J. and Eysenck, S.B. Manual of the Eysenck Personality Inventory. (University of London Press, London, 1964).

Eysenck, H.J. and Eysenck, S.B. Personality Structure and Measurement. (Routledge and Kegan Paul, London, 1969).

Goldfarb, W. Emotional and intellectual consequences of psychological deprivation in infancy: a re-evaluation. In Hock, P. and Zubin, J. (eds.) Psychopathology of Childhood. (Grune, New York, 1955).
Harlow, H.F. and Harlow, M.H. (1966). Learning to love. American Scientist, 1966, 54, 244-272.

Kagan, J., Sontag, L., Baker, C., and Nelson, V. (1958). Personality and I.Q. change. Journal of Abnormal and Social Psychology, 1958, 56, 261-266.

Kamin, L.J. The Science and Politics of I.Q. (Lawrence

Erlbaum, Potomac, 1974).

Lewis, M. State as an infant-environment interaction: an analysis of mother-infant behaviour as a function of sex. Merrill-Palmer Quarterly of Behavioural Development, 1972, 18, 95-121.

Lynn, R. An Introduction to the Study of Personality. (MacMillan, London, 1971).

McCandless, B. Children: Behaviour and Development. (Holt, Rinehart and Winston, London, 1969).

Newman, H., Freeman, F., and Holzinger, K. Twins: A Study of Heredity and Environment. University of Chicago Press, Chicago, 1937).

Novak, M.A. and Harlow, H.F. Social recovery of monkeys isolated for the first year of life: I. Rehabilitation and therapy. Developmental Psychology, 1975, 11, 453-465.

Robertson, J. Mothering as an influence in early development. Psychoanalytical Studies of the Child, 1975, 17.

Rogers, C.R. On Becoming a Person. (Houghton Mifflin, Boston, 1961).

Rosenberg, M. (1965). Society and the Adolescent Self-Image. (Princeton University Press, Princeton, 1965).

Sandler, J. and Hazari, A. The obsessional: on the psychological classification of obsessional character traits and symptoms. British Journal of Medical Psychology, 1960, 33, 113-122.

Shields, J. Monozygotic Twins. (Oxford University Press, Oxford, 1962).

Shinedling, M.M. and Pederson, D.M. Effects of sex of teacher and student on children's gains in quantitative and verbal performance. Journal of Psychology, 1960, 76, 79-84.

Taylor, C. and Holland, J. Predictors of creative performance. In Taylor, C. (ed.) Creativity, Progress and Potential. (McGraw Hill, New York, 1964).

Terman, L. and Oden, M. Genetic Studies of Genius IV. (California University Press, Stanford, 1947).

Thomas, A., Chess, S., and Birch, H. The origin of personality. Scientific American, 1970, August.

Trasler, G. In Place of Parents: A Study in Foster Care.
(Routledge and Kegan Paul, London, 1960).

Vernon, P.E. Intelligence: Heredity and Environment. (Freeman,
San Fransicso, 1979).

Witkin, H.A. The perception of the upright. Scientific
American, 1959, February.

Witkin, H.A. Psychological differentiation and forms of
pathology. Journal of Abnormal Psychology, 1965, 70, 324-336.